Australian Cinema after *Mabo*

Australian Cinema after Mabo is the first comprehensive study of Australian national cinema in the 1990s. Drawing on concepts of shock, memory and national maturity, it asks what part Australian cinema plays in reviewing our colonial past. It looks at how the 1992 *Mabo* decision, which overruled the nation's founding myth of *terra nullius*, has changed the meaning of landscape and identity in Australian films, including *The Tracker*, *Rabbit-Proof Fence*, *Moulin Rouge*, *The Castle*, *Cunnamulla*, *Looking for Alibrandi* and *Japanese Story* amongst many others. It is essential reading for anyone studying Australian cinema and for those interested in how the history wars of the 1990s have impacted on the way we imagine ourselves through cinema.

Felicity Collins lectures in Cinema Studies at La Trobe University. She is the author of *The Films of Gillian Armstrong*.

Therese Davis lectures in Film and Cultural Studies at the University of Newcastle. She is the author of *The Face on the Screen: Death, Recognition and Spectatorship*.

Australian Cinema after *Mabo*

FELICITY COLLINS AND THERESE DAVIS

CAMBRIDGE
UNIVERSITY PRESS

PUBLISHED BY THE PRESS SYNDICATE OF THE UNIVERSITY OF CAMBRIDGE
The Pitt Building, Trumpington Street, Cambridge, United Kingdom

CAMBRIDGE UNIVERSITY PRESS
The Edinburgh Building, Cambridge, CB2 2RU, UK
40 West 20th Street, New York, NY 10011–4211, USA
477 Williamstown Road, Port Melbourne, VIC 3207, Australia
Ruiz de Alarcón 13, 28014 Madrid, Spain
Dock House, The Waterfront, Cape Town 8001, South Africa

http://www.cambridge.org

First published by Cambridge University Press 2004

Printed in Australia by Ligare Pty Ltd

Typeface Minion 10.5/13 pt.   *System* LaTeX 2_ε [TB]

A catalogue record for this book is available from the British Library

National Library of Australia Cataloguing in Publication data

Collins, Felicity.
Australian cinema after Mabo.
Bibliography.
Includes index.
ISBN 0 521 83480 5.
ISBN 0 521 54256 1 (pbk.).
1. Motion pictures – Australia – History.   2. National characteristics,
Australian, in motion pictures.   I. Davis, Therese.   II. Title.
791.430994

ISBN 0 521 83480 5 hardback
ISBN 0 521 54256 1 paperback

Contents

Acknowledgments

The joyful co-authorship of this book has been a tale of two cities and a regional centre. Our friendship began in Sydney in the early 1980s when we were both students in the Communication degree at the NSW Institute of Technology. This book is grounded in those formative years when our thinking about film, media, history and culture was shaped by the many luminaries of the infamous Tower Building on Broadway. If the seeds for this book were sown in post-structuralist Sydney, the project came to fruition through the Cinema Studies program at La Trobe University in Melbourne, and the Film Studies program at the University of Newcastle. In December 1996 we participated in a seminar, *Film and Modernity*, led by Miriam Bratu Hansen, at the University of Newcastle. This seminar provided the impetus for our desire to rethink Australian cinema in terms of shock, memory and recognition. In Melbourne, the lively debate and recent flood of books and essays by local academics and publishers engaged in the history wars has created a stimulating context for our writing on the politics of memory in post-*Mabo* films. We are indebted to the Melbourne-based *Metro Magazine* and *Senses of Cinema* for their regular forums on Australian cinema, and for publishing early versions of ideas we have developed further in this book.

We thank Jodi Brooks for recommending texts on traumatic memory and for encouraging this project. Con Verevis provided Felicity Collins with the opportunity to present early work on landscape and aftershock at the Centre for Contemporary Photography in Melbourne in October 2001. The 2002 Conference of the Australian and New Zealand Film and History Association at Flinders University gave us the opportunity to road-test the metaphor of backtracking in recent Australian films. We are grateful for suggestions and encouragement from Tracey Bunda, Ann Curthoys, John Docker, John Hughes, Sylvia Lawson and Cassi Plate. We wish to thank Kim Armitage from Cambridge University Press for her enthusiasm and diligence, Joyleen Christensen for her efficiency with the bibliography and Venetia Somerset for her instructive copy editing. We gratefully acknowledge the generous support of friends, colleagues and family.

Australian Cinema
and the History Wars

1
Backtracking after *Mabo*

Backtrack: *(vb). 1. to return by the same route by which one has come. 2. to retract or reverse one's opinion, policy, etc.*

The familiar yet estranged figure of the black tracker has enjoyed a certain longevity in Australian cultural traditions for it easily corresponds with the metaphor of exile and imprisonment in a purgatorial landscape, identified by Graeme Turner as one of the key tropes of Australian fiction. However, with shifts in the Australian social imaginary that accompanied the Land Rights movement of the 1970s, the tracker receded into the background, a result, perhaps, of a critique of racial stereotypes initiated by Aboriginal activists and critics. In 2001–02 the black tracker made an unexpected return to Australian screens in two feature films, *Rabbit-Proof Fence* (Phillip Noyce, 2002) and *The Tracker* (Rolf de Heer, 2002), and a short musical film, *One Night the Moon* (Rachel Perkins, 2001). In both features, an iconic actor of the 1970s, David Gulpilil, was cast in the role of the tracker.[1] His startling, intense screen presence haunted *Rabbit-Proof Fence* and dominated *The Tracker*. After a period of relative obscurity (save for smaller roles in *Crocodile Dundee*, Peter Faiman, 1986; *Until the End of the World*, Wim Wenders, 1992; and *Dead Heart*, Nicholas Parsons, 1996), Gulpilil's return to the screen in two key films of the post-*Mabo* era, like the films themselves, can be understood as a kind of backtracking, a going over of old ground in Australian national cinema, a going over which reprises and at the same time retracts some of the seemingly intractable figures of Australian national identity.

In this book, we use 'backtracking' as a key term to describe and interpret Australian cinema (and to a lesser extent, television) in the twelve years since the 1992 *Mabo* decision overturned the nation's founding doctrine of *terra nullius* (i.e., land belonging to no one). However, from the outset, we want to be clear that this is not a book about the *Mabo* decision itself or the representation of Aboriginality in Australian cinema. It is a book about the cultural rather than political impact of a paradigm shift in Australian historical consciousness. The *Mabo* decision is central to this shift because it forces Australians to rethink 'race relations' and the colonial past as integral to what Tim Rowse describes as a morally illegitimate national identity.[2]

Australian colonial histories show that, from day one, European settlers/invaders recognised the fiction of *terra nullius*.[3] This is evident in their encounters with Aboriginal clans in possession of land, initially in coastal areas and later in the interior, which the British had presumed to be inhospitable and therefore 'empty' of human life. Yet, as Henry Reynolds argues in *Aboriginal Sovereignty*, 'the advantages of assuming the absence of people were so great . . . that legal doctrine continued to depict Australia as a colony acquired by occupation of a *terra nullius*'.[4] Racist assumptions about Aboriginal culture provided the basis for the continued non-recognition of Indigenous ownership of the land. As Reynolds puts it: settlers/invaders saw Indigenous people as primitives 'who ranged over the land rather than inhabiting it'.[5] Despite a history of Indigenous resistance to dispossession, supported at different times in the nation's past by a number of non-Indigenous Australians, the story of the nation's origin, in the occupation of land belonging to no one, remained intact until the High Court's *Mabo* decision in 1992.

This landmark legal decision to recognise the pre-existing property rights of Indigenous Australians created shock-waves across the nation as non-Indigenous Australians were forced to confront the fiction of *terra nullius*. As Justice Brennan wrote in his summation of the case: 'Whatever the justification advanced in earlier days for refusing to recognise the rights and interests in land of the indigenous inhabitants of settled colonies, an unjust and discriminatory doctrine of that kind can no longer be accepted.'[6] Events over the past decade have shown, however, that neither the *Mabo* decision nor its subsequent enactment has settled issues of land rights between Indigenous and non-Indigenous Australians.[7] On the contrary, non-Indigenous Australians find themselves on unsettled ground as we come to terms with the fact that our democratic society has a serious flaw. One public nation-wide poll done for the Council for Aboriginal Reconciliation in early 2000 showed that a large majority of people (80%) feel that the process of reconciliation is important; but they are strongly divided about how the process should proceed. For example: 'In principle, 57% agreed and 37% disagreed that a reconciliation document might help relations between Aborigines and the wider community. But only 28% favoured giving the document a legal status.'[8] In 2004, Australians remain divided on a range of post-*Mabo* issues, including: the legal and financial implications of recognition of Indigenous Australians' prior ownership and sovereignty; the idea of collective blame and the need for an official apology for past injustices; proposals for what

4

the Howard government calls 'practical reconciliation' – that is, strategies for overcoming the startling inequities in Indigenous health, employment, education and rates of imprisonment.

Politicising History

The *Mabo* decision is at the centre of an unprecedented politicisation of history in Australia. The 'history wars' are being played out in the public arena, in which competing sides attempt to explain Australia's past and determine how best to remember it. These history wars are not unique to Australia. In the wake of 20th-century genocide and other forms of atrocity, many post-industrial societies are having a similar debate, struggling for answers about how to explain unspeakable episodes from the recent past, and how to remember them. Indeed, cultural theorists see this struggle over the past as integral to the paradox of modernity whereby we valorise progress while simultaneously lamenting the loss of a safer, more secure past. In recent times, referred to as late modernity, obsession with the past has intensified, resulting in what Andreas Huyssen calls 'the globalization of memory'.[9] Huyssen's description of this culture reminds us that in daily life we are bombarded by invitations to remember the past through popular global memory of the Holocaust in films like *Schindler's List* (Steven Spielberg, 1993), a new wave of museum architecture, the rise of autobiography and memoir writing, retro fashion, the History Channel, and so on.[10] The past is, quite literally, closing in on us to produce what Huyssen calls 'an ever-shrinking present'.[11] At the same time, Huyssen reminds us that 'while memory discourses appear to be global in one register, in their core they remain tied to the histories of specific nations and states'.[12] Since the terrorist attack on the World Trade Centre twin towers on 11 September 2001, it is tempting to focus primarily on global relations. Certainly, this is something the Howard government did in the lead-up to the 2001 election. But as Huyssen argues, all nations are faced with 'the task of securing the legitimacy and future of their existing or emergent polities', and one of the main ways they do this 'is to commemorate and adjudicate past wrongs'.[13]

In Australia, the history wars have centred most intensely on past treatment of Aboriginal peoples and the politics of land since the *Mabo* decision. One of the first major acts in the politicisation of history in the wake of *Mabo* was Prime Minister Paul Keating's Redfern Park speech (1992). Keating's assertion that '*we* took the traditional lands', '*we* brought the diseases', '*we* committed murders' radically altered the terms of the nation's

5

self-understanding.[14] The Prime Minister's acknowledgment that 'we', the present generation, should take collective responsibility for colonial forms of violence and subjugation was an initial step in the process of reconciliation between settler and Indigenous Australians. But Keating's speech also outraged many Australians, especially neo-conservatives, including Opposition Leader John Howard.

To understand why neo-conservatives oppose Keating's assertions about the past, we need to go beyond the underlying concept of moral responsibility and consider the speech in the broader context of Keating's Republican agenda and his politicisation of history. Keating's aim, indeed his personal passion, was to shift Australia's identity away from a British-centred past to a history grounded in Australian experience. Earlier in 1992, Keating had accused Britain of deserting Australia in 1942 at the fall of Singapore. Mark McKenna suggests that Keating's anti-British agenda can be read as a 'useful means of transferring responsibility for the evils of colonialism from Australia to Britain'.[15] In this light we can better understand why neo-conservatives see Aboriginal reconciliation as such a threat to the nation. Keating's assertion of a moral flaw at the heart of national identity not only demands a response from present-day Australians. It also brings into disrepute the nation's British heritage upon which national identity has been so proudly based, thus revitalising the Republican call to cut all ties with Britain.

For these reasons among others, neo-conservatives sought to defend the old account of Australia's past as a nation of well-intentioned, hardworking British settlers. In his 1993 Sir John Latham Memorial Lecture, Australian historian Geoffrey Blainey introduced the phrase 'the black armband view of history', claiming that there was a crisis in Australian history: 'a swing of the pendulum from a position that had been too favourable to an opposite extreme that is decidedly jaundiced and gloomy.'[16] Howard seized this view and pillaged Blainey's speech, incorporating phrases such as 'the black armband view of history' into his own rhetoric. By the mid-1990s, the history wars were in full swing. Public debate over issues such as the Stolen Generations, frontier conflict, school curricula and the National Museum confirm that history is no longer a dying discipline in schools and universities but an issue of national importance. Individual historians such as Manning Clark and Geoffrey Blainey have become national figures, while high-profile journalists such as Christopher Pearson and Piers Akerman, and public intellectuals such as Robert Manne, Tim Flannery, Germaine Greer, Ron Brunton and Peter Howson are strongly identified with either the left-liberal or neo-conservative view on how best to explain the nation's past, how best to remember it.[17]

Cinema after *Mabo*

How then do we begin to think about Australian cinema in the post-*Mabo* era? What part does cinema play in the national process of reviewing our colonial past and rethinking the ways in which settler and Indigenous cultures can coexist? This book investigates the extent to which Australian cinema, in the aftershock of the *Mabo* decision, has reprised its role as an arbiter of national identity by going over some old ground. This backtracking is literal in the case of the landscape tradition which anchored national identity to British settlement of the land. It is also metaphorical in the case of a miscellany of films which have a common interest in the problems faced by settler and Indigenous peoples of being at home in Australia, whether home is located in the bush, the suburbs or the outback, or is conceived as local, national or international terrains of action. And whether 'being at home' after *Mabo* is understood in terms of coexistence and recognition of a sovereign First Nation within the Second Nation, on the Canadian model, or post-colonial reconciliation based on a moral rather than legal understanding of Indigenous–settler relations.

Influential writers have analysed the anxiety and ambivalence which seem endemic to Australian nationhood and to Australian cinema.[18] However, the cultural impact of the *Mabo* decision (and the peculiar forms of anxiety about the nation's past and future to which it has given rise) has not yet been analysed in terms of cinema. In this book we are preoccupied with the issue of how the Australian cinema has mediated historical memory and national self-recognition in the wake of the *Mabo* decision, as well as related events such as the 1997 *Wik* rulings on *terra nullius* and native title, the Stolen Generations report, National Sorry Day, the opening ceremony of the Sydney 2000 Olympics, and the 2001 centenary of Federation. If the false belief in *terra nullius* can no longer be maintained as the blind spot in Australian national history, how has the cinema (as the cultural flagship of national identity) begun to revise and retract its established (some would say exhausted) tropes of national self-recognition?

At one end of the media spectrum, the televised opening ceremony of the Sydney 2000 Olympic Games was a particularly self-conscious media event, integrating an Indigenous dreamtime as the pre-history of the nation. In turn, the nation's history was allowed to unfold as a montage of masculine archetypes, from the robust stockman-on-horseback to the lawn-mowing man of suburbia.[19] At the other end of the entertainment spectrum, the national cinema of 2000–02 produced a cycle of films concerned with Indigenous–settler relations.[20] Rather than a celebratory montage of national archetypes, this cycle revised certain familiar figures such as the black tracker, the lost child, the bush battler, and the Australian landscape itself. If many of these films seemed strangely belated, already out of date at the time of their release ten years after the *Mabo* decision, it was partly because the subsidised national cinema lacked the immediacy of television, radio and print media. This belated quality was partly an effect of film-funding policy. Proposals dealing with the unpopular subject of the nation's colonial past needed to overcome commercial resistance to Indigenous–settler stories in order to qualify for production funding. Further, from the perspective of national cinema, films featuring Aboriginal characters tended to revive an Anglocentric version of the social imaginary at a moment when the economy and popular culture were moving decisively into a post-national, cosmopolitan mode. However, if we look at these same films from the international perspective of late modernity, it becomes clear that Australian films dealing with traumatic events in national history have been very timely. As a genre of international cinema, Australian films have become part of a global, media-based politics of memory, where national traumas like genocide are now being understood in terms of the failures of Western modernity.[21] For us, the term 'after *Mabo*' implies a national cinema that, in various ways, tells us what it feels like to be living in the 'afterwardness' of colonialism during a moment of intense globalisation.

Key Concepts

In this book we propose that Australian cinema is one of the public spaces in which Australians have been able to experience the impact of the *Mabo* decision as a national 'shock of recognition'. We argue that cinema enables collective and intimate forms of recognition which have a different impact from legal and political recognition. Our understanding of post-*Mabo* cinema is informed by Walter Benjamin's theories of history, modernity and shock. Benjamin argues that there is a structural affinity between the montage principle of film – the rapid juxtaposition of images – and the alienating effects of modernity, making film an embodiment of the peculiar shock effects associated with the rapid changes of modernity.[22] Benjamin's understanding of film and modernity is closely related to his concept of the dialectical image and historical consciousness. For Benjamin, the past makes itself evident in dialectical moments where the past and present collide, where, in his words, 'the past flashes up in the instant it is recognized and never seen again'.[23] He cautions, however, that we should not confuse these moments of 'recognizability' with the idea of seeing the present in terms of the past, of assuming a continuity between past and present. Rather, these flashes, in which the past becomes visible, arise out of *recognition of discontinuity*. It is precisely this recognition of the *Mabo* decision as a rupture in the continuity of Australian history that informs our understanding of Australian cinema after *Mabo*. The shock of recognition of historical discontinuity entailed in the *Mabo* decision provides the impetus for us to propose a new way of thinking about the relationship between Australian cinema and a post-*Mabo* politics of recognition. This approach to a contemporary national cinema has the advantage of providing a way for us to backtrack over some well-worn debates about Australian national identity.

In their ground-breaking study of Australian cinema of the 1970s and 1980s, Susan Dermody and Elizabeth Jacka deploy the concept of a 'social imaginary' to account for historical modes of spectatorship in national cinema. In this study, we use concepts of shock, recognition and trauma to define a post-*Mabo* social imaginary grounded in memory. We refer to memory in four different ways: historical memory as the chronological ordering of events; involuntary memory as a chain of associations incited by shock; remembering the past as a work of mourning in the psychoanalytic sense; and repetitive, belated memory associated with historical trauma. In the following chapters we draw on theories of memory and trauma cinema in order to answer the question posed by Radstone and others: 'why these films now?'[24] More particularly, why these films, here, in this national cinema, now? We are interested in questions of how 'unintegrated traumatic memories may impede recognition of present traumas'; of trauma's 'internal conflict between the pre-traumatised and traumatised self'; of trauma as 'the layering of several experiences rather than the impact of one'; and of the role trauma films may play 'in their spectators' integration of trauma, mitigating individualised isolation and creating empathy with the suffering of others in the present'.[25]

Apart from the influence of current research into memory and trauma films, our concept of recognition and memory in cinema is indebted to Miriam Hansen's reprise of critical theory's approach to cinema as an intimate public sphere of experience. Drawing on the writings of Benjamin and Kracauer, Hansen's work offers an alternative to film theory's concept of cinema as a place of voyeuristic and fetishistic identification. Her historically grounded ideas are particularly useful for rethinking the ways in which history, recognition and memory continue to be so central to our experience of Australian national cinema as a 'vernacular modernity'.[26] The following readings of *Black and White*, *The Tracker* and *Black Chicks Talking* (Leah Purcell, 2002) will clarify our use of the interrelated concepts of Australian cinema as a public sphere for reprising or going back over established themes of national history, as a site for the politics of recognition, and as a trauma-tised space of public memory.

History and Storytelling in *Black and White*

At a forum to launch the Melbourne season of *Black and White*,[27] the direc-tor, Craig Lahiff, and actor David Ngoombujarra discussed two different concepts of history informing their film about the landmark 1959 trial of an Aboriginal man, Rupert Max Stuart. Whereas Lahiff was concerned with transforming complicated historical events into a feature film, Ngoombu-jarra considered Stuart's story to be just one of many 'hidden stories' waiting to be told. This contrast between history and story indicates two different possibilities for cinema as a public sphere. In his writing on storytelling, Benjamin emphasises the difference between historical remembrance (Craig Lahiff's approach) and epic memory (David Ngoombujarra's approach).[28] For us, it's not a choice between history as coherent remembrance and storytelling as epic memory, but rather a sense of how they are both oper-ating in *Black and White*.

From the factual point of view of historical remembrance, Stuart's death sentence for the rape and murder of a nine-year-old girl in Ceduna, South Australia, was commuted into a fourteen-year prison sentence after seven stays of execution. These stays were won chiefly (according to the film) through the confused, altruistic but determined efforts of his defence lawyers, Dave O'Sullivan and Helen Devaney, Christian minister Tom Dixon, and media scion Rupert Murdoch. Working with screenwriter Louis Nowra, Lahiff drew on three books about the case and on other historical mate-rial including an interview with O'Sullivan's daughter and contact with Rupert Max Stuart. This contact with Stuart led to the inclusion of a final scene (taken from a documentary film, *Broken English*, Ned Lander, 1993) which gives Stuart the last, inconclusive word in the film on the question of his guilt or innocence.[29] This scene ends the film, putting into doubt the screenplay's carefully constructed series of defence arguments, dramatised by Lahiff in the courtroom scenes as a conflict over reliable evidence and historical truth.

For Lahiff, the film represents an important legal case that changed the judicial system in South Australia. It also represents a particular moment in race relations in 1950s Australia, as race intersected with class in the Anglocentric city of Adelaide, a moment which the film seeks to bring to historical consciousness. This approach to the historical film as a correc-tive to national history understands cinema as a public sphere which can re-educate its audience by reconstructing and reinterpreting a significant traumatic event in the history of race relations. A crucial aspect of our understanding of backtracking in post-*Mabo* cinema is the way in which history, reconstructed as a courtroom melodrama in *Black and White*, speaks to the dilemmas of the present. In its depiction of flawed individuals committed to obtaining white justice for a black man in the 1950s, the film is firmly on the side of a 1990s politics of reconciliation. Yet its central courtroom drama, from which Ngoombujarra's character, Max Stuart, is largely excluded, reminds us that legal justice in the present is more important than historical empathy if reconciliation is to have any meaning. A sense of history as unfinished business pervades the film's ending, leaving the audience with an overriding sense of anticlimax, of hollow victory. This aura of pernicious, endemic failure, which surrounds all the white characters in the film, is relieved only by the documentary coda which allows Stuart to address us directly, not as a victim-survivor, nor as a 'real-life' witness to the events we have just seen dramatised, but as a kind of trickster or jester who, after all the effort of the film to clarify the facts of the case, leaves us with a bit of a riddle about evidence, truth and belief: Elvis really is dead. Isn't he?

Although the factual courtroom drama, based on the historical record, is the most prominent generic strand in *Black and White*, the film draws on several other genres, including costume melodrama, crime investigation, the modernist flashback, and even the road movie. This hybrid genre is more akin to Ngoombujarra's notion of history as epic storytelling. The mixing of genres produces a series of shifts between different emotional registers or affects. This incoherence of genre and affect has something to tell us about the limits of the historical film in communicating traumatic experience through a national cinema conceived as both a commercial-industrial and a cultural-interventionist public sphere. The incoherence of affect, together with the chronic sense of political, professional and personal failure in *Black and White*, have something to tell us about history, memory and storytelling in cinema after *Mabo*. The film's mix of the modernist flashback together with family melodrama and the crime thriller is a case in point.

In her description of 'trauma cinema' Janet Walker has described the problems that traumatic or catastrophic historical events present for memory and for the stylistic conventions of narrative film form:

> Like traumatic memories that feature vivid bodily and visual sensation over 'verbal narrative and context', these films are characterised by non-linearity, fragmentation, nonsynchronous sound, repetition, rapid editing and strange angles. And they approach the past through an unusual admixture of emotional affect, metonymic symbolism and cinematic flashbacks.[30]

Lahiff's use of the modernist flashback in *Black and White* is a gesture in the direction of Ngoombujarra's concept of cinema as a place of epic storytelling. The question of how traumatic stories are told, by whom, to whom, becomes evident in Lahiff's use of two characters as narrators of the same story from two opposing points of view. Lahiff's two narrated flashbacks are modernist in that they challenge the conventional use of the flashback to establish 'the truth' in historical films.

The modernist flashbacks, unlike the courtroom scenes in *Black and White*, belong (through the intensity of his performance) to Ngoombujarra, even though the first is narrated by his defender, O'Sullivan (Robert Carlyle), and the second by his prosecutor, Chamberlain (Charles Dance). Each flashback presents a persuasive re-enactment of Stuart's interrogation by the police. Each insists it is a truthful account of how Stuart's confession was either 'beaten out of him' by habitually brutal police (defender O'Sullivan's view), or 'laughed out of him' by wily interrogators (prosecutor Chamberlain's view). The first flashback is tied to the crime genre's ploy of challenging the defence to prove that a confession is false. O'Sullivan's naturalistic flashback represents the police as a tightly bonded working-class fraternity with a shared set of prejudices: without compunction they routinely manufacture the evidence they need to prove the guilt of the person they 'know' committed the crime; if that person is an itinerant worker and a 'half-caste', so much the better. The second flashback is less conventional, entailing a startling shift between the generic affect of the true crime story and the upper-class melodrama. While the crime thriller version, narrated by O'Sullivan, is presented as part of making a legal case for the defence of Stuart, the melodramatic version, narrated by Chamberlain, is addressed to an elegant dinner party hosted by Chamberlain's wife. Chamberlain's transgression of social etiquette brings to a head his failing upper-class marriage and his contempt for public opinion engineered by the bumptious Rupert Murdoch and his compliant newspaper editor. As the sequence intercuts between Chamberlain's flashback to the crime and the melodramatic tensions of the dinner party, the audience is offered a choice between genres. The contrast between the crime thriller and the upper-class melodrama leaves it up to our genre preference to judge which version of Stuart's confession is true: the social realist flashback of police brutality constructed from the point of view of the defence lawyer, or the melodramatic representation of Stuart's (alleged) rape and murder of a nine-year-old girl, emphatically narrated by the prosecutor to shock his high-society wife and her friends out of their media-manipulated sympathy for Stuart.

Black and White is modernist in that it leaves the viewer unsettled by this clash of genres, a representational strategy that says the truth is a matter of point of view and of storytelling conventions. In the end Stuart does not hang but he does go to gaol for fourteen years, leaving the viewer unsettled by the inconclusive outcome of the case. Ngoombujarra's award-winning performance (Best Male Actor at 2003 AFI awards) ensures that the enigma of Stuart and the pathos of his story dominate the film. However, the horror of the crime against the little girl, her story and her family's suffering, is buried in the legal and class war of attrition between the inarticulate O'Sullivan and the smoothly eloquent Chamberlain.

The intricacies of gender, class and race in *Black and White* do not resolve themselves in a seamless narrative structure. Rather, the film takes the viewer through jarring shifts in tone, mood and genre as it tries to condense the important historical facts, political stakes, and current reinterpretation of the Stuart case into the narrative conventions of commercial cinema. The resonance between the Stuart case and the history wars of the 1990s is clearly signalled in the way the film deals with two issues: language and evidence. The prosecution case rests on Stuart's signed confession and circumstantial evidence. The defence case goes through a series of changes, motivated by new evidence discovered in the course of trying to find any admissible evidence that will save Stuart from the death penalty. The testimony of an expert witness, T. G. H. Strehlow, is vital to demonstrating the non-fit between Stuart's first language, Aranda, his distinctive use of English, and the Queen's English used in the disputed confession. However, despite Strehlow's evidence, the Royal Commission remained unconvinced that the written version of Stuart's verbal confession had been unduly altered by the police. The efforts of the defence team to discredit the evidence are finally overshadowed by politics and the media's role in making Stuart a *cause célèbre*. The film's preoccupation with evidence resonates with current debates, led by Keith Windschuttle, about the fabrication of historical evidence and the whitewashing of frontier history, involving lawyers, academic experts and the media.[31] The film reverses Howard's media spin on a navel-gazing cultural elite imposing their unwelcome views on the battlers of working-class Australia. *Black and White*'s reprise of the 1950s shows an arrogant Adelaide political and social elite under pressure from the media and from the underdogs (O'Sullivan and Devaney), who insist on defending an Aboriginal man who has not been accorded a fair hearing by the police, the judiciary or the government, all of whom are white Anglo males. The history wars of the 1990s involve a similar cast of characters, disputing the facts of the past, the reliability of the evidence and the nature of post-colonial truth and justice. The difference is that in the history wars of the 1990s the roles have been reversed: those arguing for justice have been cast as the cultural elite while those defending the status quo have been cast as benign battlers.

Death and Recognition in *The Tracker*

Rolf de Heer's *The Tracker* also uses the past to refer to the present. The film's distinctive style includes contemporary painted images of the land as well as a haunting soundtrack of vivid lyrics by Aboriginal songwriter/singer Archie Roach. By depicting the Australian landscape as a mythic space, the film attempts to displace post-*Mabo* politics of recognition (with its discourse of guilt and shame) onto a set of archetypal figures and a self-consciously mythic narrative form. We argue that de Heer's attempt at a mythic account of a massacre of Aborigines during a fictional police tracking expedition set in 1922, 'somewhere in Australia', can be read as an allegory of the master–slave dynamic central to Hegel's concept of the struggle for recognition.

For Hegel, recognition is a fight to the death. The master refuses to recognise the slave in order to assert and maintain his own freedom. If the master were to recognise the slave he would risk non-recognition by the slave and therefore become the slave. This struggle is played out in *The Tracker*'s story of the relationship between The Tracker (David Gulpilil) and the police officer leading the party, named allegorically (as are all the characters) as The Leader (Gary Sweet). After becoming suspicious of The Tracker, The Leader shackles and chains him, immediately setting off a struggle between the two. In one scene, The Tracker attempts to free himself by plunging from a rocky cliff into a waterhole. Dragging The Leader with him, The Tracker tries to drown The Leader as the two men struggle in the murky water. The Tracker fails, but shortly after this incident the narrative reaches an unexpected turning point. After witnessing The Leader's summary killing of two tribal Aborigines camped in a dry riverbed, the young police officer, named The Follower, accuses The Leader of murder and arrests him at gunpoint. The Follower then frees The Tracker from the shackle and chains, using them to enchain the accused Leader. But the master–slave dynamic between The Tracker and The Leader continues as a fight to the death.

The nature of this fight for recognition is made clear in the film. As the party passes by the dead body of one of The Leader's victims, The Tracker drags the enchained Leader from his horse to the ground, forcing him to face the dead man before him. Here, a sequence of extreme close-ups of the face of the dead man, as well as reaction shots of both The Tracker and The Leader, invite the spectator to recognise the dead man's humanity as it is revealed in this face-to-face encounter with human mortality. The Leader, however, refuses to see in this way, turning instead to confront The Tracker. Biting down on his lip, he hisses that it is The Tracker who will die, for he has committed the unthinkable crime of enslaving a white man. At this point both The Tracker and the audience realise that in order for The Tracker to survive he must take justice into his own hands. This moment of realisation leads to the key question raised by the film's play with the master–slave dynamic of recognition, namely what is involved when the audience passionately wants the white leader to be hanged at the hands of the black tracker?

The film's setting up of an intense desire in spectators to see The Leader hanged marks a break in genre conventions. The conventional desire to see a 'baddie' blown away is out of character with the art cinema's commitment to ambiguity and ambivalence. More troubling, perhaps, is the fact that, in Hegelian terms, this desire for the murder of The Leader by non-Indigenous members of the audience constitutes a deathwish, a willing of themselves to be killed off. It is possible to read this desire as the dead end of white self-castigating guilt. However, we want to suggest something more positive by thinking about the audience's willingness to side with The Tracker in terms of an ethics of friendship and a principle of loyalty. This involves shifting attention away from the primary relation between The Tracker and The Leader to the relation between The Tracker and The Follower.

An essay on the ethics of friendship by Leela Ghandi is suggestive in this regard. Ghandi poses a question similar to the one raised in *The Tracker*: 'Does loyalty to "my own" liberate me of ethical obligations to all those who are not of my own nation, family, community, republic, revolution?'[32] This question, of ethical obligation to a stranger, is at the heart of The Follower's inner struggle leading up to his imprisonment of The Leader. Having made the decision to take this course of action, The Follower finds himself in a peculiar alignment with The Tracker. In the logic of spectatorship, the viewer is also positioned in this curious space: aligned with a stranger against 'a countryman' in a relation that is best described as a new friendship. Returning to the philosophers of ancient Greece, Ghandi explains that there are two classical models of the ethic of friendship. First, there is Aristotle's model of friendship based on the idea of *philia* and linked to citizenship. As Ghandi explains, citing Aristotle, in the Greek *polis*, ' "a friend is another self "; "The basis of affection between citizens is equality and similarity".'[33] In this model, friendship is at the service of the state, ensuring loyalty to the *polis* on the principle of sameness. We can see this dominant model at work, for example, in the Coalition of the Willing's declaration of war on Iraq in 2003. The second model of friendship, explains Ghandi, comes from Epicurus and is based on *philoxenia* – 'a love for guests, strangers, foreigners'.[34] This ethic of friendship 'is predicated upon a principled distaste for the racial exclusivity of the *polis*'.[35] In this sense, it is an ethic that could not abide the racial exclusivity of the Australian polity, which was founded on the White Australia policy and continues to underpin policies, such as the Pacific Solution, designed to deter and punish refugees. It is the Epicurean model of the ethic of friendship that we find most suggestive for our understanding of the spectator's dilemma in *The Tracker*.

In his decision to imprison his leader, The Follower enacts a shift in loyalty away from 'a countryman' towards 'a stranger'. Further, this shift in loyalty results in a tricky reversal of positions between The Follower and The Tracker. By aligning himself with The Tracker, The Follower commits a felony, as The Leader reminds him. Having taken the risk of becoming friends with The Tracker, The Follower becomes a stranger in The Tracker's eyes. And this is where things become most interesting, enabling a form of social recognition that takes us beyond the struggle to the death inherent in Hegel's struggle for recognition. The friendship between The Follower and The Tracker is premised on a recognition of difference but one that allows for an ethics of hospitality. The Tracker is now recognised as the one who is 'at home', welcoming The Follower to another's country where they are both strangers, or guests. Indeed, The Tracker's hospitality extends to a willingness to share cultural knowledge, opening the eyes of The Follower and the spectator to his cultural understanding of the land as 'country'. This is a relation to the land that eschews notions of ownership in favour of custodial obligation and belonging. The end of the film makes the meaning of country even clearer as The Tracker sets off on the long return journey to his own country. This scenario of hospitable exchange in another's country stands in contrast to the discourse of exile generated by neo-conservatives in the wake of *Mabo*. Responding to the Labor government's introduction of native title legislation in 1993, John Howard, then opposition leader, appeared on national television holding up a map of Australia and warning viewers that something like 90 per cent of the continent could be reclaimed by Aborigines under Keating's proposed legislation. The fear implanted by Howard was that native title legislation would make non-Indigenous Australians strangers in their own land.

On one level *The Tracker*'s mythic tale of massacre and other colonial atrocities arrives too late in the history wars, in that it is behind the times in its thinking about how best to remember traumatic colonial events. Upon its release the film did not attract the sort of attention that might have led to widespread debate of the kind generated by *Rabbit-Proof Fence*. Instead, interest in the film was limited to art-house audiences, leaving Keith Windschuttle's *Fabrication of Aboriginal History* at the centre of debates about how to explain and remember frontier massacres. On another level – and this is something we have discovered about many post-*Mabo* films – *The Tracker* comes too soon. The ethic of friendship and new forms of recognition we have read into the film is ahead of its time. Ongoing support for the Howard government's policies on national security indicates that an overwhelming majority of Australians accept friendship as a basic principle of democracy only if it is based on a notion of the friend 'as another self, as what is most similar'.

Recognition, Identity and Trauma in *Black Chicks Talking*

Historical and storytelling forms of memory and recognition are not limited to films that deal directly with the past. Cinema can invoke traumatic memories of past events in films set in the present. Leah Purcell's television program *Black Chicks Talking* is a documentary comprised of interviews between Purcell and five very different Aboriginal Australian women (identified as Deborah Mailman, Rosanna, Cilla, Tammy Williams and Kathryn). The program provides an opportunity for Aboriginal women to make a direct demand for settler Australians to recognise them as 'strong, black, beautiful women'. It does this by representing diverse experiences of being an Aboriginal woman. This diversity is linked to different regions of Australia from Bardi Jawi Country in the North Western Kimberleys, to Cherbourg in Murri State or Queensland, and Launceston in Palawa State or Tasmania. Further, *Black Chicks Talking* explores conflicts between the five women over the politics of claiming Aboriginality as an identity to be proud of. This is particularly acute in the encounters between the filmmaker and Kathryn, a former Miss Australia, who struggles to find the right words to describe her recently discovered identity as an Aboriginal woman.[36] 'I could say I'm Aboriginal or I could say I'm part Aboriginal', she tells Purcell. The issue of who is recognised as Aboriginal today is taken up by the other women as they discuss the legacy of shame attached to Aboriginality for some of their parents, and their own loss of language, culture and law.

The film intercuts on-location interviews with a gathering of Purcell and the five women at a dinner party in Sydney. This structure allows for two modes of storytelling: each woman speaks intimately, face to face, with Purcell; this contrasts with the dinner party gathering which allows the women to speak communally about their different experiences of Aboriginal identity. In addition, there is a sense in which the film is addressed to two audiences. For most of the program the address is to a racially neutral television viewer. However, there are occasions when some of the women directly address the viewer as white. One such moment is when Purcell and Mailman are in a conversation with each other about skin colour and insulting white words which were used by policymakers to separate children from their parents. Here, Mailman suddenly turns away from Purcell and, looking directly into the camera, says: 'Don't call us fucking half-caste, quarter-caste, one-eighth . . . because you're denying . . . everyone who's gone before us.' However, Kathryn, who is confronted with the absurdity of being 'one-sixteenth' Aboriginal, is unsure of what it means for her future identity to be recognised as the first Miss Australia of 'Aboriginal descent'. What she longs for is just one story from her mother that would tell her where she comes from as an Aboriginal woman.

If we apply the idea of shock and recognition to Purcell's documentary, we can explain what is at stake when the program asserts a collective Aboriginal identity, but also introduces conflict arising from radically different experiences of being a black woman in contemporary Australia. This conflict between the women themselves over how to represent their identity allows viewers to recognise the trauma of colonialism. What we hear in the interviews is a series of testimonies about being a black woman in Australia today. But we also witness at the dinner party the inexpressible anxiety that the experience of colonisation has produced about identity. This is most pronounced in the juxtaposition between Kathryn, the former Miss Australia (1999), and Cilla, young mother of six (four girls and two boys). Kathryn struggles with the question of how and, indeed, *if* she should take up 'the gift of Aboriginality', as she calls it, hitherto hidden from her by her Aboriginal mother, who remains silent on Kathryn's matrilineal heritage. On the other hand, Cilla claims she is 'not in any way special because I'm Aboriginal', bearing witness, surely, to the reality of her life as a member of one of Australia's poorest and most disenfranchised social groups. In terms of the difficulties of recognition posed for individuals by Australia's colonial history, the documentary is compelling because it allows the viewer to recognise the legacy of pain and suffering that arises from the violence of *terra nullius*. In other words, *Black Chicks Talking* makes evident a form of political identity that is grounded in the conflict between recognition (as a proud Aboriginal woman) and non-recognition (as a half-caste, quarter-caste) as Tammy says, 'reducing our culture to pigmentation'. Purcell's documentary expresses the full meaning of historical dispossession through the trauma of Aboriginal identity played out in the present.

Rethinking Australian national cinema through the constellation of terms discussed above offers new ways of understanding the relationship between Australian films and audiences in local, national and global contexts. Just as the Australian cinema of the past decade has backtracked across the well-trodden ground of national identity in order to find new paths, this book seeks to reconsider the role of national cinema in a global politics of history, memory and identity. In the following chapters we consider three key issues: the commercial and cultural strategies which shaped the response of the Australian film industry to the post-*Mabo* history wars; the aftershock of the *Mabo* decision and its impact on the landscape tradition in Australian cinema, from the iconic desert to the bush, the city, the suburbs and the beach; and the role of trauma and grief in a cinema concerned with the nation's coming of age.

Notes

1 Gulpilil's screen persona was established in *Walkabout* (Nicholas Roeg, 1971), *Mad Dog Morgan* (Philippe Mora, 1976), *Storm Boy* (Henri Safran, 1976), and *The Last Wave* (Peter Weir, 1977).
2 Tim Rowse, *After Mabo: Interpreting Indigenous Traditions*, Melbourne University Press, 1993, p. 2.
3 For a vivid account of colonial contact based on journals and letters of the First Fleeters see Inga Clendinnen, *Dancing with Strangers*, Melbourne: Text Publishing, 2003.
4 Henry Reynolds, *Aboriginal Sovereignty: Reflections on Race, State and Nation*, Sydney: Allen & Unwin, 1996, p. x.
5 ibid., p. x.
6 *Mabo and others v. Queensland (no 2) 107, Australian Law Reports* (ALR), 1992, p. 42.
7 For a concise and informative critique of legal challenges to the *Mabo* (1992) decision, including Western Australia's unsuccessful 1995 challenge, as well as challenges to the *Wik* (1995) decision, which led to the Native Title Amendment Bill (1997) (Cth) or 'NTAB', see Garth Nettheim, 'Native Title, fictions and "convenient falsehoods"', in *In the Wake of Terra Nullius*, a special issue of *Law.Text.Culture*, 4(1) 1998, pp. 70–80.
8 Newspoll, Saulwick & Muller and Hugh Mackay, 'Public Opinion on Reconciliation'. In Michelle Grattan (ed.), *Reconciliation: Essays on Australian Reconciliation*, Melbourne: Black Inc., 2000, p. 35.
9 Andreas Huyssen, 'Present pasts: media, politics, amnesia'. In Arjun Appadurai (ed.), *Globalization*, Durham and London: Duke University Press, 2001, p. 60.
10 ibid., p. 61.
11 ibid., p. 68.
12 ibid., p. 63.
13 ibid., p. 63.
14 Paul Keating, 'The Redfern Park Speech'. In Grattan, *Reconciliation*, pp. 60–4.
15 Mark McKenna, 'Different perspectives on black armband history', Australian Parliamentary Library Research Paper 5, 1997–98.

16 Geoffrey Blainey, 'Drawing up a balance sheet on our history', *Quadrant*, 37(7–8) 1993, pp. 10–15.

17 On the history wars in Australia, see Stuart Macintyre and Anna Clark, *The History Wars*, Melbourne University Press, 2003. On debates on frontier conflict, see Robert Manne (ed.), *Whitewash: On Keith Windschuttle's Fabrication of Aboriginal History*, Melbourne: Black Inc. Agenda, 2003 and *Frontier Conflict: The Australian Experience*, Canberra: National Museum of Australia, 2003. For an account of neo-conservative responses to *Bringing Them Home* (1997), the report of the national inquiry into the Stolen Generations, see Robert Manne, 'In denial: the stolen generations and the right', *Quarterly Essay*, no. 1, 2001. Also see Tim Flannery, 'Beautiful lies: population and environment in Australia', *Quarterly Essay*, no. 9, 2003; David Malouf, 'Made in England: Australia's British inheritance', *Quarterly Essay*, no. 12, 2003; and Germaine Greer, 'Whitefella jump up: the shortest way to nationhood', *Quarterly Essay*, no. 11, 2003.

18 See Susan Dermody and Elizabeth Jacka, *The Screening of Australia*, vol. 2: *Anatomy of National Cinema*, Sydney: Currency Press, 1988; Ross Gibson, *South of the West*, Bloomington and Indianapolis IN: Indiana University Press, 1992; Tom O'Regan, *Australian National Cinema*, London and New York: Routledge, 1996; William Routt, 'On the expression of colonialism in early Australian films'. In A. Moran and T. O'Regan (eds), *An Australian Film Reader*, Sydney: Currency Press, 1985; Graeme Turner, *National Fictions: Literature, Film and the Construction of Australian Narrative*, Sydney: Allen & Unwin, 1986 and 1993.

19 See Linnell Secomb, 'Interrupting mythic community', *Cultural Studies Review*, 9(1) 2003, pp. 85–100.

20 *The Tracker* (Rolf de Heer, 2002); *Beneath Clouds* (Ivan Sen, 2002); *Rabbit-Proof Fence* (Phillip Noyce, 2002); *One Night the Moon* (Rachel Perkins, 2001); *Black and White* (Craig Lahiff, 2002), *Yolngu Boy* (Stephen Johnson, 2001).

21 Huyssen, 'Present pasts'.

22 See Walter Benjamin, 'The work of art in the age of mechanical reproduction'. In Hannah Arendt (ed.), *Illuminations*, transl. Harry Zohn, London: Fontana, 1992, pp. 211–44.

23 Walter Benjamin, '"N" (re: the theory of knowledge, theory of progress)', transl. Leigh Hafrey and Richard Sieburth, in Gary Smith (ed.), *Benjamin: Philosophy, Aesthetics, History*, University of Chicago Press, 1989, pp. 43–82.

24 'Special Debate: Trauma and Screen Studies', ed. Susannah Radstone, *Screen*, 42(2) 2001, pp. 188–215.

25 ibid., pp. 191–2.

26 See for instance Miriam Hansen, 'America, Paris, the Alps: Kracauer and Benjamin on cinema and modernity'. In Leo Charney and Vanessa Schwartz (eds), *Cinema and the Invention of Modern Life*, Berkeley and Los Angeles: University of California Press, 1995.

27 Nova Cinema, Carlton, 23 October 2002.

28 Walter Benjamin, 'The storyteller: reflections on the works of Nikolai Leskov'. In Arendt, *Illuminations*.

29 *Broken English* is part of *Blood Brothers*, a Film Australia series of documentaries produced and directed by Ned Lander, Rachel Perkins and Trevor Graham.

30 Janet Walker, 'Trauma cinema: false memories and true experience', *Screen*, 42(2) 2001, p. 214.

31 Keith Windschuttle, *The Fabrication of Aboriginal History*: vol. 1, *Van Diemen's Land 1803–1947*, Sydney: Macleay Press, 2002.
32 Leela Ghandi, 'Friendship and postmodern utopianism', *Cultural Studies Review*, 9(1) 2003, p. 15.
33 Ghandi, 'Friendship and postmodern utopianism', p. 17.
34 ibid., p. 18.
35 ibid.
36 This issue opens the published interview between Purcell and Kathryn Hay in Leah Purcell, *Black Chicks Talking*, Sydney: Hodder, 2002, pp. 213–48.

2
Home and Abroad in *Moulin Rouge, The Dish* and *Lantana*

When Russell Crowe became the inaugural winner of the Global Achievement Award at the nationally televised 2001 Australian Film Institute (AFI)
Awards, he ended his acceptance speech with the provocative words, 'God
bless America'. It was not hard to imagine the assembled film and television
industry catching its collective breath. Only two years before, in 1999, the
AFI Awards had provided a public platform for the industry's attack on the
High Court's decision that New Zealand programs would henceforth qualify
as Australian content when broadcast on free-to-air commercial television.[1]
In 2003 the AFI Awards ceremony once again became a public forum for the
industry's vociferous attack on the bilateral trade agreement being negoti-
ated with the United States. For a national feature film industry struggling
to extract more than 5–7 per cent of the nation's annual box office revenue
from Australian cinema-goers, Crowe's words must have felt like a rude
betrayal of the home-grown industry that had nurtured his talent.[2] So it
is not hard to imagine a collective sigh of relief going through the audito-
rium when Crowe added, after a perfectly timed pause, 'And thank God for
Australia'. In 2002, accepting the award for his leading role in *The Tracker*,
David Gulpilil, again with impeccable timing, responded to the ovation with
a laid-back one-liner, 'Thanks. I deserve this.' Unlike Crowe, Gulpilil did
not get to deliver a preamble or elaborate on his punchline, at least to the
television viewers, who were immediately diverted to a commercial break.
It is unlikely that the startled moment of incomprehension, followed by
the laughter of recognition in response to both Crowe and Gulpilil, would
make much sense outside the context of the Australian film and television
industry and its relatively small national and international audience. Within
the genre of a televised industry awards night, Crowe's and Gulpilil's words
stand out as a kind of shorthand for issues and debates that have defined the
Australian film industry throughout its history. As a medium-sized industry
which attracts some level of subsidy and protection, Australian cinema has
to compete, at home and abroad, with Hollywood popular cinema, as well as

British and European national cinemas. At the same time, with deregulation of the Australian economy, the local production industry has become more engaged with the global market.

As a result of national recognition and international exposure, both Crowe and Gulpilil have entered the annals of great cinema talents, with *L.A Confidential* (1997) as Crowe's international breakthrough and *Rabbit-Proof Fence* (Phillip Noyce, 2002) and *The Tracker* (Rolf de Heer, 2002) as Gulpilil's return to form on national and international screens. However, the difference in the terms of Crowe's and Gulpilil's visibility raises the perennial question of how to characterise Australian cinema. Tom O'Regan makes a convincing argument that it is best regarded as a medium-sized national cinema, lacking coherence as a subsidised local industry, and as an English-language team player in international cinema.[3] Crowe is now a blockbuster star in transnational Hollywood, his career bookended by two films which represent a trajectory from the intensely local, independent Australian film *Romper Stomper* (Geoffrey Wright, 1992) to the spectacularly transnational blockbuster *Master and Commander* (Peter Weir, 2003). By contrast, Gulpilil is the canny stayer whose local career has been bookended by the European vision of directors Nicholas Roeg (*Walkabout*, 1971) and Rolf de Heer (*The Tracker*, 2002). Crowe has transcended his New Zealand birth and his Australian coming of age to become a Hollywood Oscar winner. As a star with deal-making power, his access to a range of leading roles is now unconstrained by issues of national identity. Gulpilil's international exposure has been contained within the art-house niche reserved for Indigenous Australians in world cinema. Gulpilil's screen persona has been defined by the way he has played to and undercut the Eurocentric fantasy of an exotic or mystical figure, somewhere between the canny black tracker and the noble savage. Gulpilil achieved international visibility with his comic undercutting of audience expectations of authentic tribal Aboriginality in *Crocodile Dundee* (Peter Faiman, 1986). However, the reception in January 2004 of *The Tracker* by critics in the United States as 'a decent little exercise in nativist outrage', marked by Gulpilil's 'startling authority', 'furious moral certainty' and 'mystical aura of a man . . . in touch with the earth', indicates that Gulpilil's current screen persona revives the exoticism of *Walkabout* and combines it with the post-colonial moral authority invested in an Aboriginal elder.[4] This persona has been complicated by Darlene Johnson's portrayal of Gulpilil in his everyday life in the television documentary *One Red Blood* (2002).[5] In 2004, Crowe's ever-expanding career options contrast with Gulpilil's stop-start career pattern (typical of the local industry). Given the successful export of Australian talent to Hollywood over many decades, the jury might still be out on whether Russell Crowe was the most deserving recipient of the AFI's first Global Achievement Award. However, within the genre of national cinema, Gulpilil's 'I deserve this' speaks volumes (about surviving as a *local* actor for more than three decades) to an industry conversant with its own transient history and tenuous status within international cinema. For Crowe, national identity is no hindrance to a wide range of on-screen roles, whether neo-Nazi skinhead in Melbourne, gay son of cool dad in Sydney, cop in Los Angeles, gladiator in ancient Rome, whistleblower or mathematician in America, or ship's captain on the high seas. For Gulpilil, every screen role is contained within the boundaries of a national cinema which returns at unpredictable intervals to questions about the authoritative place (mythic, historical, spiritual, cultural) of Aboriginality in Australian identity. Crowe carries no such burden in his on-screen roles, although he may be called upon to speak for the national industry off screen.

This chapter will venture into the thicket of questions to do with globalisation, local industry strategies, and national cinema by looking at three films, *Moulin Rouge* (Baz Luhrmann), *The Dish* (Rob Sitch) and *Lantana* (Ray Lawrence) which competed at the 2001 AFI awards (the year of Crowe's speech). These three films adopt commercial-industrial strategies for negotiating the local, the national and the global. The next chapter will look at a cultural-interventionist strategy developed by Bridget Ikin of SBS Independent Television (SBSi) to fund a package of films released in 2002 (the year of Gulpilil's speech). The thorniness of these issues can be felt in the nexus and dissonance between the forces that have shaped Crowe's international career ('God bless America') and fostered Gulpilil's longevity ('I deserve this'), in a financially protected but creatively independent ('Thank God for Australia') film industry. Keeping in mind that the blessings of global Hollywood have been visited unevenly upon the three different sectors (production, distribution, exhibition) of the Australian film industry, this chapter will backtrack over the idea that Australian cinema might be re-imagined as a genre (or type) of international cinema.[6] As a genre, Australian cinema is characterised by two main strategies, the commercial-industrial (mainly initiated by the private sector) and the cultural-interventionist (mainly initiated by the public sector). These strategies are broadly shaped by the way economic and cultural policies have regularly fallen out of step with each other since deregulation of the Australian economy became gospel for both major political parties in the 1980s. More particularly, this chapter looks at three films in terms of their industrial-commercial strategies within a national economic and cultural policy framework which positions Australian cinema as an international genre.

24

Australian Cinema as a Genre of International Cinema

If we think of Australian cinema as a genre, and of the 2001 and 2002 AFI awards as post-*Mabo* moments within the genre, it is possible to explain how the audience recognised precisely where Crowe and Gulpilil were coming from, locally and internationally. Genre allows us to think about the expectations and knowledge the 'generic' audience brings to an occasion like the AFI awards. This notion of a generic audience assumes there is a constellation of people with varying degrees of arcane knowledge derived from a shared history of viewing Australian film and television since the cultural renaissance of the 1970s. This concept saves us from reverting to the dubious idea that the audience for Australian cinema shares an innate sense of national identity expressed through both Crowe and Gulpilil as icons of national cinema. This view might argue that Crowe is the Australian actor who has most successfully taken the iconic Anglo-Celtic male, the larrikin-ocker of 1970s Australian film and television, and transformed it through a series of character roles into a transnational figure.[7] And that Gulpilil's performances since *Walkabout* have rung the changes in cinema's stock figure of the Australian Aboriginal, to the extent that Gulpilil stands for a type of national character, story or landscape that is specific, local, and non-transferably Australian. However, if we put national identity to one side for a moment and take up the idea of Australian cinema as an international genre, then the gap between the transnational (Russell Crowe) and the local (David Gulpilil) starts to become comprehensible as a field of play that is more flexible and more varied than the circumscribed idea of national cinema. In this playing field, economic and cultural politics are more important than the slippery slide of national identity for understanding the Australian 'accent' in international cinema.

Several things are implied in the idea of genre as a field of play. The first is that a national cinema is recognisable to audiences as a set of conventions or norms. From this perspective, Australian cinema is marked by particular types of characters (laconic males of the recessive, ocker or larrikin category); iconic landscapes (the outback, the bush, the suburbs, the beach); narrative patterns (melancholy defeat or wry acceptance of things-as-they-are); and aesthetic choices (low budget, independent, naturalistic). The second idea implied by genre is that there is a generic audience of critics and viewers who have a range of expectations of the genre based on cumulative knowledge and debate about the films and about the industry (for instance, the Australian road movie of the 1990s borrows elements from New Hollywood road movies, but it also adds local elements: the characters tend to depart from Sydney or Melbourne in a hurry, encountering an assortment of ugly Australians along the road; they reach a crisis point involving criminal misdeeds and sexual misunderstandings in the outback, often north of Adelaide or back of Bourke, and return to the coastal fringe for an ambivalent, ironic ending). The third idea entailed in genre is that genre films function for their generic audience as either mythic or ideological solutions to ongoing, unreconciled social conflicts.[8] In this sense, Australian films might appeal to particular local and international audiences for the way they backtrack over the dilemmas of a minor English-speaking nation negotiating a place for itself in global politics on the basis of its former status as a far-flung dominion of the British Empire, and, since the Second World War, as a South Pacific deputy to the current world superpower, the United States of America.[9] Shifting perceptions of nationhood entailed in the nation's social imaginary, from Anglophile White Australia, to multicultural settler nation, to cosmopolitan labour force in the Asia-Pacific region, are also part of what defines the experience of Australian cinema for its generic audience.[10]

Further, the post-*Mabo* period might be understood as a particularly *open* moment in the history of the genre of Australian cinema.[11] As well as trying to assert itself in a global economy dominated by a handful of transnational media conglomerates, the post-*Mabo* film (together with its generic audience of viewers and critics) signifies the return of unreconciled national issues, at the very moment when a cinema of national identity seems most redundant.[12] This vigorous return of a national agenda for Australian cinema is remarkable for two reasons. The first is the long history of bipartisan support for economic policies which regulate and subsidise the local film and television industry as part of a transnational media market.[13] These economic policies demand that the industry be commercial, efficient and competitive in the international market. Yet, for three decades, the film production industry (focusing on drama and documentary forms) has successfully agitated for the cultural protection of Australian stories against a flood of cheap imports which, it is argued, pose a threat to national identity, much as the imported cane toad threatens the local environment. The second is the Howard government's apparent resolve to replace left-liberals with neo-conservatives on the boards of key cultural organisations (including ABC and SBS Television and the National Museum).[14] The neo-conservative aim is to restore a strong sense of unity and pride to the nation based on an Anglocentric model of national identity, borrowed from One Nation.[15] The outcome is a post-*Mabo* cinema which is subject to a major contradiction. On the one hand, Australian cinema's international strategies display clear evidence of the bipartisan economic policies which promote a commercial-industrial ethos, despite a necessary level of government subsidy and protection. On the other, the post-*Mabo* culture war between left-liberals and neo-conservatives battling for control of the social imaginary is evident in the startling difference between the feature films that contended for AFI Awards in 2001 and 2002. The prominent films from each year represent a divide between a commercial-industrial ethos and an ethos of cultural intervention. However, as will become apparent in the next chapter, the two sides of the culture wars do not divide neatly into commercial entrepreneurs and cultural apparatchiks.

The idea of a national cinema as a field of international play has been given leverage by the clash between economic and cultural objectives since the election of Hawke's ALP government in 1983 and the defeat of Paul Keating's ALP government by John Howard's Liberal Coalition in 1996. To explore the kinds of moves that have been made in this playing field, our focus for the remainder of this chapter will shift from Crowe and Gulpilil to three films that competed at the 2001 AFI Awards, each adopting different commercial-industrial strategies within the genre of Australian cinema. The next chapter will look at two films that emerged as part of a package deal between cultural and film funding bodies in 2002 through the intervention of SBSi in the culture wars.

Commercial–Industrial Ethos and Local–Global Strategies in *Moulin Rouge, The Dish* and *Lantana*

One way of mapping the local-global as a national policy issue with textual/aesthetic outcomes is to take Baz Luhrmann's *Moulin Rouge* and Working Dog's *The Dish* as benchmark films for local engagement with New Hollywood's global blockbuster economy. If *Moulin Rouge* takes up the challenge of New Hollywood's ultra high-budget spectacle of digital effects, funded by Twentieth Century Fox, *The Dish* resorts to a low-budget, televisual deployment of a resilient populist nationalism, one that resonates wryly with Howard's oft-cited vision for a 'relaxed and comfortable' Australia and his more recent profile as junior partner to Bush and Blair in the Coalition of the Willing's war on Iraq in 2003. The film standing between the blockbuster spectacle and the populist comedy-drama at the 2001 AFI awards was *Lantana*, which stole the show from both *Moulin Rouge* and *The Dish*, reaffirming a middle-brow film industry's sceptical relation to both global Hollywood and local television as models for aspiring commercial auteurs.

The Dish and *Moulin Rouge* appear to exemplify the tension between inward-looking Australian films, preoccupied with familiar types of characters in familiar landscapes, and outward-oriented, international films that pitch themselves to an international marketplace by drawing on local talent and facilities to become a branch of the global infotainment industry. The inward-looking films tend to be low-key comedy-dramas exploring downwardly mobile or marginalised milieux in old (Anglo-Celtic) or new (multicultural) vernaculars. The global films made in Australia, such as the *Matrix* trilogy, tend to use digital effects to create imaginary cities or worlds that are ubiquitous rather than geographically located.[16] Between these two extremes, *Lantana* is more typical of run-of-the mill, outward-looking films whose budgets are eclipsed ten times over by that of Sydney Fox Studio's local blockbuster, *Moulin Rouge*. Although its locations make it a Sydney film, *Lantana* draws on the international genre of the crime thriller to explore middle-class life in a cosmopolitan rather than national context.

Although there appears to be a clear divide between the global and the local film, even the most resolutely parochial Australian films are attuned to trends in international cinema. Exemplifying the dialectic between the global and the local, both *Moulin Rouge* and *The Dish* might be considered as event films in the same way that the International Sydney Olympics of 2000 was simultaneously a global and national media event. Both films exhibit the Olympian ambition to stage the greatest show on earth, *Moulin Rouge* as spectacle and *The Dish* as allegory. However, despite a shared interest in enhancing Australia's place on the global map (through a combination of technology and concept), *Moulin Rouge* and *The Dish* adopt opposing strategies for getting into the international marketplace.

With a reported budget of US$52.5 million, *Moulin Rouge* is clearly competing offshore with the Hollywood blockbuster (it opened in Australia against Steven Spielberg's historical blockbuster *Pearl Harbor*). With an estimated (Australian average) budget of AUS$5–6 million, *The Dish*, through its distribution deal with media conglomerate Time-Warner, was clearly aiming for an independent breakthrough hit in national and international markets. Taking into account the vast difference in production and marketing budgets, *Moulin Rouge* and *The Dish* share some common ground. Both engage with the dominant New Hollywood form, the blockbuster, and both keep the European market (which now includes Britain) and cultural heritage within their sights. In the case of *The Dish*, Australia's national status is an explicit issue and informs the film's sly address to the Australian, British and American markets. In the case of *Moulin Rouge*, Australianness is effaced only to return as a hybrid, postmodern (distinctively Sydney) sensibility, one that seems entirely at odds with *The Dish*'s tongue-in-cheek style of populist nostalgia for a benignly bucolic Australia. However, both films have been produced as antipodal engagements with New Hollywood in both economic and textual senses.[17]

Spectacular Party People in *Moulin Rouge*

In an article on specularity in *Bram Stoker's Dracula* (Francis Ford Coppola, 1992), Thomas Elsaesser describes the emblematic New Hollywood film as the high concept blockbuster, directed by a 'power baby' or Movie Brat, financed and marketed by a US media conglomerate, and distributed via satellite-cable-video technologies.[18] The New Hollywood style is characterised by digital sound and image technologies, new temporal structures and 'the mania for citation'.[19] Moreover, the hybridity and intertextuality of the New Hollywood film since the mid-1970s exhibits the movie brats' 'self-conscious use of old mythologies, genre stereotypes, and the history of cinema itself'.[20] This knowledge of cinema history, expressed as an element of style, produces a double address to the spectator as both naive and ironic, innocent and knowing.[21] Elsaesser argues that in the high concept blockbuster film 'the vigorous refiguring of the text and its limits . . . joins economic with textual excess'.[22] The priority given to audiovisual impact and citation produces new temporal forms (time-travel, multi-strand narratives, open endings enabling sequels), and 'shape-shifting' rather than consistent character identity.[23] In terms of spectatorship, the New Hollywood film displaces voyeuristic and fetishistic identification in favour of aural and visual engulfment, which Elsaesser describes as 'producing a more corporeal set of perceptions' typical of 'the multimedia viewing experience'.[24] Viewers and critics are thereby deemed capable of responding in a variety of classical or post-classical ways to the New Hollywood mode, resulting in incompatible understandings and judgements of the films, clearly evident in the critical reception of *Moulin Rouge*.

Reviews of *Moulin Rouge* tend to agree on one point – the visual and aural excesses of Baz Luhrmann's follow-up to *Strictly Ballroom* and *William Shakespeare's Romeo & Juliet* (1996) produce a delirious, disorienting, sensory assault on the viewer. The effect of Baz Luhrmann's 'red curtain' style and New Hollywood's high concept blockbuster is much like the combination of ecstasy and rave parties. For some of the film's generic audience, *Moulin Rouge* is a party film, a postmodern homage to popular music and the craze for dance parties: very camp, very Mardi Gras, very Sydney. To other members of the generic audience, *Moulin Rouge* is a step forward for the local special effects industry, but it also represents a downgrading of national cinema into an offshore service industry for global Hollywood. This is reflected in the AFI awards, where *Moulin Rouge* was snubbed by the voters (key members of the generic audience for Australian cinema). A series of craft awards for special effects damned the film with faint praise. This snub by the industry followed a rejection of the investors' bid for tax concessions under 10B, with the Australian Taxation Office refusing to collude in tax avoidance schemes involving large corporations and financial institutions.[25]

Reviewers are also sharply divided in their evaluation of the film's engulfing spectacle: on the one hand the film is rejected for its banal plot, its lack of depth, its superficial characters and its music video style; on the other, it is praised for its spectacular, postmodern pastiche of images and music. Sustained interest in the film lies in the excess of both its digital effects and its layers of audiovisual sampling and citation. For some reviewers the issue of the film's Australian identity is at stake. The film has been vigorously defended as a non-American blockbuster by *Sydney Morning Herald* reviewer Paul Sheehan, who revels in the distance between *Moulin Rouge* and Australia's last international blockbuster, *Crocodile Dundee*.[26] Local defenders of the film are quick to point to the Australian creative team, Rupert Murdoch's money, Nicole Kidman's starring role, a supporting cast of Australian talent, the two British imports, Ewan McGregor and Jim Broadbent, and the one American import, John Leguizano. Further, as Sheehan argues, '*Moulin Rouge* is a brilliant extension of Australia's trademark niche in the global film industry – hypertheatre'. Luhrmann's artistic sensibility, too, has been defended as Australian in so far as he has invented, in his red curtain trilogy, a 'cinematic language' which is 'particularly Australian'.[27]

An alternative critical strategy treats *Moulin Rouge* as either an attempt to revive the musical or as a failed epic experiment on a par with the auteurist hubris of Francis Ford Coppola's *One From the Heart* (1982) and Michael Cimino's *Heaven's Gate* (1980). In this context Adrian Martin describes *Moulin Rouge* as 'the campest film folly since the days of Erich von Stroheim'.[28] Much of the criticism of *Moulin Rouge* is divided over the value of the film's rapidly edited snatches of song and dance (rather than full-length show-stoppers in the classical tradition). The film has been scrutinised for its soulless appeal to the DVD generation of 'internet squatters' and 'culture vultures in a fast-forward media environment'.[29] At the same time it has been lauded for its hybridity: 'MGM vs MTV, Busby Berkeley on ecstasy, Fred and Ginger . . . with equal measures of love and irony – on top of a mardi gras float . . . a time-travelling, medium-hopping musical'.[30]

The delirious 'time-travelling, medium-hopping' hypertheatre of *Moulin Rouge* speaks directly to Elsaesser's analysis of the specular engulfment which characterises New Hollywood. The film's temporal conceit (late 20th-century pop songs reprised in a 21st-century transnational film set in a 19th-century Paris nightclub made famous by a Toulouse-Lautrec poster) exploits cinema's ahistorical capacity, speaking to a late modern, post-national, melting pot sense of identity which takes the ubiquity of popular culture (from postcards and posters, operas and myths to Monroe and Madonna) as its reference point. Just as the cinema of specularity can be experienced as classical or post-classical, as naive or sophisticated, *Moulin Rouge* can evoke national and post-national takes on identity. In terms of economic and textual excess it is an international film, with signs of Australianness effaced in favour of signs of Sydney not as a place but as a sense of style. Although *Moulin Rouge* revels in *fin-de-siècle* Paris as the digitally re-imaged capital of 19th-century modernity, the film's own *fin-de-siècle* sensibility is grounded in Sydney as a style capital of late 20th-century modernity. The film's high concept Sydney style has been honed by the annual spectacle of the Gay and Lesbian Mardi Gras, brought into international recognition by the staging of the Sydney 2000 Olympics, underwritten financially by Sydney's Fox Studios, and enhanced digitally by special effects company Animal Logic. However, although high concept spectacle is not the only option in the international marketplace, its global influence is a determining factor for Australian film as a genre of international cinema.

Benign Battlers in *The Dish*

Although they share the same editor, Jill Bilcock, *Moulin Rouge* and *The Dish* appear to occupy opposite sides of the post-classical/classical divide which characterises contemporary cinema. However, no film which pitches itself at the American market is uncontaminated by the blockbuster. As an independent, low-budget film with a potential blockbuster theme (the American moon landing of 1969), *The Dish* deploys the blockbuster's infantilised affect of awe and wonder to emulate the boy's-own adventure films of Hollywood's original high concept brats of the 1970s, Lucas and Spielberg.[31] Although its production budget does not stretch to blockbuster effects, *The Dish* uses archival footage and pop music as well as American characters (the Ambassador, the man from NASA) to project itself into the American market (through a distribution deal with media conglomerate Time-Warner) as an antipodal or reverse image of the blockbuster film. The film expresses admiration for the blockbuster's universalising theme (world peace imagined as an international audience of television viewers united in awe, tears and wonder as an American flag is planted on the moon). At the same time, *The Dish* takes the mickey out of politics and history, producing an ironic distance from the world stage by foregrounding small-town characters who, even as they rise to the occasion, seem to have the exact measure of their place in world events. Just as the modest team of dish workers (embodied by Sam Neill's pipe-smoking, cardigan-clad, self-effacing man of science, Cliff) honours the higher purpose behind the overreaching ambition of NASA, *The Dish* honours the blockbuster, asking only to occupy the space in the American market reserved for the independent, breakthrough hit. However, just as Parkes and Honeysuckle Creek remained invisible to the international audience of 600 million television viewers as the source of the images of the 1967 moon landing, *The Dish* remained an event only in the Australian film industry. *The Dish*, like the Australian contribution to the moonwalk, is a routine event in international cinema, just one in a series of small-scale marketing events eclipsed by the saturation coverage given to the release of the year's Hollywood blockbusters.

But what kind of event is *The Dish* in Australian cinema? The geopolitical space of Australian cinema is anticipated by the film's tongue-in-cheek account of 'the greatest story never told'. The film's art-directed nostalgia for the 1960s works against any serious attempt to pinpoint Australia's coming of age as a team player in the infotainment industry. The makeshift moment of making it to the international team is cut down to size when the Prime Minister's advisor announces with succinct humour, 'We've got the moonwalk.' The television comedy group Working Dog, with hits like the ABC-TV series *Frontline* (1994–97) and its first feature film, *The Castle* (1997), has the proven ability to tap into a vein of populist national sentiment. This is achieved through its trademark self-deprecating humour combined with an affection for the battler – tapping into familiar Australian strategies for responding to an economic, cultural and political position of relative weakness, leavened by close ties to superpowers. Yet for all the newfound national pride exhibited by the film's characters at the end of *The Dish*, there is a defensive, almost apologetic tone in the film's nostalgic rendition of Australia's chance to play in the big league. This sense of being second-rate has something to do with the American market's indifference to the Australian-made product, a repetition of *The Castle*'s limited exportability, despite its home-grown success. This limited success is repeated in the local interest and international indifference which greeted Working Dog's sly attempt to go beyond the parochial in *The Dish* by borrowing an American event and marketing it to the world from a down-under perspective.

Like Australian television drama, *The Dish* did well with the national audience in 2001 (earning around $18 million compared to *Moulin Rouge's* $25.5 million, with the Hollywood animation, *Shrek*, in number one position, earning $29 million at the Australian box office in 2001).[32] Yet beyond raw box office figures (which fail to reflect key marketing factors like saturation television advertising, multi-screen release patterns, star power, distribution deals with cinema chains, and a limited release pattern for independent and foreign films in the North American market) the impact of *The Dish* on international markets is much harder to measure. However, the film itself anticipates the disparity between national aspiration and international reception. The widescreen version of the film provides a large canvas for small-town, parish-pump themes of purported universal significance. However, the film's chronic deflation of its own widescreen perspective on Australian history is evident in its repeated, awestruck shots of the Parkes radio telescope, shots which are doubly deflated by the film's ironic title, *The Dish*, and by the telescope's rural location, referred to as 'a sheep paddock'. This strategy of awestruck deflation provides an Australian perspective on Hollywood's blockbuster film industry, undercutting excess and over-achievement, valuing an optimal contribution rather than an ethic of maximum exploitation epitomised by both the NASA space program and the blockbuster. Through repeated contrasts of scale and tone between NASA and Parkes, *The Dish* makes a virtue of the necessity of being a minor player in an international league. It is in this sense that *The Dish* owes its better moments to the bumbling spirit of Britain's Ealing comedies rather than to the Hollywood high concept industry.

Anxious Flesh in *Lantana*

A curious feature of the 2001 AFI awards was the sureness with which *Lantana* stole the show from its major competitors, edging *Moulin Rouge* into the craft awards and eclipsing *The Dish* (a disappearing act in terms of film awards, despite success at home and its enviable distribution deal with Time-Warner). *Lantana*, like *The Dish*, belongs to a cluster of mundane Australian films which routinely negotiate tensions between cinematic spectacle and televisual naturalism, between a sophisticated, outward-looking spectacle and a naive, inward-looking (though canny) populism. For the purposes of this chapter, *Lantana* represents a third way, between *Moulin Rouge* and *The Dish*.

One of four crime thrillers entered in the 2001 AFI awards, *Lantana* appeals to the international market as a genre film featuring international, billable names – Barbara Hershey and Geoffrey Rush.[33] The Australian trailer is pitched at the crime thriller audience, juxtaposing the image of a woman's body (entangled in the exotic tropical weed lantana) with a montage of the key suspects in a murder investigation. In contrast, the film's press kit and reviews emphasise *Lantana*'s enquiry into the mysteries, not so much of guilt and murder, but of marriage and middle age. Adopting this dual strategy of the psychological thriller grafted onto the personal relations film, *Lantana* has tapped into a broader audience than the obvious middle-aged demographic targeted by the BBC quality mini-series, screened regularly on Sunday nights by ABC-TV. *Lantana*'s successful crossover from limited release on the art-house circuit to wide release through the suburban multiplex can be attributed to this double pitch, as well as to the collaboration between an experienced local distributor (Tait Brady at Palace) and a tenacious creative team headed by respected film producer Jan Chapman, second-feature director Ray Lawrence and theatre writer Andrew Bovell. The casting of familiar television actors in the ensemble film (particularly Kerry Armstrong from *SeaChange*, the remarkable Rachael Blake from *Wildside*, Glenn Robbins from *The Panel* and Peter Phelps from *Stingers*) and the screen adaptation of Bovell's play *Speaking in Tongues* add two further 'presold' elements to the package. However, the question remains whether these factors are sufficient to explain *Lantana*'s sweep of AFI awards, together with the coolness of the AFI voters towards the year's expected crowd pleasers, *Moulin Rouge* and *The Dish*.

Ostensibly a psychological thriller investigating what looks like a murder, *Lantana* connects internationally to the contemporary multi-strand narrative in the vein of Robert Altman's *Short Cuts* (1993). The pleasures of *Lantana* lie in its confident orchestration of the moody desires and bodily discontents of the film's ensemble of middle-aged characters as four marriages unravel amid a thicket of interlocking professional and domestic lives. Early in the film, the overweight and unfit Leon Zat (Anthony LaPaglia) struggles for breath after a morning 'I don't want to die' jog, only to be told by his wife, Sonia (Kerry Armstrong), 'You *are* going to die. Stop jogging.' Mortality, and the shadow it begins to cast over middle age, is an unpromising marketing hook for a feature film straddling the blockbuster, high concept terrain of commercial cinema. Yet *Lantana* uses the decentred, multi-strand narrative and the alibi of the thriller to pursue its low-concept themes by linking and then isolating its characters in widescreen shots which reveal the contingency of (certain kinds of) human bodies as they age. In this sense *Lantana* activates what Walter Benjamin calls the 'optical unconscious' of cinema. Through such devices as the widescreen close-up, *Lantana*, 'by focusing on hidden details of familiar objects, by exploring commonplace milieus . . . extends our comprehension of the necessities which rule our lives' and also 'manages to assure us of an immense and unexpected field of action'.[34] In *Lantana*, cinematographer Mandy Walker's medium close-ups reveal the hidden details of the mid-life body and its field of action in sensual wide shots which seem to offer a different kind of visual pleasure by touching the eye and brushing up against the ear.[35]

Along with the discontented flesh trying to break through the anaesthetisation of mid-life and its routines, *Lantana* makes visible the range of locales of middle-class life. These distinctive locales indicate the socio-economic strata of middle-class experience, as characters begin to connect with each other, as strands of space within the film begin to tangle like lantana, extending the thriller's conventional field of action into the multi-strand narrative of the art cinema. These milieux are recognisable Sydney habitats, from the inner-city renovation, to the suburban double-brick or weatherboard bungalow, to the architect-designed bushland retreat. As local habitats, *Lantana*'s distinctive houses and its ubiquitous workplaces, bars, bookshops, dance studios and nightclubs are readily exportable to an international audience sharing a similar field of action. Whereas *Moulin Rouge* imports its field of action from pictorial representations of late 19th-century Paris, and *The Dish* exports a vision of small-town Australiana unchanged by the 1960s, *Lantana* captures its generic middle-class audience where it lives in the 21st century. In this sense it is an export-oriented film, but its international cinematic reference is the quality drama we expect from independent auteurs rather than the Hollywood blockbuster of the commercial power babies.

Lantana is a deceptive film that invites its audience into the cinema by promising the tension and release of the thriller. The twist in this thriller is that there has been no murder, only a failure of trust which produces the film's opening exploitation image of a woman's corpse entangled in lantana. For AFI voters the film delivers something familiar that was crafted by the first wave of Australian auteurs (notably Beresford, Noyce, Schepisi, Weir) before they left for Hollywood at the end of the 1970s. One of the staples of Australian 'quality' cinema is the intimate ensemble film from a creative team capable of examining the necessities which shape the lifestyle of the local middle class. (Jan Chapman, Gillian Armstrong and Helen Garner might be the perfect realisation of such a team in the 1992 production *The Last Days of Chez Nous*; Andrew Knight and Deb Cox might be considered the equivalent in Australian television drama, their critical success with the mini-series *After the Deluge* in 2003 demonstrating the importance of television for the longevity of certain genres that were once the province of cinema.)

By engaging the thriller as an international calling card, *Lantana* partici-pates in one of the commercial-industrial protocols of what O'Regan calls a mundane national cinema. O'Regan insists that both meanings of mundane are pertinent to understanding the place of low-budget independent films: as 'everyday' local products of a minor national cinema and as 'worldly' products of international (albeit unequal) cultural exchange.[36] As O'Regan puts it, this is a matter of 'international form' with an Australian 'flavour'.[37]

An Australian Flavour in Commercial-Industrial Films

In their ground-breaking studies of Australian cinema of the 1970s and early 1980s, Susan Dermody and Elizabeth Jacka adopted the concept of a social imaginary rather than national identity to explain the characteristics of a second world cinema.[38] The idea of a social imaginary as a tangled undergrowth of historically shaped, cultural modes of perception and social experience is a useful one for considering the Australian 'flavour' which so many critics perceive in films as unlike each other as *Moulin Rouge, The Dish* and *Lantana*. By definition, these commercial-industrial films need to attract market interest in the form of private investment, a pre-sale or distribution deal. To increase the odds in favour of a profitable return on investment (in an international market where eight out of ten American films fail to go into profit at the box office) Australian films need to think global as well as local. What then are we to make of a persistent expectation, from the generic audience, of an Australian flavour in commercial-industrial films conceived with one eye on the international market?

In the recent history wars (see Chapter 1), Miriam Dixson has discerned 'some of the enduring patterns' of Anglo culture which linger in the nation's social imaginary even as Australians experience the intense aftershock of global corporatism.[39] For the generic audience, it may be that the three films discussed in this chapter are indicative of enduring patterns as well as shock-waves of change in the social imaginary over the last decade. *Moulin Rouge* might register the pleasures and rewards of singing and dancing for our supper in the open market, envisaged as expansively cosmopolitan in Keating's big picture, and as creatively entrepreneurial in the new digital era of infotainment corporations. The Sydney ethos of 'party harder', marketed under the banner of Mardi Gras since the 1980s, coincided with Treasurer Keating's rise to prominence as passionate advocate of the free-market econ-omy. However, in the Hawke-Keating era of economic rationalism from 1983 to 1996, the commercial ethos of the cosmopolitan entrepreneur (embodied by veteran British actor Jim Broadbent in *Moulin Rouge*) was tempered by a revived sense of Australia as 'a first rate social democracy . . . truly the land of the fair go and the better chance'.[40] In his history-making Redfern Park speech of 1992, Keating asked non-Aboriginal Australians to *imagine* the past from the perspective of Aboriginal people. He argued that reconciliation based on recognition and justice for Aboriginal Australians would take an act of imagination similar to the one that transformed the 'narrow and insular' Australia of the 1960s into 'a culturally diverse, worldly and open Australia' in a single generation.[41] For the attentive, generic audience of Australian cinema after *Mabo*, the Australian flavour in commercial-industrial films might well be those figures of landscape and character, milieu and habitat that resonate with the complex shifts in the social imaginary accompanying the shifts in economic policy and cultural rhetoric deployed under the banner of the Hawke-Keating governments. If Gulpilil and Crowe both stand tall in this social imaginary, straddling old and new ground a decade after the Redfern Park speech, then it may well be that the moral authority of Gulpilil and the commercial clout of Crowe, together with *Lantana* and *Moulin Rouge*, are outcomes of the Keating cultural and economic moment.

In this view, *The Dish* reprises the 1960s not as a decade of change but as the tail-end of the Menzies era, as the last time when Australia could happily enjoy its place in the world, secure in its identity as a benign backwater, before Britain's entry into the Common Market broke the bonds of Empire and forced Australia into a new role as a minor team player in global events orchestrated from elsewhere. The 1960s, affectionately re-imagined by *The Dish*, are uncannily similar to the prosperous, protected Australia of the 1950s, fondly remembered by neo-conservatives as a prototype for Howard's 'relaxed and comfortable' Australia in the 21st century. The fact that *The Dish* was successful at the box office but a non-event in popular culture, and that it was ignored at the AFI awards, indicates that its tongue-in-cheek homage to the more benign aspects of Howard's nostalgic vision of the 1950s failed to resonate with the changes taking place in the social imaginary. The unexpected critical success of *Lantana* suggests that the film stole the AFI awards from both *Moulin Rouge* and *The Dish* because it offered its generic audience a more complex response to the anxieties of the urban middle class, broadly represented as inclusive of suburban battlers, at one end, and the cosmopolitan literati at the other. It is this middle ground that is reshaping the social imaginary in Australia as it is courted by both sides of politics. Pundits have named it the 'aspirational class' and pollsters are reminding political leaders that voting patterns can no longer be depended on in electorates once considered rock-solid for one or other side of politics.

As an exploration of the field of action of the middle class, *Lantana* brings new tensions of home, family, work and unsatisfied longings into widescreen focus in subtle ways that do not rely on quirky comedy, grotesque suburbia or rituals of mateship for Australian 'flavour'. Rather, *Lantana* manages to integrate its cast of local media personalities (Armstrong, Blake, Colosimo, Robbins, Purcell) and its internationally recognised film actors (LaPaglia, Hershey and Rush) into a Sydney middle class indebted to Keating's economic reforms, tempted by Howard's promise of security, less enamoured of nostalgia for community than *The Dish*, and more likely to watch the Mardi Gras parade on television than to be found dancing at *Moulin Rouge*'s party.

Notes

1 New Zealand programs comprise around 20 per cent of the content on New Zealand free-to-air television. Australian programs comprise at least 55 per cent of content on Australian free-to-air television. See Roger Horrocks, 'New Zealand cinema: cultures, policies, films'. In Deb Verhoeven (ed.), *Twin Peeks: Australian & New Zealand Feature Films*, Melbourne: Damned Publishing, 1999, pp. 129–37. Horrocks outlines cultural costs and benefits of a deregulated film and television industry in New Zealand. One of the benefits is a kind of localism producing an 'Antipodean camp' aesthetic rather than nationalism's straight white macho figures.

2 For a persuasive analysis of Australia's globally integrated distribution/exhibition sector as a starting point for understanding why this situation is likely to get worse, not better, see Mary Anne Reid, *More Long Shots: Australian Cinema Successes in the 90s*, Sydney: Australian Film Commission, and Brisbane: Australian Key Centre for Cultural and Media Policy, 1999, pp. 110–29.

3 Tom O'Regan, *Australian National Cinema*, London & New York: Routledge, 1996, pp. 44–71 and 96–106.

4 Quoted in Lawrie Zion, 'Short Cuts', *Age*, A3, 30 January 2003, p. 8.

5 *One Red Blood* (Darlene Johnson, 2002) was broadcast on ABC-TV on 11 December 2002 as part of the national broadcaster's Australian documentary series *The Big Picture*.

6 See O'Regan, *Australian National Cinema*, pp. 194–6 . This concept of Australian film as a genre of international cinema has been discussed in William D. Routt, 'Me Cobber, Ginger Mick: Stephano's story and resistance to empire in early Australian film'. In Verhoeven, *Twin Peeks*, p. 37. It supports Routt's attempt to interpret an Australian silent film as an international classic rather than as a representation of national identity.

7 For a precedent in Paul Hogan, see Alan McKee, *Australian Television: A Genealogy of Great Moments*, Melbourne: Oxford University Press, 2001, pp. 117–35.

8 On nation itself as a type of genre, open to being remade in the same way that genres are transformed, see Rick Altman, 'What can genres teach us about nations?' *Film/Genre*, BFI, London, 1999, pp. 195–206.

9 For two recent literary accounts of Australia's ambivalent ties to the UK and the USA see David Malouf, 'Made in England: Australia's British inheritance', *Quarterly Essay*, no. 12, 2003; and Don Watson, 'Rabbit syndrome: Australia and America', *Quarterly Essay*, no. 4, 2001.

10 On the concept of a 'second world' social imaginary in Australian cinema, see Susan Dermody and Elizabeth Jacka, *The Screening Of Australia: Anatomy of a National Cinema*, vol. 2, Sydney: Currency Press, 1988, pp. 17–23.

11 There is something of this idea at work in the notion of 'the nation as an *open* framework for action' in Meaghan Morris, 'Lunching for the republic'. In *Too Soon Too Late: History in Popular Culture*, Bloomington IN: Indiana University Press, 1998, p. 298.

12 See Graeme Turner, 'Whatever happened to national identity? Film and the nation in the 1990s', *Metro*, 100, 1994, pp. 32–5.

13 For a succinct account of government measures to support film financing in Australia since 1970 see Ina Bertrand, 'Finance'. In Brian McFarlane, Geoff Mayer & Ina Bertrand (eds), *The Oxford Companion to Australian Film*, Melbourne: Oxford University Press, 1999, pp. 156–9.

14 For an account of such appointments to the National Museum of Australia see Stuart Macintyre, 'Working through the museum's labels'. In *The History Wars*, Melbourne University Press, 2003, pp. 191–215.

15 For an overview of the way the Howard Government has exploited One Nation supporters and the politics of race since 1996, see Robert Manne, 'The Howard years: a political interpretation'. In Robert Manne (ed.), *The Howard Years*, Melbourne: Black Inc. Agenda, 2004, pp. 3–53.

16 See Tom O'Regan and Rama Venkatasawmy, 'A tale of two cities: *Dark City* and *Pig in the City*'. In Verhoeven, *Twin Peeks*, pp. 187–203.

17 O'Regan describes the Australian 'antipodal condition' as a permanent structure of unequal cultural exchange with the dominant film cultures of USA, UK and Europe: *Australian National Cinema*, pp. 106–10.

18 Thomas Elsaesser, 'Specularity and engulfment: Francis Ford Coppola *and Bram Stoker's Dracula*'. In Steve Neale and Murray Smith (eds), *Contemporary Hollywood Cinema*, London: Routledge, 1998, pp. 191–208.

19 ibid., pp. 191–2.

20 ibid., p. 195.

21 ibid., p. 193.

22 ibid., p. 197.

23 ibid., pp. 200–1.

24 ibid., p. 204.

25 *Encore*, 19(8) 2001, p. 6.

26 Paul Sheehan, '*Moulin Rouge* is all it was hyped up to be – and more', *Sydney Morning Herald*, General News Section, 6 June 2001, p. 26.

27 Stephanie Bunbury, 'Luhrmann says his film's strictly Australian-made', *Age*, General News Section, 11 May 2001, p. 3.

28 Adrian Martin, Review of *Moulin Rouge* in *The Age*, Today Section, 24 May 2001, p. 5.

29 Deirdre Macken, 'So superlatively superficial', *Australian Financial Review*, General News Section, 26 May 2001, p. 2.

30 Vicky Roach, 'Dancing feet a sight to see', *Daily Telegraph*, Supplement, 24 May 2001, p. 8.

31 See Justin Wyatt, *High Concept: Movies and Marketing in Hollywood*, Austin TX: University of Texas Press, 1994.

32 *Encore* 19(8) 2001, p. 14. Figures based on totals to 1 August 2001.

33 The other three crime thrillers released in 2001 were *The Bank* (Robert Connolly), *The Monkey's Mask* (Samantha Lang) and *Risk* (Alan White).

34 Walter Benjamin, 'The work of art in the age of mechanical reproduction', in Hannah Arendt (ed.), *Illuminations*, transl. Harry Zohn, London: Fontana, 1992, p. 229.

35 This sensual experience of viewing particular kinds of film images is explored in Laura U. Marks, *The Skin of the Film: Intercultural Cinema, Embodiment, and the Senses*, Durham & London: Duke University Press, 2000, pp. 138–53.

36 Tom O'Regan, *Australian National Cinema*, pp. 136–7.

37 ibid., p. 218.

38 Dermody and Jacka, *The Screening of Australia*, vol. 2, pp. 17–23.

39 Miriam Dixson, 'Identity: history, the nation and the self'. In Joy Damousi and Robert Reynolds (eds), *History on the Couch: Essays in History and Psychoanalysis*, Melbourne University Press, 2003, pp. 123–5.

40 Paul Keating, 'The Redfern Park Speech'. In Michelle Grattan (ed.), *Reconciliation: Essays on Australian Reconciliation*, Melbourne: Black Inc., pp. 60–4.

41 ibid., p. 63.

3

Elites and Battlers in *Australian Rules* and *Walking on Water*

Australian cinema, perceived as an international genre, brings to mind iconic landscapes, characters and stories which take hold in the memory as *visual* images. However, in *Australian Rules* (Paul Goldman, 2002) and *Walking on Water* (Tony Ayres, 2002), it is the voice and the breath that linger in the memory as *aural* images. In *Australian Rules* there is a transformation from a polyglot of vernaculars in the opening sound sequence to one clear voice-over at the end. In *Walking on Water*, everything important hinges on the breath, from Gavin's last strangled gasp to the breakdown and recovery of each of the characters involved in Gavin's final expiration. This chapter will explore the loss of identity and recovery of the voice, and the breath, in *Australian Rules* and *Walking on Water*. Between them, the two films draw our attention to the reshaping of a transplanted Anglo-Celtic social imaginary in Australian cinema. Miriam Dixson argues that 'Australian identity still carries the marks of yesterday's British connection'.[1] David Malouf qualifies that assertion by arguing that an experimental and open sense of identity characterises the Australian social imaginary because 'we are a bit of the motherland set down in a new place and left to develop as the new conditions demanded, as climate, a different mixture of people, changes in the world around us, and our reaction to them, determined'.[2]

This reshaping of the social imaginary by new conditions involves a politics of identity in a national context informed by tensions between the claims of history (the past) and social mobility in the new economy (the future). In both films, change in the social imaginary (and recovery from its most brutal exclusions) is evident in the merging vernaculars of 'bush battlers' and 'cultural elites'. It is also implied in the context of an international, media-based politics of memory which speaks to contemporary experiences of dislocated identities based on nation, class, race, ethnicity or gender. Both films make it difficult to imagine a future built on a resurgent, populist desire for a unified national identity based on a whitewashed version of the British heritage.

Before addressing these issues, however, we need to recover some old ground in film politics in terms of the stand-off between culture and commerce, art and industry, explored so thoroughly by Dermody and Jacka in their formative study of 1970s and 1980s Australian cinema.[3] *Australian Rules* and *Walking on Water* were released in 2002 as part of a reprise of a cultural-intervention strategy by the public sector in political circumstances that do not favour left-liberal initiatives. In partnership with the 2002 Adelaide Festival of the Arts, SBS Independent television (SBSi) initiated a package of feature films which contest neo-conservative ideas of national identity, recent history and media memory. This intervention followed the success of *Unfinished Business: Reconciling the Nation*, a ground-breaking package of programs broadcast nationally on the multicultural television channel SBS over ten days from 25 May to 3 June 2000. This package included nine new dramas and documentaries, six existing films, and live coverage of the Sydney Harbour Bridge walk. As a work of cultural intervention, *Unfinished Business* was compiled and broadcast to coincide with Corroboree 2000, Reconciliation Week and National Sorry Day.[4] It was an ambitious and partisan moment of cultural intervention which had its origins in the release in 1997 of *Bringing Them Home*, the report of the Human Rights and Equal Opportunity Commission on the Stolen Generations.[5] *Unfinished Business* was the brainchild of SBSi's general manager, Bridget Ikin, a feature film producer best known for her work with Jane Campion. Ikin worked with commissioning editor John Hughes (an activist filmmaker who has since the 1970s worked across a range of genres inflected by political modernism) to put together *Unfinished Business* in conjunction with local filmmakers. During this period, SBSi made a significant shift in its conception of multicultural broadcasting, going far beyond its origins in multilingual radio programming aimed at non-English-speaking ethnic communities. This shift entailed a rethinking of nationhood in terms of Indigenous, white settler and migrant experiences which cannot be assimilated into a unified national identity or be contained within multicultural identity politics.

In 2001–02, Ikin followed up SBSi's success with *Unfinished Business* by negotiating an ambitious package of five feature films with Peter Sellars, controversial artistic director of the 2002 Adelaide Festival of the Arts. With the backing of SBSi and the Adelaide Festival, these low-budget feature films attracted funding from a variety of public sources including the AFC, SAFC, NSWFTO and FFC, taxpayer-funded organisations which are an essential part of the infrastructure of commercial film production in Australia.[6] However, rather than a market-driven, commercial-industrial strategy, the SBSi-Adelaide Festival package is remarkable for its renewal of a 1970s strategy of cultural intervention under the auspices of multicultural television and a regional arts festival. This feature film initiative is all the more remarkable for attracting public funding under the neo-conservative Howard government, whose attack on left-liberal 'cultural elites' has been institutional as well as rhetorical. One of the reasons SBSi was able to implement a left-liberal strategy for cultural intervention in a neo-conservative climate has been its multicultural charter, which requires it to represent a diversity of voices, including Indigenous and non-Anglo voices which are, by and large, absent from commercial television and even the ABC.

The SBSi-Adelaide Festival strategy of bringing together a variety of culturally motivated partners from the public sector (with some commercial commitment from the distribution sector) involves an activist ethos and an aesthetics of poor cinema.[7] By adopting an interventionist rather than commercial ethos, the strategy reinvents a cinema of *erfahrung* (a cinema of reciprocal experience between filmmakers and audiences). This notion of cinema as a public sphere involving mutual recognition emerged in independent cinema in West Germany, the United States and Britain from the late 1960s. It helped shape an alternative, independent cinema of social activism, identity politics and personal experience in Sydney and Melbourne through the Filmmakers Co-operatives and other independent organisations during the 1970s.[8] Three decades later, *Unfinished Business* and the SBSi-Adelaide Festival initiative revive this commitment to a dialectical exchange between filmmaker and audience, engaging with issues of national history, personal memory and identity politics of race, gender, ethnicity and class. At the same time, looking beyond the national, SBSi participates in the growing international phenomenon of a postmodern politics of memory and experience which, in late modernity, is more interested in 'present pasts' than in modernism's 'present futures'.[9]

This chapter argues that, between the resurgence of a cinema of reciprocal experience (or *erfahrung*) and a recent boom in media memory in traumatic and entertainment forms, the social imaginary of Australian identity and what Dixson calls its 'anchoring Anglo-Celtic core' has undergone significant shifts.[10] Some of these shifts are evident in the way the past intrudes on the present in the contemporary settings of *Australian Rules* and *Walking on Water*. Unlike the majority of films in the 2000–02 cycle of Indigenous-settler-national history films, *Australian Rules* and *Walking on Water* are contemporary films set in recognisable locations, the former in a struggling South Australian fishing town, the latter in the affluent eastern suburbs of Sydney. These places are 'locales' in the sense that characters and events typical of those locales (for instance, a football Grand Final between the sons of sheep farmers and the sons of fishermen, won by the sons from the Aboriginal mission) are bound up in vernaculars which originate in those very times and places. In this sense, although the two films might appear to represent a conservative opposition between 'bush battlers' and 'city navel-gazers', both are concerned with the emergence of new vernaculars – as idiom and architecture of post-national identities.[11]

Finessing with the Anglo-Celtic Social Imaginary in *Australian Rules*

Australian Rules was adapted from the coming-of-age novel *Deadly, Unna?* by Phillip Gywnne. The decision to change the title for the release of the film is a risky one, given that most Australian films tend to play down their national origins in order to compete for the attention of the multiplex cinema audience. The change in title also risks an instant turn-off for non-football fans, who recognise the title as a reference to the AFL code, favoured over Rugby codes in the southern states and known colloquially as Aussie Rules. A film title which threatens to critique national identity by taking a metaphoric look at the rules governing boys and football promises an update on mateship as the core of Anglo-Celtic identity. *Australian Rules* literally goes over this parched ground, examining the cracks of race, gender and class which appear as the thin topsoil of white working-class mateship is eroded by Indigenous, middle-class and feminine vernaculars. The blend and clash of different vernaculars in the film was paralleled by the media controversy over the protocols for white filmmakers borrowing stories and characters from an Aboriginal community. The sustained debate over who has the right to tell Indigenous stories, or to give permission for those stories to be told, is one indication that contemporary mateship, conceived as a level playing field with no special privileges for non-male, non-white Australians, can no longer pass itself off as an inclusive, anchoring core of national identity.[12]

In an effort to explain the persistence and cultural transmission of the 'anchoring Anglo-Celtic core' of Australian identity in the face of multicultural and global influences, feminist historian Miriam Dixson has turned to philosophers Paul Ricoeur and Cornelius Castoriadis. Ricoeur describes the social imaginary as 'an opaque kernel' 'beyond or beneath the self-understanding of a society', a 'foundational mytho-poetic nucleus' that precedes cultural representations or ideas.[13] For Castoriadis the social imaginary is dynamic and creative, instituting and conserving patterns of meaning. Dixson extends the idea of nation as an imagined community by adopting Castoriadis's view that the social imaginary bestows on each historical period 'a quite specific . . . mood'.[14] In Dixson's view, 'the experience of convictism, the originary power of an authoritarian, centralised state, Anglo-Irish rancour, and race and sex relations' give the Australian social imaginary its 'unique patterning'.[15] This idea of the persistence of an apparently outdated Anglo-Celtic social imaginary is useful for understanding *Australian Rules* as a post-*Mabo*, perhaps post-national project under the auspices of SBS multicultural television.

There is a turning-point moment in *Australian Rules* when an outsider, a talent-spotter for the national AFL competition, makes a speech about football and opportunity and mateship. Like the viewer, he is a silent witness to the entrenched codes of race, class and gender that rule Prospect Bay's footy club. However, he is there to support the local club and its transmission of the values of Australian mateship through the AFL code. As a beneficiary of the social mobility offered by sport, he believes that 'when men get together wonderful things happen'. Speaking from experience, the ex-champion says of football, 'It's kept me alive. Taken me places.' But his attempt to inspire a new generation of players is interrupted by Pretty Boy from the back of the hall: 'More gunyah bullshit.' Pretty Boy no longer believes in the inclusiveness of the white man's code of mateship. His words are timely and economic: they mark his vernacular as dissident and Aboriginal. The real bullshit occurs seconds later when the ex-champ is pressured into presenting the best-on-ground medal to the coach's son, taking it away from match-winning goal-sneak Dumby Red. This is an injustice that no amount of self-serving racism among the townspeople can deny and it leads directly to Dumby Red's tragic death.

The gap between whitefella faith in the ethos of Australian mateship and blackfella anger at 'gunyah bullshit' is represented in the opening shot of the film in a close-up of the bare, cracked earth of the local football ground, well past its glory days. This eroded playing space is the meeting ground on which white working-class wordsmith Gary Black ('Blacky' to all except his Mum) and Dumby Red ('Dark Prince' of the Aboriginal players from the Mission) get under each other's skin with shared fantasies of sporting and sexual feats. The opening sound bite, a rich polyglot of voices calling out across the oval, invents a vernacular of friendship which thrives on differences of race and gender. The film revels in these vernacular spaces, opening the listener's ear to the language not only of the footy clubroom ('no more finessing', 'go the guts') but also the pub ('a *lemonade* for the boys'), the pier (supernovas, the universe and sweet talking), the street ('now you're even talkin' like one of them') and the embattled home ('gutless fucking wonder', versus 'we don't use those words in this house').

There are two spaces in the film that are marked out as no-go areas for Gary Black and the film viewer. What we hear from these spaces, and what we glimpse of them, disturbs the familiar, generic Australian vernaculars of club, pub and pier. The first off-limit space is the Mission, place of origin of the film's tongue-in-cheek (Dumby Red) and political (Pretty Boy) Indigenous vernaculars. The boys from 'the Mish', together with Dumby's sister, Clarence, and father, Tommy, enter the town spaces, making themselves seen and heard as a distinctive community, but not an exclusive one. Gary (Blacky) is addressed by Tommy, with affection, as 'you little black bastard', while Dumby Red says to Gary 'you plenty blackfella too', after explaining the niceties of team-play based on not 'shaming' your cousin. However, Gary is not a blackfella and that's made clear towards the end of the film when he has to front up to Dumby Red's funeral, prompted unexpectedly by his foul-mouthed mate, Pickles. Gary's right of entry to the Mission, renamed Aboriginal Land, is not automatic. Only Tommy can give Gary the nod to enter, after Clarence vouches for him. Although Tommy is relegated to the back bar of the pub in town, his authority in his community is a marked contrast to that of Gary's Dad.

The problem of discredited white authority in *Australian Rules* dovetails with the doubt the film sheds on the anchoring core of Anglo-Celtic identity in Australia, the creed of egalitarianism, fair go, mateship. The most disturbing and profoundly unresolved space in the film, where white male authority is put to the test, is in Gary's family home. The off-limit space in the home is the parental bedroom where something violent and ugly is going on between the parents. The muffled sound of sexual and emotional violence is tormenting for the children and, through the soundtrack, for the viewer. The father's authority, symbolised by the forbidden block of chocolate in the fridge, is enforced by this muted undercurrent of trauma in the family. When the father finally asks Gary to close ranks, to choose sides over Dumby Red's shooting, even the mother (who has encouraged Gary's development as a footballer, but more importantly as a literary wordsmith) agrees – 'He *is* your father.' The film has several options for finding its way through this impasse between new forms of friendship (evident on the footy field where Gary and Dumby Red lead the team to an unlikely victory orchestrated by Gary's Mum) and old forms of white male authority (enforced in the home and in the football club by the father, the publican and the coach).

The first option is the slap. Clarence, the clever girl from the Mish (Aboriginal Land) who moves fluently between her brother's street talk and Gary's love of literary language, knows where to draw the line. When Gary wishfully declares, in a moment of private eulogy, that Dumby Red's light will shine forever, Clarence slaps him back into reality: 'Shut up. He's dead.' Yet Gary cannot take sides with her against his father, who shares the town's deep sexual ambivalence towards women from the Mish as 'gins', 'sluts', and 'black velvet'. The second option is the paternal look. A 'gutless fucking wonder' in his father's eyes, a 'little black bastard' in Tommy's more affectionate gaze, Gary is caught between these two paternal figures. When Tommy drops Gary home after Dumby Red's funeral, Tommy (Dumby's father) and Gary's father (Dumby's killer) exchange an intransigent look that contains a history of death as the irreconcilable ground between white settlers and Indigenous Australians. As a coming-of-age film, *Australian Rules* is unable to go further with this historically charged look between an Aboriginal father and the man who shot his son, but the moral authority belongs to Tommy.[16] Again Gary is unable to go against his father in this moment, but when Tommy drives away, the showdown between father and son finally begins. As the third option, Gary's resistance to his father's authority takes a physically passive form, echoing his survival tactic against the Thumper in the Grand Final. Encouraged by his younger brother's silent, pleading, fraternal look, Gary (like his mother) takes a beating from his father, and (like Tommy) wins a moral victory. This victory leads directly to the emergence of Gary's voice as the narrating voice and author of the story. However, his lone voice on the soundtrack comes at the cost of the mixed vernaculars that opened the film. In the end scene at the pier, Clarence and Gary jump into the sparkling water together. We see them frolic, but it is Gary's voice, tutored by his mother, that we hear, alone, in the final voice-over. Gary speaks for Clarence when he declares, 'We're leaving. There's nothing here for us in this tidy town.' Although the film has taken us into rich territory for reshaping Australian identity, this ending restores something of the status quo. Clarence's voice (female and Aboriginal) is silenced by Gary, just as Dumby Red has been forever silenced and Gary's mother's voice has been quietened by the father's violence. We cannot help wondering what Clarence might have said if she had been given the last word, or if her voice had been allowed to overlap with Gary's. It is hard to believe there is nothing there for her after what we've glimpsed and heard of her community at the Mish. This cultural erasure of Clarence's experience, in favour of the male protagonist honing his voice as a young writer, takes us back to the footy ground, now silent and deserted, its polyglot vernaculars dead and buried with Dumby Red and the Best-on-Ground medal. The possibility of a new politics of open-ended identity based on the interplay of Indigenous, white settler and literary vernaculars (which might even have found a way to include Gary's stoned and racist mate, Pickles, and the angry, articulate Pretty Boy) is lost. What is gained, however, is a genuine discrediting of One Nation's nostalgia for an anchoring core of 19th-century Anglo-Celtic mateship. In the world created by *Australian Rules* the social imaginary has tempered its benign affection for canny battlers from the bush. The long-standing ethos of mateship as the core of national identity is revealed as corrupt and exclusive. For women, for Aboriginal men, and for young male writers interested in the fertile ground of cultural mingling, mateship is a shorthand code for a parched, violent, non-viable form of national identity. Part of the non-viability of this form of male authority is the economic and cultural changes demanded of the populace as Australia moves from its beef, wheat, wool and minerals-based economy of the 19th century to join late modernity's transnational service and infotainment-based economy in the 21st century. In this borderless economy, identities, like people, have become commodified, readily exchangeable in the flux of the marketplace where authority has become more corporate and less fraternal-paternal.

Recovering the Keating Years in *Walking on Water*

If Clarence and Gary manage to get away from Prospect Bay it is conceivable that they might turn up somewhere in close proximity to the floating populace of Sydney's cosmopolitan beachside suburbs. This dislocated milieu is given a transnational or borderless identity through a local experience of living with the AIDS crisis in *Walking on Water*, a film that might be understood as a long recovery party after a big night out at *Moulin Rouge*. If *Australian Rules* is grounded in a recognisable Anglo-Celtic social imaginary disturbed by the intermingled identities of working-class, white settler and Indigenous Australians, then *Walking on Water* imagines post-national identity as something entirely provisional, utterly experimental. In this socially mobile milieu, characters slip the noose of class, ethnicity and gender. What binds them together is guilt and grief within contingent communities which act a little like families, a lot like friends. These communities include the local pub with its meat tray raffle, the shared household performing the last rites for AIDS sufferer Gavin, the streets and clifftops of the Bondi-to-Bronte stretch of lifestyle suburbs, and the gay dancefloor where no one has authority and it's up to you to handle your drugs, your gender issues, and your sexual orientation. This milieu has its own vernacular, a post-national one that owes something to Keating's vision of an outward-looking, cosmopolitan Australia where the ockers and larrikins, shearers and Anzacs, footballers and lifesavers have long been transformed into mere icons of Australian popular culture, irrelevant to daily life but suitable for opening and closing the Sydney Olympics in a true Mardi Gras parade of kitsch or camp style.

Although the view that Australia is a British-derived diaspora has been under attack since multicultural nationhood became a matter of government policy in the 1970s, the emergence of Pauline Hanson and One Nation in the mid-1990s has led to a populist revival of support for a return to Anglo-Celtic forms of national identity. This nostalgia for Australia as a

provincial outpost of the British Empire was gently probed in *The Dish*
(Rob Sitch, 2001) with its bumbling but well-intentioned locals keen to put
on a good show for the Americans in an English village kind of way. Focusing
on the emergence of *style* as a defining element of Australia, Malouf takes a
different angle from Dixson on the Anglo-derived social imaginary. Looking
at Australia from the vantage point of Britain, Malouf sees a shift from the
19th-century concept of Australia as the antipodean 'underworld' to a 20th-
century romance with Australia as a provisional place 'of perpetual *lightness*'
where 'your own freer self might suddenly break loose'.[17] From the vantage
point of Australia, the view is slightly different for Malouf. He argues that
the debt to the mother country is not so much Australia's founding settler
figures (of convicts and squatters, land selectors and gold-diggers) but the
ongoing international connections Australia enjoys with other outposts of
the former British Empire. The passport and currency linking these outposts
is a late Enlightenment, post-civil war form of English as the metaphorical language of Shakespeare and the 'reasonable' language of parliamentary
democracy.[18] Defining the social imaginary of settler societies (whether
long-standing, like Britain, or recent, like Australia) as 'experiential rather
than essentialist',[19] Malouf locates Australian independence from Britain
two decades after the Second World War alliance with the United States
in the Pacific. Britain's hands-off approach to the transplanted bit of itself in
the antipodes finally forced Australia out of its Commonwealth comfort
zone and into contact with new trading partners when Britain joined the
European common market in the 1960s.[20] This places the emergence of the
cosmopolitan moment earlier than 1970s multiculturalism and much earlier than the Hawke-Keating floating of the currency and deregulation of
the banks which signalled the end of an isolated economy in the 1980s. For
Malouf, Australia was always an experimental place, 'Made in England', but
cut loose in the 1960s to improvise its way into an independent and ultimately enviable style of Mediterranean living, shaped by old entanglements
and new opportunities.[21]

This experimental style of living, featured in *Walking on Water*, has its
origin in changes in Australian culture dating from the 1960s. The historical
mood of that era was sustained until the demise of Keating's Labor government and the election of Howard's neo-conservative coalition in 1996. The
death knell of left-liberal cultural influence was sounded by the triumphant
xenophobia of the *Tampa* crisis which ensured the re-election of Howard in
2001 on the grounds of his border protection and Pacific Solution policies
on refugees and asylum-seekers.[22] *Walking on Water* was produced in the
aftermath of this decisive defeat of left-liberal agendas which had been in
ascendance since the late 1960s. Although the film's characters appear to

belong to an urban elite who have forsaken family ties as the mainstay of their lives, they have been toughened by everyday adversity as AIDS forces them to invent new ways of dealing with unprecedented situations. Living in Sydney's perpetual lightness, they are simultaneously immersed in an underbelly of grief. Their emotionally shell-shocked state is a response not only to the continuing catastrophe of AIDS but also to the populist attacks on 'elite' forms of cosmopolitan identity. These attacks on 'political correctness' were effectively launched in the 1990s by Pauline Hanson's One Nation party of bush battlers and displaced workers protesting against Asian immigration, funding of special programs for Aboriginal communities, and the eclipse of Anglo-Celtic Australia by multiculturalism.

The underbelly of grief in *Walking on Water* goes deeper than the AIDS crisis and its effect on gay communities in cosmopolitan Western cities defined by their place in late modernity's global infotainment and service economy. In the context of SBSi and its multicultural charter, *Walking on Water* mourns a 1960s cosmopolitan ethos of open-ended experiment with identity and lifestyle. This experiment shifted in the 1990s from excitement and opportunity in the service economy to something closer to a daily grind. Charlie works in the hospitality industry; Anna and Gavin were partners in a design business; Gavin's family from the industrial town of Whyalla run a laundromat. As Anna puts it, in the new work hard, party harder economy, she is 'Workaholic. Alcoholic'.

The SBSi package of feature films is involved in a shift in identity politics from ethnic diasporas maintaining their language and connections to their homelands, to an oppositional multicultural and Indigenous aesthetic aimed at unanchoring the core Anglo-Celtic imaginary. *Walking on Water* takes this shift a step further. Anna (Maria Theodorakis) and Charlie (Vince Colosimo) are friends who inherit the beachside house they share with Gavin when he dies. His death brings his mother, brother, sister-in-law and niece to Sydney from remote industrial Whyalla. This narrative premise of the family gathering at the deathbed has obvious potential for a drama of identity politics around class, gender, ethnicity and sexuality. However, ethnicity is unmarked in the film, except through the names and contrasting appearances of the actors. Anna and Charlie have no back-story in Greek and Italian immigrant families to contrast with Gavin's Anglo family from the country. Gavin's family are Northern European blonde, but his closest friends are Southern European brunette. The film treats this difference as unremarkable. Neither does the film dramatise AIDS and homosexuality, or class and gender, as the cause of family strife. Its finely nuanced conflicts (for which Roger Monk won the 2002 AFI award for Best Original Screenplay) are post-identity issues to do with shared social and symbolic experiences.

The nuances of who shares these difficult experiences, and how, are registered in the film as much through the breath as through a hard-boiled cosmopolitan vernacular.

In *Walking on Water* the breath dominates the soundtrack at the climactic moment of Gavin's death. This climax comes early in the film; the rest is a long denouement, a protracted moment of holding grief and guilt inside, like holding the breath and waiting for a moment of release in order to breathe out. For those who witnessed Gavin's last, strangled breath, grief is blocked by guilt and blame which cannot be spoken because, in a sense, the botched manner of Gavin's death is not the point. And neither is his homosexuality. For Charlie, the trauma of suffocating Gavin with a plastic bag returns as the traumatic sound of Gavin fighting for breath, his body defying the gift of a morphine-assisted death. For Anna, the blame for Gavin's undignified death is shifted to Charlie, giving her the moral authority to carry out Gavin's last wishes to the letter, culminating in her insistent removal of wisps of white baby's breath from amid the red roses on his coffin.

For Simon, the death of his brother opens up a liminal space which he attempts to cross by trying on aspects of Gavin's lifestyle. Sending his wife and daughter back to Whyalla with his mother, Simon stays behind to collect the ashes. While Charlie doses himself up with the last of Gavin's morphine and faces the end of a love affair, Anna and Simon seek release in sex, drugs and alcohol. Grief breaks out of the contained body first for Simon. On the dancefloor with Anna at a gay nightclub, he finds that it takes considerable emotional fortitude to handle his brother's party-hardened lifestyle. He breaks down, and Anna takes him home and puts him on the phone to his wife. We hear the breath return to his body as the stranglehold of tightened emotions is released through sobbing.

For Anna, there is no refuge, after all, in controlling Gavin's funeral or in uncontrolled partying with Simon. A long-standing denizen of the Sydney designer lifestyle, she knows how to handle herself all too well. Her grief comes in a solitary moment of sobbing in the car, that modern space of isolated sorrow, after she drops Simon, with Gavin's ashes, at the airport. For Charlie, grief and guilt bring loneliness and a moment of despair, taking him out to the clifftops where he contemplates the drop into the ocean crashing on the rocks below. Putting aside their quarrel, Anna comes looking for Charlie and draws him back into connection. This moment of tenderness between the estranged friends brings Charlie some relief and he too breaks down.

Only Margaret, Gavin's mother, cannot find a place to ease the bodily weight of her grief. Desperate to escape Anna's tight control of the official spaces of mourning, Margaret retreats to a hotel room, longing to sink into that other place of solitary grief, the warm bath. But there's only a cold, tiled shower in her hotel room so Margaret's grieving is limited to her defiant theft of souvenirs from Gavin's bedroom. Grief in *Walking on Water* is tangible, tactile. It can be felt in Gavin's things as each of the characters takes something to remember him by. Simon wears his shirt, Charlie swallows the last of the morphine, Anna has his will at her fingertips, and Margaret pockets the chipped ornament that Gavin once hurled at a lover. In these sensual contacts between bereaved bodies and objects once touched by Gavin, the past becomes vividly tangible in the present.

What unites these otherwise solitary mourners is their shared sensual experience of grief in a milieu where living (in perpetual lightness) is a bit like walking on water: impossible, but somehow the only option for displaced cosmopolites, whether from the country or the city. Although Gavin's family does return to Whyalla, to their laundromat business, there is no nostalgia for a simpler life involved in their return home. Nor are they cordoned off from cosmopolitan ways of experiencing the unanchored, floating quality of modern life. *Walking on Water* refuses to put them in the role of battlers from the backblocks casting a disingenuous eye over the pretensions and shenanigans of city folk. The relaxed and comfortable Australia of the 1960s, wryly celebrated in *The Dish*, is nowhere in evidence in the party city that produced *Moulin Rouge* and *Walking on Water*. At the beginning of the new millennium, there is only the recovery party to survive, and an open future to contemplate, at the end of the film, when Gavin's house is put up for sale/lease. Although Anna and Charlie's cosmopolitan world belongs more to the outward-looking Wiggles (a hugely successful local export for children's television cited in the film) than to the inward-looking code of Aussie Rules, it is a world whose mood is imbued, like *Australian Rules*, with an urgent sense of the recent past. It is this urgent mood, of the past pressing in on the present, that raises the question of how historical consciousness can be perceived in films which appeared to be deeply embedded in the present and whose endings look to the future.

Memory and the Mood of the Times

As *Australian Rules* and *Walking on Water* make clear, there is an argument to be made that cinema is a throwaway consumer product which touches lightly on contemporary experience and makes it recognisable through the genre of Australian film. In this genre, identity is contingent. It is lightly assumed in an amnesiac culture where social mobility and endless opportunities to reinvent yourself, to leave your past behind, to discard restricting identities of class, race, ethnicity, gender and nation, are taken for granted as one of the benefits of modernity and the transnational economy. Yet a mood of sustained loss, of unresolvable grief pervades both films, implying that memory and identity, rooted in particular locales, are not so easily discarded. And that living within modernity's new global coordinates of imagined experience through the media, the internet, and free-flowing consumer goods under bilateral trade agreements, requires something more than a resilient adaptation to the future as it arrives in the form of jobs in the service, lifestyle or infotainment industries. If *Australian Rules* shows how hard it is to relinquish white male authority underwritten by mateship, *Walking on Water* shows how hard it is to keep your footing in the global melting pot where authoritative forms of identity have long been dissolved in favour of corporate teams, sole contractors, and their clients. Yet through their sense of locale, their use of local vernaculars as a shorthand for the succinct ways in which film characters (and the generic audience for Australian films) 'get' each other, both films convey the particularity of experiences which are local and transnational in flavour. It is this flavour or mood which defines historical consciousness in the present.

If the SBSi/Adelaide Festival feature film deal of 2002 begs to be considered as a form of cultural intervention, we might expect it to enjoy a different relationship to the audience from the commercial-industrial film product discussed in Chapter 2. The concept of *erfahrung*, or reciprocal experience, is useful for describing the intimacy between filmmakers and audiences whose experience and expectations of cinema are grounded in 1960s social movements that have their residue in the ethos of cultural intervention as it appears in the 1990s at SBSi and other film sites like Film Australia. The cinema produced in this activist milieu might claim to be offering the audience an experience which has more local flavour, more depth and more authenticity than the commercial-industrial cinema (most of which is imported from global infotainment conglomerates running the film production arm of their business out of Hollywood). A common charge against the commercial-industrial product is that it offers its audience a fleeting form of experience, *erlebnis*, which serves as a momentary distraction, a consumer event which fails to leave a trace in memory or consciousness. Further, the ubiquity of *erlebnis* as the dominant mode of experience in commodity culture leads to a kind of amnesia or instant forgetting based on infotainment overload. As Andreas Huyssen suggests, the peculiar feature of postmodern media overload is not so much the instant forgetting inherent in information updates, redundant technology, or retro fashion, but Western modernity's increasing preoccupation with the past, whether as historical memory of 20th-century traumas like the Holocaust or as entertainment memories in blockbusters like *Titanic* (James Cameron, 1997).[23] Huyssen argues against the conservative view that sees a boom in memory practices since the 1980s as compensation for the loss of traditional values grounded in stable communities and nations, nostalgia for that which defines Western modernity. Rather, Huyssen advocates a shift from a 'discourse of loss' to one 'that accepts the fundamental shift in structures of feeling, experience, and perception as they characterize . . . our present'.[24] In this formulation it is not memory of the past which is compensatory, nor is it a matter of opposing a quality cinema of *erfahrung* to a commodity cinema of *erlebnis*. Rather, what is at stake in the proliferation of memory practices, from museum villages to family histories, is historical consciousness as a component of postmodern identity. For Huyssen postmodern identity is informed not just by endless recoding, recycling and citation of past forms but by the desire or necessity to act and speak from within the present structures of experience.[25] These acts may be shaped by the transnational yet they are necessarily local, regional and national. And they are shaped by 'differently paced modernities' in terms of the fragmented forms of local experience with which they are entangled.[26]

From this perspective, 'differently paced modernities' produce different structures of experience which are historically and geographically grounded in the local, regional and national. The issue of identity politics in Australian film might not be a matter of opposing interventionist films from the multicultural imaginary to commercial-industrial films indebted to an anchoring Anglo-Celtic imaginary. It is possible to argue that the doggedly commercial project, *The Dish*, shares the same modernity as the interventionist project, *Australian Rules*. In this modernity, small-town Australia (of the 1960s) is on the cusp of change and only those who can leave behind the embattled identity of the little Aussie footballer will gain a foothold in the bigger playing field beyond the town limits. The structures of perception in both films are decidedly those of the white male making a shift from the rough code of 19th-century bushmen to a more polished code of 21st-century corporate fraternity. Similarly, the low-budget urban drama, *Walking on Water*, the quality multi-strand thriller, *Lantana*, and the blockbuster digital FX musical, *Moulin Rouge*, share the same Sydney-based experience of Western modernity as urbane, cosmopolitan, middle-class. The structures of perception and feeling in these films are shaped by genre, as well as by time and place. In *Walking on Water* and *Lantana* identity is shaped by the exigencies of middle-class life in an open economy. Here, the national suddenly counts for less than it used to, as do the imperatives of gender, sexuality and ethnicity. In *Moulin Rouge*, although the setting is a digitised, hypertheatrical Paris at the end of the 19th century, the mood and feel belong to the

Sydney 2000 Olympics and its year-long hyper-party to mark the end of the millennium.

Together, these films achieve a sense of what it feels like to be living, tenuously, in the globalised present, in a cosmopolitan place which derives its lifestyle from transnational consumer culture, and its vernaculars, in part at least, from the Anglo-Celtic social imaginary of *The Dish* and *Australian Rules*. For the generic audience with a long-standing interest in Australian film, these different modernities share a common feature. They are imbued with a discourse of loss, whether repudiation of an exclusive and outdated brand of mateship as the basis of national identity in *Australian Rules*, or nostalgia in *The Dish* for the benign moment before the 1960s heralded a change of era, or acceptance of an underlying feeling of loss as endemic to modernity's cult of social mobility and perpetual change in *Walking on Water*, *Lantana* and *Moulin Rouge*. Unlike the explicitly post-*Mabo* films (*The Tracker*, *Black and White*, *Rabbit-Proof Fence*, *One Night the Moon*, *Yolngu Boy*, *Beneath Clouds*), Australian films with contemporary settings tend not to register their historical consciousness by dramatising historical injustices. Rather, their historical consciousness is registered in the way they take an interest in finding cinematic devices for evoking in the audience the structures of feeling and perception that speak to the experience of an era of change which Huyssen and others call late modernity.

The final question for this chapter is the short-lived role of SBSi in reviving a 1960s activist, interventionist ethos – to open up spaces for understanding some of the structures of contemporary experience, feeling and perception in Australia. Under the leadership of Bridget Ikin, SBSi was able to anticipate political events in its programming policies during the first two terms of the neo-conservative Howard government. By supporting programs which contested that government's deprecation of 'navel-gazing cultural elites', SBSi insisted that the past is not over and done with in Australia.

From a cultural-interventionist perspective, policy frameworks are bound up with aesthetic and ideological issues. We are arguing that film and television industry policy in the post-*Mabo* period is shaped by and reshapes the social imaginary of the nation, which is itself undergoing fiercely contested redefinition in the era of globalisation, courtesy of the bipartisan policy of economic rationalism and the divided cultural politics of the history wars. We approach these issues directly through our reading of films (rather than of policy papers, industry reviews, funding practices).

How do we explain an apparent contradiction in films during the Howard government's third term in office? On the one hand, film and television policy is formulated by a neo-conservative federal government keen to refute the black armband view of Australian history in favour of an oft-quoted 'relaxed and comfortable' ethos, a government keen to dismantle the institutions which have been a platform for left-liberal agendas since the Whitlam era, and keen to attract the votes of those disaffected by bipartisan economic policies. On the other hand, the years 2000–03 have seen an unprecedented cluster of feature films taking a left-liberal approach to the history and present impact of British colonisation of Australia, at the same time that these films have adopted various strategies for negotiating the misfit between global and local moments of experience. The ability of SBSi to go against the political grain shows that the discrepancy between global-scale actions (shaped by transnational corporations and the United States as superpower) and responses to local situations has opened up spaces for different vernaculars, each of which participates in a media politics of memory.

The dismantling of the left-liberal cultural agenda has gathered momentum since the 1996 election, impacting on the independent filmmaking community whose values were formed in the 1960s social movements and counterculture. This impact goes beyond ideological defeat of a cinema of *erfahrung*. It has been institutionalised, particularly through a series of conservative appointments to the cultural organisations which owe their existence to the changes that started to happen in the late 1960s as middle Australia blasted its way out of the mindset of the British-loving Menzies era. As this chapter has argued, there is common ground between cultural-interventionist and commercial-industrial films in Australian cinema. It is likely that this common ground will become stronger as the industry deals with the fear that local histories and stories that can only be remembered and narrated in the Australian context will be swamped by a flood of cheaper imports under the bilateral free trade agreement. This agreement was finalised between Australia and the United States on 9 February 2004, arousing further anxiety that free trade will spell the end of Australian content in cinemas, pay TV, and future digital media delivery systems. Partnerships between free-to-air public television and commercial broadcasters in the production of feature films, mini-series and documentaries will rely even more on the pragmatic activism of board members, bureaucrats and programmers, with SBS Independent as one recent model of a cinema of cultural intervention.[27]

Notes

1 Miriam Dixson, 'Identity: history, the nation and the self'. In Joy Damousi and Robert Reynolds (eds), *History on the Couch: Essays in History and Psychoanalysis*, Melbourne University Press, 2003, p. 120.

2 David Malouf, 'Made in England: Australia's British inheritance', *Quarterly Essay*, no. 12, 2003, p. 64.
3 Susan Dermody and Elizabeth Jacka, *The Screening Of Australia*, vol. 1, Sydney: Currency Press, 1987.
4 Belinda Smaill, 'SBS Documentary and *Unfinished Business: Reconciling the Nation*', *Metro*, 126, 2001, pp. 34–40.
5 Human Rights and Equal Opportunity Commission, *Bringing Them Home*. Report of the National Inquiry into the separation from their families and communities of Aboriginal and Torres Strait Islander children, Canberra, 1997.
6 The SBSi package of feature films included *Australian Rules, Beneath Clouds, The Tracker, Yolngu Boy* and *Walking on Water* (all released in 2001–02).
7 James Ricketson, 1979, 'Poor movies, rich movies'. In Albert Moran and Tom O'Regan (eds), *An Australian Film Reader*, Sydney: Currency Press, 1985, pp. 223–7.
8 On cinema as a public sphere of *erfahrung* see Thomas Elsaesser, *New German Cinema*, London: BFI, and Basingstoke: Macmillan, 1989, pp. 157–9.
9 Andreas Huyssen, 'Present pasts: media, politics, amnesia'. In Arjun Appadurai (ed.), *Globalization*, Durham: Duke University Press, 2001, p. 57. Thank you to Nathalie Brillon for drawing this article to our attention.
10 Dixson, 'Identity', p. 120.
11 Stuart Macintyre, *The History Wars*, Melbourne University Press, 2003, pp. 3–4. Macintyre argues that while Keating as Prime Minister asked 'egalitarian' Australians to look outward to Asia and the global economy, Howard promoted the notion of a 'self-indulgent elite' as 'a foil for the battlers'.
12 A session at the November 2002 Conference of the Australian and New Zealand Film and History Association held at Flinders University in Adelaide raised the complex issues of procedures for working with the appropriate people in Aboriginal communities to ensure that the right to tell a story has been granted in line with filmmaking protocol devised by the Australian Film Commission.
13 Quoted in Dixson, 'Identity', p. 120.
14 ibid., p. 128.
15 ibid.
16 The moral authority of Tommy, the father, is a reminder of the moral authority of the grandfather in the New Zealand film *Whale Rider* (Niki Caro, 2002). However, *Whale Rider* emphasises the poignancy of the grandfather's struggle to transmit Maori culture when he takes to his bed, beaten by disappointment, opening the way for a mythic solution, rather than one that addresses the historical reality shown in the film.
17 Malouf, 'Made in England', pp. 62–3.
18 ibid., pp. 46–49.
19 ibid., p. 59.
20 ibid., p. 63.
21 ibid., p. 65.
22 For an account of the cumulative impact of the Howard Government on the left-liberal political agenda in place since the election of the Whitlam Labor Government in 1972, see Robert Manne, 'The Howard years: a political interpretation'. In Robert Manne (ed.), *The Howard Years*, Melbourne: Black Inc. Agenda, 2004, pp. 3–53.
23 Huyssen, 'Present pasts', p. 67.

24 ibid., p. 71.
25 ibid., p. 73.
26 ibid., p. 54.
27 Meaghan Morris has produced a subtle reading of the committee-based forms of activism which have brought about the cultural changes now under attack from the neo-conservatives appointed by Howard's government. See Meaghan Morris, 'Epilogue: future fear'. In M. Morris, *Too Soon Too Late: History in Popular Culture*, Bloomington IN: Indiana University Press, 1998, pp. 219–34.

4

Mediating Memory in *Mabo – Life of an Island Man*

Since the High Court's judgment in *Mabo and others v. The State of Queensland (No 2) (1992)*,[1] 'Mabo' has become a household word in Australia. In his commentary on the cultural implications of the decision, Jeremy Beckett, anthropologist and witness for the plaintiffs, claims that media and politicians have added a new word to the Australian vernacular.[2] '"Mabo"', he says, 'has come to stand for the whole issue of Aboriginal land rights, as in "Mabo law", "Mabo deal", "Mabo show" and of course, "Mabo madness"; if it has not already become a verb, it soon will.'[3] For Beckett, the over-use of 'Mabo' in popular discourse has, among other effects, 'overshadowed' the fate of the leading litigant.[4] Put simply, 'Mabo' is *a name without a face*. This cultural oversight, this gap between a judgment and a historical subject, prompted the making of the award-winning biographical documentary film *Mabo – Life of an Island Man* (Trevor Graham, 1997). In this chapter we undertake a close analysis of this film, considering the role it has played in mediating public recognition of both the *Mabo* decision and Mabo 'the man'. We are interested in how this documentary has become a popular history of *Mabo* and what this success tells us about shifts in documentary filmmaking in Australia in the 1990s and the forms of spectatorship they can enable.

Up Close and Personal

In the past fifteen years we have witnessed major changes in all areas of independent documentary film: funding, production, style, distribution and reception. These changes can be broadly attributed to the shift away from the cinema as the key site of independent documentary film to television. The new emphasis on narrative and personalisation, typified in successful television documentary series such as *Australian Story* (ABC-TV), has generated debate, much of which tends to be framed by old familiar oppositional terms, such as fact and fiction, critical intervention and entertainment, the personal and the social.[5] But some commentators are more open in their thinking on this shift towards television. John Hughes, filmmaker and former Commissioning Editor for SBS Independent (1998–2001), suggests that we have in fact reached a stage where the desire of public sector television networks to develop new ideas in the area of documentary 'is occupying some of the territory that has previously been occupied by filmmakers themselves in producing critical or observational intervention in the culture'.[6] A survey of successful 'breakthrough' documentaries – the kind that get people talking – shows that many use a mix of techniques associated with television, such as a strong sense of narrative, drama and character and a focus on the personal, while still allowing for critical insight into social processes: *Facing the Music* (Robin Anderson and Bob Connolly, 2001), *Ordinary People* (Jennifer Rutherford, 2002), *Rats in the Ranks* (Robin Anderson and Bob Connolly, 1996), *The Good Woman of Bangkok* (Dennis O'Rourke, 1991), *Losing Layla* (Vanessa Gorman, 2001). It follows then that what is required is a critical practice that can go beyond conceptual oppositions such as those mentioned above, addressing how these documentaries and others position the spectator and what forms of social recognition are enabled by these new modes of appeal.

One of the most successful documentaries of the past decade is *Mabo – Life of an Island Man*. When it was first screened at the 1997 Sydney International Film Festival it received a standing ovation that lasted more than five minutes and was voted Best Documentary Film. Since then, it has won numerous other national and international film awards, including history and cultural awards.[7] It had a successful national theatrical release and has been screened several times in prime time on national television (ABC Australia), while Currency Press recently published the script – a publishing first in Australia. Reviews indicate that this phenomenal success is largely due to the distinctive personal style of the film.[8] John Ryan, for example, writes: 'Moving away from his earlier treatment of Mabo-the-case, Graham's film has brought Mabo-the-Man much closer to us.'[9] The film uses first-person narration, recounting throughout details about the making of the film and the relationship between the filmmaker and its subject. It uses personal testimony by family members and friends, and it also includes a number of dramatisations of events, including Bob Maza's outstanding readings of Eddie Mabo's love letters to his wife Bonita. A number of reviews and feature articles suggest that this intimate style of filmmaking brings us closer to the significance of the historic judgment than a more conventional documentary could. Tom Ryan encapsulates this view in his description of the film as 'an intimate history'.[10]

But what exactly is an intimate history? What is at stake when conventional historical discourse is replaced by 'up close and personal'? Or to put it slightly differently, what are the implications of a history designed to move its audience? We raise these questions because although the film's director claims to diverge from the documentary principle of (assumed) objectivity, the film is nevertheless fuelled by the ideal of national education. *Mabo – Life of an Island Man* serves in many contexts as an official history of the case, including many secondary and tertiary curricula.[11] In doing so, this intimate film fulfils the requirements of the traditional social role of the documentary, that is, the 'task', as Terry Morden describes it, of 'guid[ing] citizens through the complexity of modern life towards an active role in the democratic processes'.[12] But it also deploys the language and techniques of intimacy to organise non-Indigenous spectators into a particular affective response to the death of Eddie Mabo.

In media reports at the time of the release of his film, Graham often states that his aim was to tell a personal story and to move people. These sentiments are reiterated in the introduction to the published screenplay of the film, where he writes: 'The success of the film in Australia indicates that there is a willingness amongst Australians to embrace reconciliation and social justice, *provided* the issue can be made to touch them personally' (emphasis added).[13] This attitude accords with what Lauren Berlant identifies as 'forms of intimate attachment' – attachments that are, she argues, increasingly replacing and transforming former relations between the public sphere and the private.[14] Berlant claims that forms of intimate attachments such as those between 'nations and citizens' or 'churches and the faithful', or even more mundane forms such as 'the intimacy between people who walk dogs or who swim at the same time each day', have generated 'a specific aesthetic'. On the nature of this aesthetic, she makes the point that intimacy is an expression that relies on or is a response to what she describes as 'shifting registers of unspoken ambivalence'.[15] She gives the example of lovers: 'When things become ambivalent between lovers', she says, 'they resort to the intimacy of talking about the relationship'.[16] Likewise, she continues, 'when citizens feel that the nation's consented-to qualities are shifting away' they also seek the 'language of intimacy'.[17]

In the rest of the chapter we show how in order to mediate social recognition of both the *Mabo* decision and its namesake, Graham's film *Mabo – Life of an Island Man* generates a form of intimate attachment between the film's spectators and its subject. Moreover, we will show how it does so largely by provoking the particular range of emotions associated with tragedy. First we examine the film's use of techniques of faciality, such as biography and portraiture, to create an intimate picture of Eddie Mabo as a tragic hero. Then we argue that the film can also be understood as generating a second kind of intimate proximity, one in which the gap between the name and face of Mabo is made visible as a series of traumatic defacements.[18]

The Mask of Tragedy

On one level, *Mabo – Life of an Island Man* is a straightforward biography: it organises the events of Eddie Mabo's life into more or less chronological order and in such a way that the narrative unifies these events into a single purpose in life, namely Mabo's struggle for land rights. By using the trope of the face as the means of mediating social recognition of Mabo, the film is also a portrait machine. It combines archival material and interviews with Mabo's family members, friends and political allies to trace out the contours and features of Mabo's unique personality. We learn that he was 'family-orientated', 'generous', 'humorous', 'egotistical' and 'proud'. These testimonies are intercut with numerous family snaps and other sources of photographic close-ups of Mabo's face, including footage from *Land Bilong Islanders* (1990). Together, these techniques 'flesh out', as one reviewer put it, a recognisable face for the hitherto faceless name.[19] At times the film brings us so relentlessly close to the face that we find ourselves, like ancient physiognomists, scrutinising Mabo's facial features as evidence of his true nature. Certainly this is what film critic Evan Williams does when he concludes Mabo was a 'hero-martyr': 'in that magnificent broad countenance, with its grey, wiry mane, there was something of the sage, the prophet, the visionary. He looked the part.'[20]

About three-quarters of the way into *Mabo – Life of an Island Man*, the metaphoric defacement of 'Mabo', which the film aims to redress, is suddenly literalised in the shocking image of a racist attack on Eddie Mabo's grave. This attack occurred in June 1995, immediately after a Torres Strait Islander tombstone-unveiling ceremony held in Townsville to commemorate Eddie Mabo and to celebrate the High Court judgment.[21] We learn that while Indigenous and non-Indigenous members of Mabo's community joined together with representatives from federal and state governments in a cultural celebration, unknown attackers spray-painted Mabo's grave with racist graffiti, including two large swastikas and the racist epithet 'Abo'. The attackers also prised a life-size bust of Mabo from its central position on the headstone, leaving in its place a large gash in the otherwise smooth marble surface. In an interview after the release of the film, Graham describes his personal response to the attack: he says, '[I] was . . . absolutely horrified and devastated . . . I fell into a crumbling heap.'[22] He also explains that the desecration of the grave is the 'real reason' for making the film: 'Bonita [Mabo] was pestering me to go and film the tombstone opening . . . so I got a crew together who went up to Townsville to film the tombstone opening and the celebrations. Then, of course, the day after the grave was trashed . . . the real reason for making the second film was a sense of outrage about his grave being trashed.'[23] At this point in the film we discover that the deface-ment of the grave is the true origin of the film. In the light of this image, this violent origin, the film's stated aim of 'giving the name a face' takes on deeper significance.

As an attack on the sacredness of the dead, defacement of a grave is a powerful act of hate. In 1990, when graves were attacked by a small group of anti-Semitic demonstrators in the Jewish cemetery at Carpentras, France, 100 000 people gathered in Paris to protest. They marched through the streets of Paris, joined by the then president, François Mitterrand. But while in France the racist attack on Jewish graves sparked widespread direct action, here the violence of defacement was swiftly subsumed in a struggle of com-peting ideologies or what Graham aptly describes as 'a media battle of sym-bols'.[24] In the *Daily Telegraph Mirror*, conservative columnist Piers Akerman claims that the defaced grave represents 'a wedge between black and white', the embodiment, in his mind, of the *Native Title Act*.[25] *The Australian* takes a more personal approach, using a large photograph of Bonita Mabo and her two grandsons crouched on the edge of the defaced grave to complete its neo-liberal point of view of the family as tragic victims. In what we might call a 'metropolitan' point of view, *The Australian* report takes a strong moral stance only to locate the cause of the attack 'elsewhere', namely in rural Australia, in the deep recesses of the psyches of 'a handful of racists'.[26]

Graham's film actively engages in this battle of symbols. In its documen-tation of the unveiling ceremony, the commanding black marble headstone is framed as a symbol of Reconciliation. The dream of a unified nation is captured in the figures of Bonita Mabo and Annita Keating (the latter rep-resenting the then Prime Minister, Paul Keating) reflected side by side in its shining surface. The reflective surface of the headstone serves as a mir-ror in which spectators can narcissistically insert themselves into a positive vision of the future. After the attack, however, this image of unity becomes an impossible point of view. The slow pans and jerky camera movements across the disfigured grave mimic the dazed faces of those at the scene. No longer able to reflect the symbolic space of a unified nation, the defaced headstone is, literally, bereft of messages. De-metaphorised, the headstone is visible for the first time in its literal sense – that is, as a marker of the site of death. It is mute in a way that only death is: silent and silencing. This confrontation with the physical fact of death is never more forceful than in the sequence of images that document the disinterment of the coffin: the sounds and images of the manual labour required to exhume the casket, the sight of the hole in the ground in Townsville's cemetery where Mabo's body once lay. From this point onward, viewing is not simply an act of social recognition but a rite of bereavement.

The final section of the film is primarily a documentation of the family's renewed mourning and the reburial of Mabo's body on his island home. Here, the narration becomes even more intimate as Graham explains that after the attack on the grave he had no choice but to continue filming. We would argue that it is also at this turning point that we begin to understand the film as a 'work of mourning': it repeats the scene of death as a way of working through it and inevitably moving beyond it. But it is also in this final 'act', titled 'Journey home', that we are reminded of the close association between mourning and tragedy. The final section reproduces the devastation of the attack and subsequent reburial by way of redeeming the suffering incurred in this unexpected resurfacing of death. It does the latter by shaping the events of the attack and reburial into the easily recognisable final act of a tragedy – the Hero's Return. In *Cinema Papers*, editor and co-producer Denise Haslem is quoted as saying that when she and Graham were editing the film, 'they recognized that the three acts fell into a Greek tragedy so easily, there was no other way to edit it'.[27] Following the structure of classical tragedy, the film is, its director claims, a case of 'life imitating art'. Graham says: 'the film is very much like the hero's journey. I keep comparing it to Luke Skywalker going out to conquer the universe. He's battling the empire, but the tragedy is, unlike Luke, he dies before his great victory.'[28]

As a tragedy, the affective experience of this film is grounded in spectators' recognition of a generic plot structure, rendering 'the face behind the name' as the face of a tragic hero.[29] To see Mabo through the lens of tragedy allows us to interpret the circumstances of his death as 'dignified endurance' of an injustice, while the reburial on Murray Island becomes 'poetic justice': Mabo, who spent his life fighting for land rights, finally returns home. While this structuring of the events of Mabo's life creates a powerful and moving cinematic experience, we need also to consider the limitations of recognising Mabo, and by association the *Mabo* decision, in the terms of tragedy. Take, for example, Evan Williams's review. He writes: 'His [Mabo's] premature death has enshrined him as a legend, a mythic figure more potent than he was in life.' Here, Williams suggests that as with all tragic heroes, Mabo is more powerful dead than alive. Indeed, Williams goes on to suggest that had Mabo survived, had we seen him in his moment of victory, the film might not have been as good as it is. Or, to use his term, it might have been 'spoiled', by which he means 'gloatingly heroic' rather than 'gentle, elegiac'. This is the thing about tragic heroes: death is not only their fate but also their nature.

As with so many others, Williams is moved by the way in which the film ends – 'on a note of exquisite sadness', to use his words. Responding to this film's tragic mood, he also implies a certain kind of fatalism. With its emphasis on fate, tragedy can serve to mask historical reality.[30] The 'sounds of traditional music' Williams refers to in his review, for example, are in fact the sacred Malo dance, which was performed by Murray Islanders in honour of Eddie Mabo. Filmed at night, the spectacle of the towering turtleshell Malo mask, combined with the dirge-like rhythms of traditional drums, enhances the drama of this act of commemoration. But to see the performance only in terms of the eternal time of tragedy is to overlook its historical specificity. What the film does not tell us is that this was the first time this dance has been performed in more than eighty years (that is, nearly the entire duration of the colonisation of the Torres Strait Islands.) In her in-depth study of the *Mabo* judgment, Nonie Sharp convincingly argues that the resurrection and performance of the Malo dance in honour of Eddie Mabo is an historic act of 'cultural revival and resistance'.[31]

Likewise, by constructing the reburial of Mabo on Mer as a Hero's Return, the film overlooks the fact that the state also played an important role in Mabo's 'journey home'. The then federal government funded the reburial of Mabo's disinterred body on the Murray Islands, concerned that if the grave were to remain on the mainland it could easily become an ongoing target for racist opposition to native title legislation. As Graham says in his narration, Mer is, possibly, the right place for Mabo to be buried, but for all the wrong reasons. The final shot of the film is a silent, grainy image of Mabo spear-fishing in the shallow waters of Mer. He is a commanding, tragic figure. But we are mistaken if we interpret Mabo's reburial on his island home as compensation for the violence of defacement, as some kind of mythic equivalent to the recognition of land rights.

The Trauma of Non-recognition

So far we have argued that *Mabo – Life of an Island Man* makes Eddie Mabo recognisable as a tragic hero. But this is only one form of recognition enabled by this complex film. The gap between name and face, judgment and historical subject, which the film seeks to conceal, also provides an opening for a second and arguably more radical perspective on the defacement of Mabo's grave. Unlike tragedy, which, as we argued, can mask historical specificity,

Walter Benjamin's philosophy of the image offers a way of understanding this image of defacement as an aesthetic experience that jolts us into a historical form of recognition – that is, a remembrance of the traumatic history embedded in the name.

Benjamin was fond of Karl Krauss's observation that 'the closer the look you take at a word, the greater the distance from which it looks back'.[32] When we see our name, or the name of a loved one, perhaps, misspelled, out of context, or, as in this case, defaced, the familiar name stares back at us like the face of a stranger. Constructionist theories of language tell us that what we grieve on these occasions is the loss of the concept of self. That is to say, the strangeness of the name exposes the arbitrariness of the sign. In Benjamin's philosophy of language the sign is never arbitrary. On the contrary, the inherent difference between name and thing made visible in moments of alienation, such as those mentioned above, reveals the fetishistic nature of words. Benjamin was fascinated by what he perceived as the 'magic of language': the way in which words and things interpenetrate and in time come to resemble each other.[33] Following on from this, we could say that the gap between name and self created by the defacement of the name is an actualisation of the original loss of the particularity of the thing in its moment of coming into being as a name. And in this way, the severed name becomes what Benjamin calls 'a dialectical image', an image in which 'the Then and Now come together in a constellation like a flash of lightning' to illuminate current concerns.[34]

As a dialectical image, the cinematic image of Mabo's defaced headstone reveals the origin of the history embedded in *Mabo*. Here, the shock effect of the image of 'Mabo' disfigured by swastikas and the word 'Abo' renders the name faceless and unrecognisable. The name is depersonalised. But it is also true to say that having been obliterated and estranged, the defaced name *actualises* the unspeakable history of defacement that attaches to this name – that is, *terra nullius*, the original non-recognition of Indigenous Law and culture. In this sense, the film is not only a historical record of race hatred but also a cultural form that enables historical recognition and public memory of Australia's particular history of defacement.

As a recurring image, the defacement of 'Mabo' takes the form of a traumatic experience. Cathy Caruth defines trauma as 'an overwhelming experience of sudden, or catastrophic events, in which the response to the event occurs in the often delayed, and uncontrollable repetitive occurrence of hallucinations and other intrusive phenomena'.[35] On several occasions in this film members of Mabo's family allude to the repetitive nature of the violence of non-recognition. In an over-the-shoulder shot we see Bonita Mabo being interviewed by a young television reporter at the Townsville cemetery immediately after the discovery of the racist attack. In contrast to the image in *The Australian*, she does not appear tragic or pitiful. To the contrary, she answers the reporter's banal questions in a steeled, almost automated mode of response. When the reporter asks how the attack makes her feel, she replies: 'It's like a nightmare, starting all over again.' In a following scene, Mabo's son also implies that the attack on the grave is something already experienced when he explains how it has 'opened up old wounds'. History and trauma come together then as we recognise the images of defacement in this film as a traumatic presence. This trauma is, as we see, unspeakable, and it is in its precise irruption in and disruption to language that the defaced name expresses or actualises the history of the effacing violence of non-recognition embedded in it.

Seeing the History *in* the Name

This second view of 'Mabo', in which we face the gap between the name and face rather than foreclose it as a tragedy and thereby veil the historical specificity of the event, opens up a different view of the name and naming. From this perspective, it is possible to 'read' the life story presented in the film through the history of the name. We learn that Mabo was born on Murray Island in 1936, the son of Robert and Paipe Sambo. When his mother died shortly after his birth, he was adopted by Benny (his maternal uncle) and Miaga Mabo. He was raised and educated on Murray Island until 1957 when the Murray Islander Council of Elders exiled him to the mainland, where he lived under two names. He was known as Eddie Mabo by most people, but also as Koiki, his Meriam (Islander) name by other Islanders and close friends. Already, the history of Mabo's name reveals the traces of colonial contact.

Taking a closer look, we can also see how the apparent fluidity of 'Mabo' became an issue in the hearing of the *Mabo* case. Reproducing large sections from the earlier film, *Land Bilong Islanders*, this film provides the only audio-visual documentation of the *Mabo* hearings. In his commentary on the case, Beckett reminds us of the well-known fact that the High Court's recognition of the collective native title rights of the Meriam people of the Murray Islands was extended to all Indigenous Australians.[36] He also brings to our attention the less known fact that Mabo's 'own claim to land was dropped in the final stages of the case'.[37] This 'terrible irony', as Beckett refers to it, occurred because in the determination of facts and issues of the case conducted by the Supreme Court of Queensland, Justice Moynihan found Mabo's claims to be 'invalid'.[38] Moynihan concluded that Mabo was not the adopted son of Benny and Miaga Mabo and therefore not entitled to make his claim. In addition, Moynihan believed Mabo was 'an unreliable witness' and described Mabo's explanation of Meriam inheritance custom as 'self-seeking'.[39] Moynihan's refusal to recognise Mabo's land claim was in effect a refusal to recognise his name. The film implies that Mabo never really recovered from the shock of this act of non-recognition. Bonita Mabo recalls her husband's reaction to this news. 'He was devastated', she says. We also learn that Mabo died a few months later, aged fifty-five. In the days leading up to his death he wrote a long, detailed genealogy of his name.

As with the film and Beckett's commentary on the case, Nonie Sharp's cross-cultural analysis of the Murray Islander's land case defends Mabo's credibility. She analyses the extraordinary demands placed on Mabo to explain himself during the hearing of evidence in the determination of the facts and issues of the case, reporting that 'In the first fourteen days of the hearing of Eddie Mabo's evidence . . . 289 objections were made by Queensland'.[40] She argues that the demand for Mabo to explain himself, along with the subsequent non-recognition of his claim, is part of the wider trivialisation of Meriam Law that occurred throughout the case. She explains how the case ignores the significance of adoption and fostering of children, as well as the wider system of name-holders, including the inherent code of secrecy and specific modes of oral performance of this particular system of inheritance.[41] She argues that when Justice Moynihan deemed Mabo's claim to be 'self-serving' he was also refusing to recognise a crucial principle in Meriam Law: to claim to own the land is 'to be responsible for it', including the responsibility of passing it on. In Meriam Law, a claimant is 'a name holder on behalf of the group who are the joint owners'.[42]

These kinds of suspicions and trivialisation of Indigenous culture are not new. Underlining the non-recognition of Mabo's family name and the subsequent refusal of his claim to native title is the racist supposition that Mabo was not a 'proper native'. Beckett notes how many of the legal and cultural commentaries on the judgment focus on the fact that the case differentiated between Islander and Aboriginal cultures.[43] If, however, we read the history of non-recognition *in* Mabo's name, we can see that both the Queensland Supreme Court and the High Court's treatment of Mabo are a *repetition* of the state's past treatment of Aboriginal culture and its current *reinstatement* of that attitude of suspicion in the form of the strict procedures and criteria of the *Native Title Act* (1993) (and its subsequent amendment). The recent Yorta Yorta claim exemplifies the limitations of native title as a form of legal recognition. When Justice Olney of the Federal Court ruled against the Yorta Yorta native title claim to land in northern Victoria and southern New South Wales, he put the view that the 'tide of history' had washed away the group's native title: 'Notwithstanding the genuine efforts of the members of the claimant group to revive the lost culture of their ancestors, native title rights and interests once lost are not capable of revival.'[44] Thus the terrible paradox of native title: the very history the *Mabo* judgment promised to overturn is precisely 'the tide' used by judges such as Olney to deny claimants their native title rights.

The traumatic history of non-recognition revealed in the shock of Mabo's defaced name reminds us of the material and social aspects of naming. In modern self-oriented societies, the proper name is considered sacred, but only because it is widely regarded as equivalent to what is called 'the essence of self'. It is a view that works to conceal the inherent sociality and power of naming. It is also a view that excludes other cultural conceptions of sacredness. In the opening of his oral history, Mabo talks about his proper name as something he was 'assigned'.[45] He also explains how 'Mabo' is the name he 'grew under'. Here, the name is not given some transcendental identity with self but recognised as part of a social practice that places, obliges and even limits the bearer in relation to others. We are also reminded by Mabo's understanding of naming that, far from being primarily about notions of self, a proper name is that which *entitles* us to property and land rights. Not the name as a bearer of the concept of self but what Judith Butler calls 'the action of names': to have a name is, she argues, to have the potential power to name another.[46] Eddie Mabo knew this about names, and it was because of this knowledge that the Australian courts regarded him with suspicion. Graham's film portrays Mabo as an activist, an archivist, and an expert in colonial histories and law, all of which the courts perceived as too *white-faced*. As Beckett observes: 'It is ironic that while anthropologists became credible expert witnesses by writing, "natives" render themselves inauthentic by reading: tainted with literacy it seems they can't go home again!'[47] And as the film shows, Mabo did not go home again until after his death, until after his name was defaced, yet again.

In this chapter we have shown how *Mabo – Life of an Island Man* makes Eddie Mabo recognisable to Australian audiences as a face, indeed as *the* face of native title. We have also tried to show how this intimate portrait of 'the man behind the name' also enables another kind of recognition. We argued that the close-up detail of the events following the commemoration service in Townsville shocks us into a recognition of the other face of *Mabo*, the underside of the mask of tragic hero, if you like, made visible in a series of traumatic defacements: the gaping hole at the centre of the marble headstone where Eddie Mabo's bust was once attached, the entirely unfillable hole in the ground in Townsville's cemetery where Mabo's body was once buried, the racist erasure of Mabo's name by swastikas and the epithet 'Abo'. In these images we can, we believe, recognise the origin of the traumatic history of non-recognition of Indigenous Australians, that is, the effacing violence of *terra nullius*. Most importantly, the film allows us to see how this particular violence repeats itself even now in current forms of non-recognition of Indigenous Australians, such as the procedures and implementation of native title legislation that regard all Indigenous Australians with suspicion.

Notes

1 This chapter is a new and developed version of Therese Davis's article 'The name and face of Mabo: questions of recognition', *Metro*, 127 and 128, 2001. On the *Mabo* decision, see *Mabo – The High Court Decision, Discussion Paper, June 1993*, Canberra: Australian Government Publishing Service. Also see Noel Pearson, '*Mabo*: towards respecting equality and difference'. In Gillian Cowlishaw and Barry Morris (eds), *Race Matters: Indigenous Australians and 'Our' Society*, Canberra: Aboriginal Studies Press, 1997; Murray Goot and Tim Rowse (eds), *Make A Better Offer: the politics of Mabo*, Sydney: Pluto Press, 1994; W. Sanders (ed), '*Mabo' and Native Title: Origins and Institutional Implications*, Canberra: Centre for Aboriginal Economic Policy Research, Australian National University, Research Monograph, no. 7, 1994.

2 Jeremy Beckett, 'The Murray Island land case and the problem of cultural continuity'. In '*Mabo' and Native Title: Origins and Institutional Implications*, p. 7. Many thanks to Tim Rowse for recommending Beckett's article and Nonie Sharp's cross-cultural analysis, *No Ordinary Judgement – Mabo, The Murray Islanders' Land Case*, Canberra: Aboriginal Studies Press, 1996.

3 ibid., p. 7.

4 ibid.

5 For an overview of these debates, see Steve Thomas, 'Whatever happened to the social documentary', *Metro*, 134, pp. 152–160.

6 Paul Davies, '"Between fact and fiction": speculating on the documentary with John Hughes', *Metro*, 136, pp. 108–9.

7 Other film awards and nominations to date include: Third place, Certificate of Creative Excellence for the categories Documentary, Current Events, Special Events, United States International Film and Video Festival, 1998; Finalist, Best International Documentary, 'Hot Docs', Toronto, Canada; Winner, Best Documentary Award, Australian Film Institute Awards, 1997; Winner, Best Script Award, NSW Premier's Literary Award, 1997.

8 See: 'The man behind the name' (*Cairns Post*); 'Mabo family album' (*Daily Telegraph*); 'A portrait of the man who was the Mabo case' (*Age*); 'Mabo the man' (*Herald Sun*); 'Powerful portrait of Mabo' (*Age*).

9 John Ryan, 'Mabo – Life of an Island Man', *Artery*, 6(8) 1997, p. 5.

10 Tom Ryan, 'Mabo – Life of an Island Man', *Sunday Age* (Melbourne), 10 August 1997, C2.

11 In 1997 the film won the NSW Premier's Audio-Visual History Award. It is a highly sought after educational resource, distributed by Film Australia, along with accompanying teaching notes and a bibliography on native title. The film has been a set text on the NSW HSC curriculum. The screenplay, published in 2000, is also a set

text. Finally, the film forms the basis of a comprehensive, sophisticated CD ROM and website production on *Mabo* by Film Australia.

12 Terry Morden, 'Documentary. Past. Future?' In Patricia Holland, Jo Spence and Simon Watney (eds), *Photography/Politics II,* London: Comedia and Photography Workshop, 1986, p. 69.

13 Trevor Graham, *Mabo – Life of an Island Man, Original Screenplay,* Sydney: Currency, 1999, p. xx. It is interesting to note that this is the first documentary screenplay to be published in Australia, perhaps, the world, providing further evidence of the film's function as a historical record of *Mabo.*

14 Lauren Berlant, editorial, *Critical Inquiry,* 24, Winter 1998, p. 284.

15 ibid., p. 286.

16 ibid., p. 87.

17 ibid., pp. 286–87. Also see Elizabeth A. Povinelli, 'The state of shame: Australian multiculturalism and the crisis of indigenous citizenship', *Critical Inquiry* 24, 1998.

18 This analysis of defacement is indebted to Michael Taussig's conceptualistion of the term in *Defacement: Public Secrecy and the Labour of the Negative,* Stanford University Press, 1999. We also gratefully acknowledge his helpful comments on an earlier draft of this chapter.

19 Veronica Matheson, *Sunday Herald Sun* (Melb), 'TV Extra', 9 November, 1997, p. 3.

20 Evan Williams, 'Enough redemption already', *Weekend Australian,* 'Review', 19 July 1997, p. 11.

21 For more detail on the unveiling ceremony and *Mabo* Day celebrations in Townsville, see Noel Loos and Koiki Mabo, *Edward Koiki Mabo: His Life and Struggle for Land Rights,* Brisbane: University of Queensland Press, 1996.

22 Jim Schembri, 'A portrait of the man who was the Mabo case', *The Age* (Melbourne), 30 July 1997, p. 7.

23 Deborah Niski, 'No man is an island', *Sunday Age,* 27 July 1997, C5.

24 ibid.

25 Piers Akerman, 'Black man's burden', *Daily Telegraph Mirror,* 6 June 1995, p. 11.

26 Fiona Kennedy, 'Racists desecrate Mabo's gravestone', *Australian,* 6 June 1995, p. 1.

27 Margaret Smith, *Cinema Papers,* 119 (August, 1997), p. 38.

28 Jim Schembri, 'A portrait of the man who was the Mabo case', *Age,* 30 July 1997, p. 7

29 Aristotle, *Poetics* (52a, pp. 2–4), as quoted in Stephen Halliwell, *Aristotle's Poetics,* London: Duckworth, 1986, p. 171.

30 See Walter Benjamin, *The Origin of German Tragic Drama,* transl. John Osborne, intro. George Steiner, London: Verso, 1977, p. 62.

31 Sharp, *No Ordinary Judgement,* p. 41.

32 Walter Benjamin, 'On Some Motifs in Baudelaire'. In Hannah Arendt, *Illuminations,* transl. Harry Zohn, London: Fontana, 1992, p. 196.

33 Walter Benjamin, 'On language as such and the language of man'. In Peter Demetz (ed.), *Reflections – Essays, Aphorisms, Autobiographical Writings,* transl. Edmund Jephcott, New York: Schocken Books, 1986, p. 330.

34 See Walter Benjamin, '"N" (Re: the Theory of Knowledge, Theory of Progress)', trans. Leigh Hafrey and Richard Sieburth. In Gary Smith (ed.), *Benjamin: Philosophy, Aesthetics, History,* University of Chicago Press, 1989, pp. 42–83.

35 Cathy Caruth (ed.), *Trauma: Explorations in Memory,* Baltimore and London: Johns Hopkins University Press, 1994. We gratefully acknowledge Dr Jodi Brooks whose

work introduced us to trauma theory and who has been extremely helpful in her comments on this chapter.

36 Beckett, 'The Murray Island land case', pp. 12–13.

37 ibid., p. 7.

38 In his judgment, Justice Moynihan wrote: 'I was not impressed with the credibility of Eddie Mabo. I would not be inclined to act on his evidence in a matter bearing on his self-interest . . . unless it was supported by other creditable evidence', as quoted in Beckett, 'The Murray Island land case', p. 18.

39 Noel Loos and Koiki Mabo, *Edward Koiki Mabo: His Life and Struggle for Land Rights*, Brisbane: University of Queensland Press, 1996, p. 16.

40 Sharp, *No Ordinary Judgement*, p. 41.

41 ibid., p. 78.

42 ibid.

43 Beckett, 'The Murray Island land case', pp. 8–10.

44 See 'Native title claim "washed away"', *Sydney Morning Herald*, 19 December 1998, p. 1. For an Indigenous perspective on developments in the Native Title debate, see 'Native Title and Wik: The Indigenous Position: Coexistence, Negotiation and Certainty', position paper, National Indigenous Working Group, ATSIC, Canberra, 1997.

45 Loos and Mabo, *Edward Koiki Mabo*, p. 26.

46 Judith Butler, *Excitable Speech: A Politics of the Performative*, New York and London: Routledge, 1997, pp. 28–38.

47 Beckett, 'The Murray Island land case', p. 22.

Landscape and Belonging after *Mabo*

5

Aftershock and the Desert Landscape in *Heaven's Burning, The Last Days of Chez Nous, Holy Smoke, Serenades, Yolngu Boy, The Missing*

The impetus for this chapter comes out of a particular viewing experience which we are calling 'aftershock'.[1] For us, this experience is associated with the unbearable weight of history embedded in the Australian landscape film of the 1990s. The landscape cinema of the 1970s established Australian film as an international genre. The 'AFC genre', as it was christened by Susan Dermody and Elizabeth Jacka, was defined by the period film which became the flagship of an inward and backward-looking national identity through quality films like *Sunday Too Far Away* (Ken Hannam, 1975), *Picnic at Hanging Rock* (Peter Weir, 1975) and *My Brilliant Career* (Gillian Armstrong, 1979).[2] However, after a decade of official support through the Australian Film Commission, the period film was repudiated as the nation's standard-bearer during the commercially oriented 1980s, particularly after the first two *Mad Max* films (George Miller, 1979, 1981) reclaimed the landscape for a contemporary, outward-looking cinema. The cinematic landscape has re-emerged as a more complex figure of national identity in the 1990s, after the High Court ended the nation's sustaining myth of *terra nullius*.

Writing about the landscape tradition in Australian feature films of the 1970s, Ross Gibson argues that 'the majority of Australian films have been about landscape'.[3] They participate fully in the 200-year-old landscape tradition whereby non-Aboriginal Australia, 'underendowed' with myths of belonging, tried 'to promote a sense of the significance of European society in the antipodes'.[4] Gibson emphasises a myth of belonging structured around an unknowable, untamable landscape, viewed as 'an awesome opponent' rather than 'a nurturing mother', a 'primitive . . . storehouse of some inexhaustible and ineffable Australianness'.[5] Taking the *Mad Max* trilogy as a turning point in the landscape tradition, Gibson argues that from the end of the 1970s, as official Australian culture became more open to contamination by international popular culture, there was 'a conscious intent to revise the old myths' of a 'flawed but marvellous' society taking on the character of a 'flawed but marvellous' continent. Gibson concludes by suggesting that, given the rapid pace of economic and cultural internationalisation evident by the late 1980s, these well-established 'national myths are also altering'.[6]

With hindsight, more than a decade after Gibson's essay was written, it is possible to argue that *national* events have been as significant as international contamination in the rewriting of national myths, and in the renewed force of the landscape tradition evident in the cycle of Indigenous–settler films released in 1999–2002. This extraordinary cycle includes nine feature films: *Australian Rules* (Paul Goldman, 2002), *Beneath Clouds* (Ivan Sen, 2002), *Black and White* (Craig Lahiff, 2003), *The Missing* (Manuela Alberti, 1999), *One Night the Moon* (Rachel Perkins, 2000), *Rabbit-Proof Fence* (Phillip Noyce, 2002), *Serenades* (Mojgan Khadem, 2001), *The Tracker* (Rolf de Heer, 2002), and *Yolngu Boy* (Stephen Johnson, 2001).

For us, the landscape films of the 1990s provoke shocks of recognition of a continent which has been anything but the sublime void of European projections. Rather, there is now a popular awareness that the continent has been written over by Indigenous languages, songlines, dreaming stories and Law for 40 000 years or more. Since the *Mabo* decision at least, the image of the outback landscape in cinema provokes recognition of historical amnesia (rather than an unknowable, sublime, interior void) as the founding structure of settler Australia's myths of belonging.

In this chapter we are interested in how a familiar icon of Australian cinema, the landscape (in particular the desert landscape, the outback), is suddenly made strange (unbearable even) by a historic event and how this raises questions to do with historical amnesia, shock and memory in a national cinema. Although the image of the Australian red centre as a vast and empty space is ubiquitous in television and advertising, we will confine our argument to particular moments from seven feature films which, in different ways, are symptomatic of the fresh impact of a familiar icon occasioned by the *Mabo* decision. The persistent return of the landscape is evident in a range of contemporary Australian genre films, whether the period film, the road movie, the identity quest, or outback melodrama. Some of these films have had critical recognition. Most of them have been routinely produced and consumed within the protocols of what O'Regan calls 'a mundane national cinema' which has no expectation of dominating the box office in its own market.[7]

In order to sneak up on this post-*Mabo* experience of aftershock, we want to place these films in relation to three critical categories which have been important in making sense of the ad hoc diversity of Australian films.[8] The first is the landscape tradition, closely associated with the AFC-funded period film which, although less popular than the urban ocker films, defined Australian national cinema from the mid-1970s into the 1980s. The 1998 release of Gillian Armstrong's adaptation of Peter Carey's 1988 novel *Oscar and Lucinda* revives the 1970s period film and tries to compensate for the historical amnesia, or national innocence, of the genre. A notable exception to the genre's myth of innocent settlement of unoccupied territory is *The Chant of Jimmie Blacksmith* (Fred Schepisi, 1978).

The second category is the purgatorial narrative of failure and defeat whereby a melancholic male protagonist merely survives (rather than conquers or transforms) a pitiless natural landscape and an exiled, insular society.[9] If the loner-hero in *Mad Max* is the ultimate figure of subsistence, the survivor-heroes of *Sunday Too Far Away* and *Gallipoli* (Peter Weir, 1981) are emblematic of the bush battler's ethos of making a virtue out of defeat. The non-viable landscape of the outback and the defeated, melancholic male are revived by Russell Crowe and Ray Barrett in the operatic, deterritorialised road movie *Heaven's Burning* (Craig Lahiff, 1997). Some elements of the ethos of survival are also evident in two contemporary Indigenous stories, *Yolngu Boy* and *Serenades*. But in the full-blown melodrama *The Missing*, outback redemption from European angst comes at such a price that the modest ethos of survival begins to look like good sense rather than moral failure.

The third category, to which less critical attention has been devoted, is comedy as the popular face of Australian cinema. The popularity of comedy stretches from the larrikin humour of *The Sentimental Bloke* (Raymond Longford, 1919), to the backblocks farce of the Hayseeds and the Rudd families of the 1930s and 1940s, to the urban ocker films of the 1970s, to the globe-trotting Paul Hogan in *Crocodile Dundee* (Peter Faiman, 1986), to the quirky suburban comedies of *Strictly Ballroom* (Baz Luhrmann, 1992), *Muriel's Wedding* (Paul J. Hogan, 1994) and *The Adventures of Priscilla, Queen of the Desert* (Stephan Elliott, 1994). The suburban grotesque is revived and transported to the outback in *Holy Smoke* (Jane Campion, 1999), deflating the spiritual aspirations embodied by the film's international stars, Kate Winslett and Harvey Keitel. The suburban wasteland, and its particular forms of family strife, provide the motive for a trip to the desert by a middle-aged woman and her father in *The Last Days of Chez Nous* (Gillian Armstrong, 1992). Their trip is more like a Sunday drive than a road movie, but like *Holy Smoke*, the prevailing ethos is down-to-earth deflation of any impulse towards the sublime brought on by the expanse of the desert.

If we take the High Court's *Mabo* decision of 1992 as a historic event which caused a paradigm shift in our thinking about identity, the land, and belonging in Australia, then our relation to landscape, as the template of national identity in Australian cinema, might also be undergoing a paradigm shift. In order to understand the effect of this paradigm shift on the impact of the landscape film after Mabo, we use the terms 'shock', 'aftershock' and 'afterwardness'.[10] The shock recognition of *terra nullius* as a myth breaks through the protective shield of historical amnesia, but at the same time the shock itself entails a protective numbing effect. The initial recognition of the historical truth behind the 1992 *Mabo* decision came as a shock to the nation as it reassessed its founding myth. But the shock did not become traumatic until the rise of One Nation and the beginning of the history wars in the mid-1990s. The historical event only becomes traumatic *afterwards*, through the process of left-liberals and neo-conservatives repeatedly going back over what 'really happened' in the past without being able to agree on what it means now. This process of going back over historical events is experienced as traumatic because the highly contentious revision of the nation's past activates unconscious fantasies which, by definition, cannot be directly acknowledged.[11]

Shock of Secular Modernity in *Oscar and Lucinda*

Thinking about history in terms of modernity, rather than postmodernism and the end of history, entails questions of memory and the peculiarly modern sensory experience of montage and shock. This aesthetic experience of shock is associated with the technologies which shape industrial and urban experience, from the factory assembly line to the phantasmagoria of the city with its tenement living, congested traffic, advertising billboards, theme parks and crowded cinemas. The modernity paradigm, taking its cue from Walter Benjamin, approaches cinema as an 'optical unconscious' which brings reality closer.[12] Cinema's framing and editing system is not unlike the visual montage of modern life seen from the moving window of a bus or train or car. The framing and editing of everyday life as a series of montages (which give us a close-up or a bird's eye view of what is normally unseen) offer a radical rethinking of history as the source of national identity through national cinema. Rather than identification with a national past imagined by a flagship national cinema, Benjamin's concept of cinema as an 'optical unconscious' insists on cinema's capacity to produce shocks of recognition of the past in the present in a dialectical image, not of the past as it really was, but of 'a memory as it flashes up at a moment of danger'.[13] Michael Taussig argues that this 'flash of recognition' and its 'numbing aftermath of shock' depends crucially on a 'singular act of *recognition* of past in present' a fleeting act of recognition which depends on 'the perception of similarity'.[14] However, the similarity between past and present is not based on continuity or cause-effect. Nor is it a matter of history repeating. Rather, history flashes up 'as a sudden rejuxtaposition of the very old with the very new', as a 'resurgence' of the old in 'the (Euroamerican) culture of modernity'.[15] The resurgence of the image of the desert landscape in Australian films at the end of the millennium is a case of the image of a pre-historic, empty landscape suddenly becoming recognisable, post-*Mabo*, as a land with a history.

As Laura U. Marks argues, official history 'actually shields consciousness from experience . . . It takes a shock to *unroot* a memory, to create a flow of experience'.[16] The return of landscape cinema, after *Mabo*, provokes a shock recognition of an unburied, unreconciled national history. This unrooted memory of a traumatic colonial past has decisively displaced cultural nationalism's bush legend and its ethos of mateship as the origin of an egalitarian nationhood. A key instance of this shock of recognition occurs in Gillian Armstrong's period film *Oscar and Lucinda*. The story is set in the colonial period from 1848 to 1870 and culminates in a wager between Lucinda, an Australian heiress (whose fortune derives from her mother's subdivision of land), and Oscar, an English clergyman and obsessive gambler, estranged from both his father's puritanical religious sect and his adopted Anglican brethren. The wager between Oscar and Lucinda involves transporting a modern church of iron and glass from Sydney to Bellingen through 'unmapped country'. The delivery of the church to a bush town in northern New South Wales takes Oscar on a journey from Christian faith to secular enlightenment and costs him his life. The scene of Oscar's death by drowning in the sinking church entails a 'shock of recognition' for the viewer whereby the past corresponds with the present, not only as a revision of colonial history but as an unrooting of collective or social memory. It is this unrooted memory of the past that endures after the film, and after the historical event in the present to which the film corresponds. The shock that creates a flow of memory, through which we recognise history in the present, comes from the dislocated sound of Oscar's prayer. This prayer for forgiveness seems to echo out over the landscape. However, the familiar landscape of the 'untamed' Australian bush is transformed by the fantastic image of the floating glass and iron church as it slowly cracks and fills with water. Oscar's prayer, together with the image of the sinking church, remind us of the bloody cost of his wager, and of colonial settlement: the massacre of the Kumbaingiri tribesmen and the murder of the treacherous leader of Oscar's expedition. The pictorial stillness of the landscape, its supposed 'emptiness', is profoundly disturbed by Oscar's prayer: 'Forgive me. Forgive me. Forgive me for my pride. Forgive me for my ignorance.' The aura of untarnished history embodied in the untouched landscape of the 1970s period film is brought to light in this scene as we hear the words that, at the time of the film's release in 1998, were intimately tied to the politics of recognition (or non-recognition) of the belated traumatic effects of *terra nullius*. When the weight of European modernity and Christianity, both represented by the glass church, entombs Oscar, there appear to be no witnesses. But in an earlier scene, as the church floats down the river to its destination, the amazing sight is witnessed by Aboriginal children. Through these silent witnesses, *Oscar and Lucinda*, like Paul Keating in his Redfern Park speech, asks us to imagine the shock of colonial history, not only as we recognise it now, belatedly, but as Indigenous Australians continue to experience it in the present.

It is the belatedness of the shock of recognition that changes the meaning of history in *Oscar and Lucinda*. It makes us ask what is the real historical event taking place here in our viewing of the film? This is a different question from how the past is represented in the film. The timing of the film's release in 1998 meant that the shock effect of the *Mabo* decision had begun to shift from recognition of the myth of *terra nullius* to fears about native title (Howard's Ten Point Plan was announced amid controversy at the 1997 Reconciliation Convention). Oscar's prayer for forgiveness also corresponded with Howard's refusal at the same Convention to apologise as Prime Minister of Australia to members of the Stolen Generations whose stories had caused waves of belated shock and grief in Indigenous and settler communities after the release of *Bringing Them Home*.[17] There is a further belated context for understanding the film. With a budget of around $16 million, *Oscar and Lucinda* was one of the first features to be produced out of Sydney's Fox Studios and distributed by Twentieth Century's art-house subsidiary, Fox Searchlight. Shot partly in England, the film, like *Gallipoli* (Peter Weir, 1981), was able to exploit Australia's historical ties to Britain, and to extend its market appeal by casting Ralph Fiennes in the role of the benighted Oscar, as well as launching the international career of Cate Blanchett, the Australian actor who went on to star as the English queen in *Elizabeth* (Shekhar Kapur, 1998). In this sense, the film looks outward to reclaim a place for the Australian period film in international cinema, and backward in time to Australia's origins in British colonial policy. The film's remembrance of the British origins of settler Australia came at a time when Australian nationhood was well entrenched in two post-Anglo-Celtic modes: the multicultural and Indigenous mode whereby acceptance of ethnic diversity had been official policy for twenty years; and the melting pot mode which had long made a virtue of a cosmopolitan identity forged by enthusiastic consumption of international brands, alongside local products. By the time Armstrong's film was released in 1998, the shock of recognition of the landscape, not as something timeless and natural but as a sign within an Indigenous cultural system, had started to become familiar, not only in cinema but also through international recognition of Aboriginal culture, particularly through dance, art and music. This sense of a familiar shock of recognition, of being shocked again, of becoming unshockable as more and more landscape images after *Mabo* evoke a traumatic colonial history, is what we mean by aftershock. Our use of the term to describe post-*Mabo* cinema implies that Indigenous and settler Australians alike are still living through the unresolved trauma of colonial settlement.

Aftershock in *Heaven's Burning, The Last Days of Chez Nous* and *Holy Smoke*

Aftershock in contemporary films is the space of everyday life and its fantasised revision of the desert landscape to fit new historical circumstances. This repeated recognition of constellations between past and present states of trauma in landscape films is best understood in terms of what Patrice Petro describes as the 'aftershock' of late modernity rather than the shock of early modernity that Benjamin and other critical theorists grappled with in the 1920s and 1930s.[18] In aftershock, recognition does not pass in a fleeting moment; it endures through repetition, replacing the numbness of shock with the everydayness of a jaded kind of recognition, akin to boredom. Petro connects boredom with the non-eventful repetitions of everyday life and the remakes of popular culture.[19] She argues that the remake 'has more to do with repetition and duration – with a history in which nothing happens – than with transformation and change'.[20] When a national cinema routinely remakes its nationalist myths through repetition of landscapes and characters, we are in the temporality of the everyday, of the present, of aftershock, where, as Petro argues, nothing much that is new happens. The everyday, in this schema, is opposed to the temporality of history where change occurs as an *event* which can be documented.[21] In this version of history, the *Mabo* decision is an event, something that can be documented as official history. However, it is the duration of the effect of the event over time, its aftershock, that concerns us here. How does the Australian landscape signify the enduring repetition of the past for those characters (and viewers) who journey into the dead heart of the continent in films with contemporary rather than historical settings?

Landscape films set in the present draw on a range of genres, including melodrama, the road movie, the personal relations film, and the adventure-quest. The post-*Mabo* effect can be understood in these films in terms of the everyday dislocations and mundane repetitions of aftershock as a benumbed or bored state. Many of the landscape films of the 1990s seem to be preoccupied with what Jacka argued for in 1988, that is, 'reconceptualising the nation', not in terms of costume drama but 'according to the vicissitudes of everyday life'.[22] The turn to genres other than the period film indicates a national cinema interested in taking up the dislocations of contemporary life. One way of thinking about a post-*Mabo* cinema of dislocation might be to think about how, in the *aftershock* of *Mabo*, the outback is no longer available for the kind of Romantic locationism extolled by Charles Chauvel.[23] For Chauvel, the land was a source of an Australian national identity for Europeans. His location films, particularly *Sons of Matthew* (1948) (set in the Queensland bush) and *Jedda* (1954) (set in the Northern Territory outback), have had a lasting impact on the landscape tradition, exemplified by *Night Cries – A Rural Tragedy* (1989), Tracey Moffatt's acclaimed remake of *Jedda*.

When characters traverse the outback landscape in an Australian road movie, the desert is confirmed as an utterly natural location for the spiritual crises of a secular society suffering the aftershock of modernity and its colonial underpinnings. As Roslynn Haynes has established, the desert landscape has been invested with a range of meanings in Australian art, film, literature, travel writing, tourism and environmental studies. Explorers, missionaries and anthropologists, as well as nation-building miners, irrigators and pastoralists, have variously seen the desert as a wilderness to be mapped, redeemed or exploited; a recalcitrant Nature defeating heroic human endeavour; or a timeless, numinous landscape inciting awe and fear. Under British colonialism, scientific modernity separated the knowing subject (usually masculine) from the land as object (usually feminine).[24] This rational, scientific view is incomprehensible in terms of Aboriginal Law, defined as a ceremonial body of knowledge based on reciprocity between ancestors, the land and all physical beings.[25] In the European view, the desert without an oasis was an ungodly void, a stark reminder of paradise lost. In the Indigenous view, natural landmarks, visible everywhere, were fully alive with indwelling spirits and the Law.[26]

The ascendancy of the alienated European view of the landscape has been challenged in the 1990s, especially in films which deal with conflicts between two laws, Indigenous and settler. This issue is taken up in Chapter 6.

What's interesting about the contemporary journey to the desert, in the films we discuss below, is how the purgatorial narrative is undergoing a transformation, a remake, as white masculinity faces a crisis of non-viability and white femininity faces a spiritual crisis. It is the downright ordinariness of these crises, their origin in the stifling sameness of suburban life, barely relieved by the monotonous duration of the endless road journey through vast expanses of unpopulated space, that points to the phenomenon of aftershock as a facet of contemporary Australian road movies.

In the 1990s, the trip to the desert has been undertaken by alienated urban dwellers, their journeys motivated by a crisis, usually with the law or the family. The landscape films place their protagonists in classic outback settings – mostly a flat, dry red earth where the road and the car (or motorbike) are the only signs of modernity's toehold on a vast, inhospitable continent. Although none of these films shares *Oscar and Lucinda*'s historical revision of the nation's origins, each of them takes the secularity of modernity as a central concern. In these films the desert landscape functions as the fantasy setting or *mise-en-scène* for a secular approach to the sacred (projected onto the Aboriginality of the land) through negation. This negation of the sacred is endemic to the spiritual quest in Australian cinema. It speaks to the problem in modernity of the spiritual as something pre-modern which becomes easily realigned with 20th-century fascism or 21st-century religious fundamentalism. In the Australian vernacular this negation is a recurring refrain best articulated as 'there's nothing out there' by Sophie Lee in Jane Campion's *Holy Smoke*, echoing Bill Hunter's 'There is no god' in Gillian Armstrong's *The Last Days of Chez Nous*. This negation of the sacred is paradoxical in that it both recognises and negates the landscape as sacred. It is as if the characters who journey into the outback are held captive by a secular modernity which allows the nation to continue to deny native title despite the *Mabo* and *Wik* cases.

Heaven's Burning

One of the most internationally contaminated road movies to emerge from the pack in the 1990s was *Heaven's Burning*. More than any of the genre's critical or popular successes, including *The Adventures of Priscilla, Queen of the Desert* (Stephan Elliott, 1994), *Doing Time for Patsy Cline* (Chris Kennedy, 1997), *True Love and Chaos* (Stavros Efthymiou, 1996), *The Goddess of 1967* (Clara Law, 2001) and *Kiss or Kill* (Bill Bennett, 1997), *Heaven's Burning* remaps the Australian landscape to speak directly to the experience of international contamination. Moreover, it does so with the distinctive local accent of playwright and screenwriter Louis Nowra, keen observer of the legacy of Hawke-Keating's deregulated Australia.

Heaven's Burning is a reprise and an update of the landscape tradition for several reasons: it retains an acute, critical sense of Treasurer Keating's deregulated Australia even as it tries to exploit the Asian film market; it remaps the Australian landscape for a tourist gaze and a corporate takeover even as it peoples it with the road movie's cast of outlaws, ratbags and no-hopers; its characters are beyond integration into a multicultural ideal; three out of four of its father-son couples are spectacularly non-viable; and Russell Crowe takes the recessive Australian hero (Colin) to a new level of passivity while Youki Kudoh's inspired rendition of Midori's transformation from Japanese honeymooning bride to hostage, bank robber and romantic outlaw upstages the Hollywood action heroine.

Heaven's Burning consciously exploits the landscape tradition for a tourist gaze and for an elusive Southeast Asian film market. But it does so in ways that emphasise Australia's dislocated place in a deregulated global economy. The familiar cinematic landscapes are deterritorialised in the film's remapping of Australia. This road movie's deranged map makes a geographical impossibility of Midori and Colin's escape route from the international tourist city of Sydney via the eerie flatness of South Australian saltpans, through the red dust outback of New South Wales, and then, somehow, back to the unlocatable beach for the film's Wagnerian finale.

The four father-son figures in *Heaven's Burning* are divided into two aesthetic types: active comic book avengers (a Japanese salaryman armed by his hapless boss, and an Afghan father who teaches his son a thing or two about torture) who cannot be integrated into a residual ideal of Australian multiculturalism; and passive icons of Anglo-Australian masculinity (the drought-stricken farmer and the city cop) whose limited capacity for action cannot hold death at bay for the young couple on the run. This stand-off on the frontier of masculinity leaves the field of action wide open for the heroine, Midori. *Heaven's Burning* opens with an extreme close-up of Midori's eye, looking for a way out of the art-directed, corporate landscape in which she finds herself playing the role of the demure Japanese bride, honeymooning in Sydney. Midori's first act is to rescript her role by staging her own kidnapping. Her plans come undone and she finds her genre in the road movie, learning to improvise, saving Colin, stealing a truck, and staging a second, more successful bank robbery. With her heroic credentials established, Midori takes charge of her own make-over, providing the costumes, make-up, hairstyle and setting for her final transformation into an incendiary image of *l'amour fou*. Colin's passivity and his father's hostility cannot dampen her spirit – in the outback she can breathe. Right up to her final breath, Midori contaminates the film with an ethic of daily self-invention in the space of the Australian road movie whose only border is death.

If the opening shot of the film belongs to Midori, so too does the film's inspired finale which begins at a Bachelor and Spinster ball and ends in apocalyptic flames on the beach. At the beach, the viewer is rewarded with three telling shots. The first is a sublime close-up of Midori's face shimmering through the flames as she farewells Colin and puts the gun to her head in a final, assured act of self-possession. The second is of the police officer, Bishop, and his rookie offsider, on the beach, witnessing the explosion of the car. The overturned car burns as Bishop sits on the beach with his arms around his knees and looks out to sea. The film leaves him there as the camera cranes up and away from the beach, pulling out to sea to reveal the coastline of an island – a place to leave behind, to depart from by air. Unless you are on that plane, however, you are still here, implicated in Bishop's contemplative gesture of survival – sitting on the beach looking out to sea as heaven burns.

Heaven's Burning is deeply ambivalent about the future of this island-continent in the Asia-Pacific region. The final shot raises the possibility of abandoning the project of Australia altogether. The film has shown its land-scape to be a montage of images peopled by blind, stoned and otherwise ill-equipped figures, most of whom are male. Fathers have nothing to hand on to their sons except outmoded technology and fundamentalist ethics. When Midori holds the gun to her head and squeezes the trigger, the narrative comes to a spectacular end. Her eye, which opened the film looking for a way out, is transferred to Bishop looking out to sea, and then to the viewer contemplating the final shot of the receding coastline. Like Bishop, we sit and contemplate the scene, sidelined from the field of action which opened so briefly for Midori.

The Last Days of Chez Nous and *Holy Smoke*

In *The Last Days of Chez Nous* the trip to the desert, which occurs in the middle of the film, presents the landscape as a tourist attraction and a site for everyday squabbles and unfinished business between a middle-aged writer, Beth (Lisa Harrow), and her father (Bill Hunter). The resolute secularity of everyday life in Australia is embodied by Hunter as the laconic Aussie bloke whose trip to the desert affirms the sacred through negation – if this trip is purgatorial then this is the purgatory of the family sedan and the Sunday drive. In the early stages of the desert journey the rising tension between father and daughter enclosed in the moving car is contrasted with the release of erotic energies at home between Beth's husband and her sister. However, although it costs Beth her marriage, the trip to the centre of Australia opens up a new vista for Beth. Alone in the family sedan with her father, having the same pointless fight they've been having for twenty years, it seems they are more alienated than ever. They end up in separate hotel rooms, watching TV alone. Whatever their intentions, they are isolated and numbed by the repetition of suburban family rites in the desert, just as they were in the city. However, when Beth and her father finally leave the car to walk companionably in the desert (her filial love declared and his parental voice silenced), Beth is able to put to him taboo questions about God and death that the suburban Australian male rarely encounters in cinema. Surrounded by the expanse of red earth that has become symbolic of the Australian psyche, this good Aussie bloke does his best with the question of God, recalling a visit to a cathedral in Budapest which left him 'unconvinced' about God. However, on the fear of dying he enters a wry plea, 'Oh, fair go.' This laconic conversation is the highlight and endpoint of a journey which is filmed as resolutely uneventful and secular. Beth's questions are posed in the empty space between the domed cathedral in Budapest and the sacred rock (Uluru) at the heart of the Australian continent, both unseen in the film. What *is* represented, from Beth's suburban verandah, is an unassuming church spire, barely visible among the trees and rooftops of the inner city. The image of the spire turns Beth's mid-life crisis into a spiritual quest. The spire refers us back to European culture, which has articulated its metaphysical questions of death, God and the soul in relation to the father. When Beth sets off to find the spire in the last shot of the film, the spiritual quest in Australian cinema is brought home from the purgatorial desert to the secular suburbs.

By contrast, Jane Campion's *Holy Smoke* maps the spiritual wasteland of suburban space onto the exotic desert landscape, exaggerating the incongruity between identity and place which is characteristic of Australian films. *Holy Smoke* begins and ends its spiritual quest in India. In between, the Australian outback (filmed in a manner reminiscent of Albert Namatjira's paintings) becomes the gothic backdrop not for the usual purgatorial quest, but for both a desecration and a comic deflation of the spiritual aspiration. The plot involves a suburban family kidnapping their daughter Ruth so that cult-exiter PJ can negate her ecstatic faith in Indian cult leader Baba. Rather than total negation of the sacred, the film's deflation is aimed squarely at Australian suburbia and its secular indifference to the desert (imagined as something between a pub crawl, an ostrich farm and a theme-park motel). Locked together in a spiritual and sexual battle, Ruth (British star Kate Winslet) and PJ (American star Harvey Keitel) are slyly defeated, not by their inner demons or by the desert, but by the intrusion of the suburban grotesque in the form of Australian television personality Sophie Lee. The kaleidoscopic desert landscape provides the *mise-en-scène* for a desecrating encounter between secular and spiritual fantasies of seduction. The contrast between Ruth and her sister-in-law Yvonne (Sophie Lee) is indicative of the way the film invites a double gaze at two familiar figures in the desert landscape: that of the sophisticated foreigner and the naive local. Ruth's key scene involves stripping naked in a desert landscape bathed in moonlight. At a moment of spiritual crisis, she becomes abject, urinating in distress before seducing PJ. By contrast, Sophie Lee's kitsch Yvonne visits PJ at night, indifferent to the outback location. Dressed in suburban *froufrou* from K-Mart, she naively narrates her sexual fantasies about Hollywood film stars before giving PJ a casual blow job. When Lee's character says, towards the end of the film, 'I've thought about it and there's nothing out there', she negates the desert as a purgatorial space in the Australian metaphysical imaginary. It is this negation of the sacred, the perception of the outback in terms of nothingness, that reprises a staunchly secular view of Australian interiority in the above films, refusing the re-enchantment of modernity sought by films like *Serenades* and *Yolngu Boy*, and the Aboriginalisation of the sacred in *The Missing*.

Afterwardness in *Serenades, Yolngu Boy* and *The Missing*

If shock, in Benjamin's sense, is associated with singular and fleeting acts of recognition, with flashes of involuntary memory which 'slip by' provoking a chain of correspondences or associations, then aftershock (which endures rather than flashes by) might be thought of in terms of a mode of revised memory that Susannah Radstone calls 'afterwardness'.[27] In her essay on history, memory and fantasy in *Forrest Gump*, Radstone makes a distinction between the historical recovery of repressed traumatic events and the psychoanalytic understanding of traumatic memories as symptoms of unacknowledgable primary fantasies. Whereas historical approaches to memory focus on the tension between official history and popular or unofficial memory (presented in a narrative of historical events in a cause-effect pattern), psychoanalytic approaches reject linear temporality in favour of the psychic temporality of 'afterwardness'. For Radstone, afterwardness 'refers to a process of deferred revision'[28] whereby 'the analysis of memory's tropes can reveal not the truth of the past, but a particular revision prompted by later events'.[29] A further difference between history's use of popular memory and the Freudian concept of memory is the role of primary fantasies (of origins, of desire, of sexual difference) in shaping experience in such a way that memories (always formed in terms of fantasies) cannot be mapped onto historical events in any straightforward way.

Thinking about post-*Mabo* landscape films in relation to this account of 'afterwardness', the landscape in non-history films (whether the deterritorialised road movie, the art-house relationship drama, the full-blown exploitation melodrama or the adventure-quest) is the *mise-en-scène* of contemporary, everyday fantasies of origins (where do I come from?), desire (what do I want from the other?) and difference (how do I understand the enigma of the other?). If Australian film is a genre of international cinema noted for its landscapes (the outback, bush, suburbs, beach), then memory in contemporary Australian films is spatial (prompted by place) as well as temporal (historical event). The continuing process of 'deferred revision' or 'afterwardness' informs our definition of a post-*Mabo* cinema as a kind of backtracking through the cinematic landscapes of pre-*Mabo* cinema.

Serenades and Yolngu Boy

Two adventure-quest films released in 2001 borrow from the landscape tradition that was inaugurated by *Walkabout* (Nicholas Roeg, 1971). Both films contribute to a contemporary multicultural cinema concerned with the transformation of Australian identity and memory. *Serenades* and *Yolngu Boy* are both concerned with the way identity can be remade in the many intersections between tradition and modernity. In this sense the two films are deferred revisions (or fantasised memories) of the archaic as it resurfaces in modernity. At one level, the two films construct an argument, from a present-day multicultural perspective, about what happened to traditional identity in the wake of British colonialism. But more than this, they struggle to express the archaic in the modern through cinema's adventure-quest genre whereby the protagonist is forced to leave home and undergo a number of ordeals before returning home and being recognised as the hero. The hero's identity is confirmed in the adventure-quest through the slaying of the dragon, sea monster or behemoth (something primeval or archaic) which threatens the social order. The conundrum for the protagonists of *Serenades* and *Yolngu Boy* is that it is their Aboriginality which is aligned with the archaic, while the threat comes from the behemoth of modernity. In this sense, the films revise the desecration of the archaic which led to the death of the unrecognised hero (David Gulpilil) in *Walkabout*. The films also lend credence to the idea that outback films which Aboriginalise the land as timeless and untamable are inevitably remaking Chauvel's *Jedda*.

Unlike the films discussed above, *Yolngu Boy* and *Serenades* use the desert landscapes of central and northern Australia as authentic locations for coming-of-age stories of Aboriginal characters forced to negotiate between different cultural traditions and legal frameworks. Both films are propositional: their schematised characters and plots present an argument as well as an adventure-quest narrative, with central and northern land-scapes as backdrops rather than expressive characters in their own right. There is a sense that both the lyrical and the melodramatic potential of the two films are held in check, refusing the stunning exoticism of Roeg's vision in *Walkabout* and the romantic locationism of Chauvel's vision in *Jedda*.[30] Cinematic excess is avoided in favour of a judicious argument in favour of revised Aboriginalities based firmly in modernity, not relegated to the primitive, the exotic or the archaic.

Although *Serenades* is set in central Australia in the 1890s and draws on historical research by Christine Stevens into the meeting points between German Lutheran missionaries, Aboriginal women and Afghan cameleers, it has a weaker historical sense than the contemporary drama of three paths taken by three young men in *Yolngu Boy*. In *Serenades*, although the story is located in time and place, the landscape itself appears unlocated and dehis-toricised. As a set of horizons which hem in Jila (Alice Haines), the outback becomes mythic and poetic rather than bound up with culture and history. The film was written and directed by first-time filmmaker Mojgan Kha-dem, whose family was forced to leave Iran in 1978 to save her mother from being executed for her activities on behalf of Iranian women. As an allegory of a young woman trying to find her own identity within the confines of three paternalistic religious cultures, *Serenades* is not unlike Tom Cowan's infamous feminist allegory *Journey Among Women* (1977). Both films res-onate with contemporary feminist understandings of decolonisation and the nexus between gender, race and sexuality. Yet both films retain a radi-cal feminist sense of the Australian outback as a space beyond civilisation where universal themes of freedom can be reprised and myths of female links to the earth can be reincarnated. The final image of Jila returning to her birthplace to dance out her own identity in relation to the land rejects the patriarchal rule of Aboriginal, Christian and Muslim cultures. Unlike *Yolngu Boy*, however, Jila cannot find a solution to her identity in the Abo-riginal culture that allowed her Afghan father to win her Aboriginal mother (for a single night) in a card game. By isolating Jila in the landscape, rein-venting her identity through her feet in contact with the earth, *Serenades* revives an autochthonous fantasy of woman having sprung from the land itself. Unlike Khadem's family who took the historical option of becoming refugees, *Serenades* opts for a universal myth of origins, forgetting history (and the different predicaments of women in a range of religious cultures) by ending outside time and place.

By contrast, the location of *Yolngu Boy* in Yolngu country is essential to the meaning of the story. The film conveys an essential belief about the con-nection between the land, identity and the Law through Baru/Maralitja Man (performed by Yolngu dancer Mangatjay Yunupingu). Here, knowledge is a matter of initiation into the Law, not a matter of individual desire to invent a new identity. The spectacular landscapes of North East Arnhem Land, from Yirrkala, through Kakadu National Park, to the city of Darwin, provide a variety of challenging obstacles in the adventure-quest undertaken by three Yolngu boys facing initiation into different futures. While the landscapes in this context are spectacular and mythic in line with genre conventions, they are also culturally specific in ways that are not immediately translatable. The land is clearly inhabited, not by a timeless people but by the Yolngu people whose ties to country now centre on Yirrkala, best known as the home ground of the popular band Yothu Yindi.

Yolngu Boy breaks with images of the desert as an inland, unliveable place by revealing Arnhem Land's proximity to the sea and by assuming that the land is able to sustain its people, physically and spiritually. The film is a hybrid of an adventure-quest film mixed with the strong cultural and historical coordinates of social realism. Rather than the typical adventure-ordeal (established in *The Back of Beyond*, John Heyer, 1954, and remade in *Walkabout*) of children lost in the outback waiting to be found, the boys' journey is a quest for the right path through the hazards of modernity. One of the sly jokes in the film occurs in the last part of the journey through Kakadu when the boys' idyllic swim in a waterhole is interrupted by the arrival of a busload of tourists, who give the boys a lift into Darwin. This is one of the many ways the film reprises the fantasy of a timeless Indigenous culture under threat of seduction by the behemoth of modernity.

If *Serenades* is historically dislocated as an outback melodrama in which Jila is exchanged between Aboriginal, Christian and Muslim men, then *Yolngu Boy* is firmly anchored in the proposition of two laws/three pathways for young Aboriginal men in the remote communities of northern Australia. The decolonisation process proposed by *Yolngu Boy* is more literal than the symbolic ending of *Serenades*. Botj (Sean Mununggurr) is driven by petrol-sniffing and petty crime to suicide; Milika (Nathan Daniels) opts for integration into modernity through a professional career in AFL football; and Lorrpu (John Sebastian Pilakui) chooses initiation into traditional Aboriginal Law. Although the choices might appear clear-cut, the untranslatable aspects of Yolngu culture are also evident in the challenges faced by the boys. If Botj shares the tragic fate of many on the frontier between two cultures, then Lorrpu and Milika represent two paths towards a more reconciled future where the Law into which they are being initiated stands for self-determination and difference within modernity. Although untranslatable difference is carefully respected in the collaborative process,

Yolngu Boy refuses to position Yolngu Law as something archaic threatened with extinction by modernity.

The Missing

At the end of the Mabo decade, as the impact of landscape begins to soften into something less keen, it comes as a shock to see the return of European fantasies of the outback as an archaic source of primitivism which can redeem modern alienation and spiritual angst. In the dream-like logic of *The Missing* (Manuela Alberti, 1999), the archaic becomes the antidote for the spiritual ills of Tommaso, a Vatican priest sent back to Australia by his wise superior to rediscover 'true values'. In contrast to the disenchanted negation of the desert as sacred in *Holy Smoke*, the priest's journey to the desert in *The Missing* seeks spiritual rebirth through an encounter with the Aboriginal spirit-world (projected onto the antipodean landscape by the European imaginary). Although this kind of appropriation of Aboriginal culture is often seen as insensitive exploitation, it can also be seen as part of a gradual process of the Aboriginalisation of settler identity. The controversial nature of this process is evident in the mixed reception of Germaine Greer's proposal that, as a political act, Australians need to rethink their identity in terms of 'becoming Aboriginal'.[31] However, David Tacey, among others, argues that left-liberal critiques of 'becoming Aboriginal' are misguided and that 'spiritual convergence is a fact' in contemporary Australia.[32]

The Missing is an unabashed exploitation film with a European art-house sensibility. It revives stock figures of the antipodean imaginary, including Tommaso, the lugubrious priest who has lost his faith, and the exotic figure of the black tracker (David Ngoombujarra) who moves between two laws. Writer/director Alberti adds several tabloid figures to the mix: the truck-driving serial killer (a throwback to Spielberg's cult telemovie *Duel*, 1971); a missing teenage daughter in search of her origins; and a pious, churchgoing mother whose guilty sin is about to be punished. The style of the film is established in the opening contrasts between the dark interiority of Vatican politics and the shimmering horizons of antipodean animism. Mysterious and occult images of the archaic begin to impact on Tommaso's mind, culminating in a rapid montage sequence of extraordinary primitivism, indebted to voodoo and zombie movies of the 1930s. The archaic intensity of these images peaks when Tommaso is surrounded by a frenzied circle of white-painted Aboriginal faces and speared in the knee as payback for his unwitting role in the deaths of a young Aboriginal boy and the tracker. This sequence is quickly followed by a gratuitous action sequence of the serial killer's truck bearing down on Tommaso, only to jacknife over the embankment and explode in a fireball. Tommaso is saved from his death struggle with the driver by a hefty spear thrown by the ethereal spirit-man whose image is then absorbed back into the heat haze.

The desire to exploit the archaic in *The Missing* vies with the competing impulses of the action flick, art-house angst and the supernatural thriller. As a recent remake of the white man's purgatorial ordeal in the desert, the film is remarkably indifferent to contemporary concerns about cultural insensitivity and the projection of fantasies of guilt and desire onto the enigmatic other. Four characters, including his illegitimate daughter, die so that Tommaso can be redeemed. The film seems unconcerned about these bodies it leaves behind in the Australian outback. The final scene celebrates Tommaso's rediscovery of true values, an epiphany that takes him from the Vatican to the streets of southern Italy to play soccer with young boys. Whether his ordeal in the desert, and the deaths of those he came closest to, will bring on a further round of traumatic memories seems doubtful.

These deferred revisions of the outback landscape involve a post-Mabo recognition of what Taussig calls 'the surfacing of "the primitive" within modernity as a direct result of modernity . . . [and] its everyday rhythms of montage and shock . . . made possible by . . . the camera and the movies'.[33] In other words, in the cinematic journey to the desert we see the makings of a post-*Mabo* fantasy of an autochthonous origin for Australian nationhood. This fantasy incorporates the aftershock of *terra nullius* for Indigenous and settler Australians. It means that the landscape is no longer the template of an untroubled national identity grounded in European modernity. Rather, identity politics, based on post-*Mabo* awareness of the land's living history, can no longer be satisfied by innocent images of unsullied desert landscapes.

Notes

1 Our use of 'aftershock' is indebted to Patrice Petro, 'After shock/between boredom and history'. In Patricia Petro (ed.), *Fugitive Images: From Photography to Video*, Bloomington IN: Indiana University Press, 1995, pp. 265–84.

2 On the period film or 'AFC Genre' see Susan Dermody and Elizabeth Jacka, *The Screening Of Australia: Anatomy of a National Cinema*, vol. 2, Sydney: Currency Press, 1988, pp. 28–37.

3 Ross Gibson, *South of the West: Postcolonialism and the Narrative Construction of Australia*, Bloomington and Indianapolis IN: Indiana University Press, 1992, p. 63.

4 ibid., pp. 64–5.

5 ibid., p. 71.

6 ibid., p. 81.

7 Tom O'Regan, *Australian National Cinema*, London & New York: Routledge, 1996, p. 113.

8 See ibid., pp. 167–88, on the diverse projects, pathways, and unstable identity of Australian cinema.

9 See Graeme Turner, *National Fictions: Literature, Films and the Construction of Australian Narrative*, Sydney: Allen & Unwin, 1986, pp. 49–52.

10 In this chapter the concept of 'afterwardness' is indebted to Susannah Radstone, 'Screening trauma: *Forrest Gump*, film and memory'. In *Memory and Methodology*, New York and Oxford: Berg, 2000, pp. 79–107.

11 See Jean Laplanche, 'Notes on afterwardsness'. In John Fletcher and Martin Stanton (eds), *Jean Laplanche: Seduction, Translation, Drives*, London: ICA, 1992, pp. 217–23.

12 Walter Benjamin, 'A small history of photography'. In *One-Way Street and Other Writings*, transl. Edmund Jephcott & Kingsley Shorter, London: New Left Books, 1979, pp. 240–57.

13 Walter Benjamin, 'Theses on the philosophy of history'. In Hannah Arendt (ed.), *Illuminations*, transl. Harry Zohn, New York: Schocken, 1969, p. 255.

14 Michael Taussig, *Mimesis and Alterity: A Particular History of the Senses*, New York: Routledge, 1993, pp. 39–40.

15 ibid., p. 20.

16 Laura U. Marks, 'A Deleuzian politics of hybrid cinema', *Screen*, 35(3) 1994, p. 258.

17 Human Rights and Equal Opportunity Commission, *Bringing Them Home*. Report of the National Inquiry into the separation from their families and communities of Aboriginal and Torres Strait Islander children. Canberra, 1997.

18 Petro, 'After shock', p. 265.

19 ibid., p. 276.

20 ibid., p. 279.

21 ibid., p. 265.

22 Elizabeth Jacka, 'Australian cinema: An anachronism in the '80s?'. In Susan Dermody & Elizabeth Jacka (eds), *The Imaginary Industry: Australian Film in the Late '80s*, Sydney: Australian Film, Television and Radio School, 1988, p. 126.

23 See Stuart Cunningham, *Featuring Australia: The Cinema of Charles Chauvel*, Sydney: Allen & Unwin, 1991.

24 Roslynn Haynes, *Seeking the Centre: The Australian Desert in Literature, Art and Film*, Cambridge University Press, 1998, pp. 3–4.

25 On Aboriginal Law, kinship and landscape see Eric Michaels, *For a Cultural Future: Francis Jupurrurla makes TV at Yuendumu*, Melbourne: Artspace, 1987, pp. 28–34.

26 Haynes, *Seeking the Centre*, pp. 12–15.

27 Radstone, *Memory and Methodology*, p. 85.

28 ibid., pp. 85–6.

29 ibid., p. 86.

30 On Roeg's landscape vision in *Walkabout* see Louis Nowra, *Walkabout*, Sydney: Currency Press, 2003. On Chauvel's locationism in *Jedda* remade in the studio by tracey Moffatt in *Night Cries*, see Meaghan Morris, 'Beyond assimilation: Aboriginality, media history and public memory', *Aedon*, 4(1) 1996, pp. 12–26.

31 Germaine Greer, 'Whitefella jump up', *Quarterly Essay*, no. 11, 2003. For a range of responses to Greer see 'Correspondence', *Quarterly Essay*, no. 12, 2003.

32 David Tacey, 'Spirit place'. In John Cameron (ed.), *Changing Places: Re-imagining Australia*, Sydney: Longueville Books, 2003, pp. 243–8.

33 Taussig, *Mimesis and Alterity*, p. 20.

6

Coming from the Country in *Heartland, Cunnamulla* and *Message from Moree*

At the end of *The Tracker* (Rolf de Heer, 2002) David Gulpilil's character, mimicking the lone hero of the Western, rides off into the far distance towards the horizon, leaving behind the young follower who will make his own way back to civilisation, a more civilised man after his enlightening encounter with the violence of the frontier between two laws.[1] In this sense *The Tracker* re-imagines the frontier violence of the colonial encounter by suggesting, through the figure of The Follower, that there is an alternative national history to the 'self-innocenting narrative casting our national forebears as caring, Christian civilisers motivated by concern for the hapless natives'.[2] Two things matter here. The first is what will *happen afterwards*, after the return to civilisation, after the end of the frontier wars. The second is how these events, these violent conflicts on the frontier between two laws, will be *understood afterwards*, how they will be translated by the surviving generations of both sides of the conflict who will, at some point, face each other in the post-colonial context of the nation. The key claim here is that founding colonial or 'frontier' conflict lives on, *afterwards* in the nation's actions and in subsequent translations of an unreconciled history between Aboriginal and settler Australians. Through *Mabo, Wik* and native title legislation, conflict over the meaning of an unreconciled national history (the history wars) has continued to be about land and its possession, about who is entitled to possess or repossess the land, and to name it, under what system of law.[3] There are other strands in the conflict over the meaning of reconciliation which also come into play. These strands have to do with the recognition of Aboriginal sovereignty through treaty, apology, compensation and self-determination under two laws, between which there is no adequate system of translation.[4]

In cinema, the difficulty of rendering the Aboriginal meaning of occupation and possession of the land is everywhere in films about place, particularly places which in different discourses are called 'the country', 'the bush', or just plain 'country'. The first term belongs to the victors in the frontier wars, the settlers with their British laws of claiming, leasing and owning the land. The last term belongs to Indigenous Australians for whom the Law and Country confer identity, culture and tradition, even where the violence and trauma of colonialism have disrupted continuous possession. The middle term, 'the bush', has been invented and reinvented by settler Australians at moments of crisis in national identity, the first being the 1890s and its cruel economic recession coinciding with cultural nationalism, the bush legend and the move towards Federation.[5] The second is the neo-conservative revival of the figure of the bush battler by One Nation and then by the Howard government in the 1990s as part of a populist backlash against native title, asylum-seekers and 'handouts' to minorities. The battler is a key figure in what Mick Dodson calls Howard's 'triumphalist view of Australian history' based on 'brave settlers conquering a people and a landmass: the victory of a superior way of life'.[6] A fourth term, 'the environment', has also entered the debate, tying environmental catastrophe to issues of national history through the work of Tim Flannery on the way that environmental disasters caused by the myth of *terra nullius*, colonial patterns of settlement and postwar nation-building schemes have created a crisis about the sustainability of current living standards in Australia.[7] An Indigenous critique of the environmentalist idea of 'wilderness' as uninhabited land has also been developed by Fabienne Bayet-Charlton, who has challenged the green movement to deal with the impact of the *Mabo* decision on green ideology and on notions of ecotourism as the future for non-urban Aboriginal people.[8] At stake in these different versions of land and landscape is the national shift (whether gradual or sudden, embraced or denied, whimsical or profound) entailed in the thought, recommended as a morning mantra for every Australian by Germaine Greer, that we are living in an Aboriginal country.[9] This is a shift in the social imaginary legally enshrined in the Mabo decision, ending the myth of *terra nullius*.

The focus of this chapter is on the ways that the ABC-TV mini-series *Heartland* (1994), Dennis O'Rourke's auteurist documentary *Cunnamulla* (2001) and Film Australia's documentary *Message from Moree* (Judy Rymer, 2003) send a message to the viewer about what's going on in the country. The assumption that life in the country (as opposed to the city) is shaped by what happened after the frontier wars is axiomatic for these programs. In the 1990s, reconciliation policies at the national level have influenced film narratives about the survival of Aboriginal communities and the various ways that settler and Indigenous Australians have intermingled in the country. However, these narratives have found their way through the public film-funding bodies (Film Finance Corporation, Australian Film Commission and Film

Australia) to ABC Television, and can thus be construed as contributing in some way to the national interest rather than to the commercial-industrial sphere of entertainment. In the commercial sphere, feature films like *No Worries* (David Elfick, 1992) and *The Bank* (Robert Connolly, 2001) revise and update the familiar trope of the innocent goodness of the country versus the sly corruption of the city, long established in the Dad and Dave comedies of the 1930s, as well as in pastoral family melodramas tied to a celebration of the nation's primary industries, such as the classic Cinesound film *The Squatter's Daughter* (Ken G. Hall, 1933).

However, although it has a bush tradition,[10] Australian cinema has no genre to compare with the Hollywood Western, through which American cinema has explored its founding mythology of wagon-train pioneers violently engaged in the Manifest Destiny of Westward expansion through Indian territories. As Mark McKenna has shown in his history of encounters between Aboriginal and settler communities in the Eden–Monaro region, pioneer histories have had a vested interest in projecting frontier violence onto others (other pioneers or warrior tribesmen) in order to preserve a benign family vignette of pipe-smoking forefathers reminiscing, from the comfort of their vine-clad verandahs, about the hard slog of settling the land.[11] This vision has been maintained in films exemplified by the ABC-TV mini-series *The Farm* (Kate Woods, 2001) about cockies doing it hard on the land inherited from their pioneering forebears. These narratives attack new policies of deregulating the banks and dropping tariffs and trade barriers which protected primary producers and small business from the vagaries of the international market. In this kind of film, the history of taking the land from its original inhabitants has been erased from the family album and national archive alike. Alternative, politicised images which endeavour to overcome historical amnesia and remember the origins of the 'the bush' in Aboriginal dispossession have come from the public sector with the input, again, of the Film Finance Corporation, Film Australia and ABC Television.

Although the desert as a vast inland tract has served as a template for national identity in Australian landscape cinema, it is usually represented as a liminal space, a threshold of experience for characters on a journey from the city to someplace else. The 'country' or the 'bush', by contrast, is inhabited by stock characters such as shearers, jackaroos, pastoralists, farmers, publicans, soldiers, squatters, footballers, miners, wives, girlfriends and barmaids. 'Coming from the country' can mean several things in Australia: it can mean coming from the land (usually a large, remote pastoral lease in the outback), coming from a farm (wheat, dairy, sugar, cotton) likely to be located on the fertile coastal fringe or a little further inland), coming from a rural industrial area like Wollongong or Whyalla, or coming from one of the many small towns on the fringe of the continent which service the surrounding farming district. It means *not* coming from the city or from the suburbs. It can include the fishing town-cum-beach resort featured in films like *High Tide* (Gillian Armstrong, 1987) and *Mullet* (David Caesar, 2001), but only if you came from there in the first place, not if you moved there from the city as in the popular comedy-drama series *SeaChange* (Artist Services and ABC-TV, 1998–2001). And not if you're a Pitt Street farmer growing avocadoes, macadamias or coffee in the north, or running a boutique vineyard in the south or west. And not if you're an Indigenous Australian for whom country might be a site of memory and identity and a basis for renegotiating settler definitions of Aboriginality.[12]

When city folk go to the country they are usually in some kind of trouble, existential or with the law, but when country folk arrive in the city (Mick Dundee in New York at the end of *Crocodile Dundee*, or Cathy Duncan in Canberra at the end of *Message from Moree*, for example) they usually manage to impress the urban sophisticates who underestimate their resourcefulness. If earlier Australian films (before the revival of the industry through government subsidy in the 1970s) were mostly concerned with Australia's ambivalent relation of dependency on the British motherland, films set in non-urban areas since the *Mabo* decision display different levels of awareness of historical debate about the legacy of violence on the frontier during the colonial years. The trauma of a settler family losing the farm has been explored in feature films (*No Worries, The Bank*) and in mini-series (*The Farm*) in terms of the deep attachment to land handed down from one generation of pioneers to the next. The frontier wars have been erased from memory in these *terra nullius* films: the enemy here is usually nature in the form of bushfire, drought, flood or pest, joined more recently by the deregulated banks and their promotion of foreign currency loans.

In films funded for broadcast on national television, however, there is a new kind of message coming from the country. In *Heartland*, a mini-series produced just after the 1992 *Mabo* decision and screened on ABC-TV in early 1994, before the *Wik* and native title legislation of 1996, issues of Aboriginality, identity, law and belonging are explored through social melodrama. Although the story is contemporary, the historical consciousness of the series stretches back before modernity and colonialism, and forward into a future based on a difficult and piecemeal process of reconciliation within families and communities, if not at the national level. In *Cunnamulla*, released in 2001, a small outback Queensland town at the end of the railway line appears to reprise the ugly working-class outback town featured in *Wake in Fright*

(Ted Kotcheff, 1971). Decades later, this prototypical remote town, once enlivened by male rural workers, appears to be socially and economically non-viable, at least as it is reprised in *Cunnamulla*. However, it is the enigma of everyday experience, etched into bodies and faces, and the endurance of habitual ways of thinking and living in towns like Cunnamulla, as the nether world of colonial and global processes, that captures O'Rourke's attention in his auteurist documentary. In *Message from Moree*, broadcast on ABC-TV in 2003, the documentary form enables a relatively transparent argument about practical reconciliation based on a mix of talking heads and observational footage.[13] But the message itself retains something enigmatic, something untranslatable in the experience of Aboriginal administrator Cathy Duncan as she takes over the running of Moree's Aboriginal Employment Service, set up by white cotton farmer Dick Estens, in a northwest New South Wales cotton town notorious for its overt racism.

If there is something enigmatic and untranslatable in the messages coming from these films, the enigma has nothing to do with exoticising the other or the country. Rather, we draw on Jean Laplanche's argument that 'the message from the other' is enigmatic because the other (as a *subject* in Freud's sense) is already possessed by an unconscious history.[14] The sense of something enigmatic, of something that is difficult to translate in these films, might be traced back to whatever the camera, as an optical unconscious, has picked up of the *afterwardness* of traumatic frontier histories buried in different parts of the country where the films were shot. On the peculiar temporal structure of trauma as belated and repetitive, Laplanche has insisted that traumatic experience involves two moments: 'it must be internalised, and then afterwards relived, revivified, in order to become an internal trauma'.[15] Further, Laplanche argues that although the memory of the original event can be reinterpreted afterwards, there is always something enigmatic or untranslatable in traumatic experience.[16] The enigmatic aspects of what we see and hear in these films will be considered here as messages from a repressed or not fully conscious past which has left memory traces in land, landscapes, faces, voices and bodies.

The untranslatable aspect of these messages, revealed in the unconscious optic of cinema (its close-ups, its *mise-en-scène*, its montage), arises from different understandings of what country might mean to Indigenous and non-Indigenous Australians. These differences occur within the dynamic context of two laws: Law underpinning traditional Aboriginal societies and laws imposed by the transplanted British colony. The lack of a treaty between settler and Indigenous Australians means that the living system of two laws has never been officially recognised. The ABC-TV mini-series *Heartland* operates precisely in this territory, using the heightened morality play of melodrama to bring the shifting and permeable frontier between black and white Australia into view. The mini-series is a significant breakthrough as a collaborative project between the national film-funding bodies and the national public broadcaster, matched only by the mini-series *Women of the Sun* (1982) in its capacity to break new ground in television through its sustained attention to what Marcia Langton has defined as 'Aboriginality': an intersubjective space created by Indigenous and non-Indigenous Australians, not only at the level of collaborative production but also as a viewing experience.[17]

Laying Down the Law in *Heartland*

Social melodrama, in its mundane television mode, is characterised by polarised moral conflicts accompanied by heightened emotional affect. In melodrama the family is often the site of intense moral and emotional conflict around issues of difference, whether of class, gender, age, race, ethnicity, sexuality or religion. These differences are usually polarised into a struggle between good and evil, and the resolution usually comes at some cost or involves some sort of sacrifice. *Heartland* begins with the generic sacrifice of a young Aboriginal woman who is brutally murdered on the beach in the rural town of Brooklyn Waters. The overarching plotline of the series is then organised around the efforts of Aboriginal police liaison officer Vincent Burunga (Ernie Dingo) to prove that Ricky (on remand in Sydney's Long Bay gaol) did not kill his girlfriend, despite his drunken confession to the crime. The second plotline involves the development of a love affair between Vincent and a white woman, Beth (Cate Blanchett), a radio producer who has left her husband in Sydney and arrived in Brooklyn Waters to settle her deceased uncle's estate. Beth discovers that her uncle Jock had a relationship with an Aboriginal woman from the Mission (the 'Mish') and that the gate between her uncle's house and the Mish is always open. From this basic plot material *Heartland* generates a number of subplots. The first is to do with Vincent discovering his place within (or between) two laws by returning to his outback community. The second revolves around a family from the Mish finding a lost son who had been removed to a white foster family thirty years earlier. The third is to do with Beth returning to her seductive, designer lifestyle in Sydney and seeing her husband and former colleagues in the radio world through new eyes. Each of these subplots generates a series of moral dilemmas which are also dramas of origins, desire and difference (see Chapter 5).

As social melodrama, in the form of the mini-series, the various subplots can be read as secondary elaborations of Freud's primary fantasies of origin and desire. As secondary fantasies, the conflicts and dilemmas of *Heartland* are ways of imagining and refiguring racial, sexual and generational differences in Australia. The linchpin of this refiguring is Vincent, the lead character who stands between two laws. If the young Aboriginal woman is sacrificed in order to initiate the narrative of racial hatred and injustice in a small town, in the end it is the town's reasonably well-intentioned white cop, Phil, who is sacrificed so that order can be restored. The restoration of law comes after racial tensions explode in the town, forcing a reluctant Vincent back into the role of go-between. In an ending which reprises the figure of the black tracker, Vincent catches one of the serial killers, then carries Phil, his severely wounded mate, out of the scrub. Despite Vincent's desperate efforts, Phil dies in his arms in the back of the police car. Vincent literally lays the white law to rest in this scene. The series ends with Alf, the Aboriginal elder from the Mission, passing on what he knows of Country and Law to Ricky and young Jason, while Vincent and Beth contemplate their future together. As Vincent suggests with a sly look, this future might include 'breeding out the white'.

Heartland's reshaping of the social imaginary has the quality of *afterwardness*, of historical consciousness or cultural memory of colonial conflict, being reshaped in the present.[18] Such re-imagining of the past in terms of the law is built into *Heartland*'s preoccupation with the difference between 'our way' and 'your way', a difference which entails unequal but shifting power relations between two laws. This difference is often untranslatable, so characters constantly find themselves caught up in an effort to explain and understand someone else, often in the context of heightened emotions of fear, desire and distrust.

The question of where the heartland of Australia might be located, geographically and culturally after the *Mabo* decision, is central to the exploration of the conflicts created by the plotlines in *Heartland*. Here Aboriginal characters interact with their own mob and with the white laws and practices that protect the ingrained racist habits of the settler community and normalise entrenched, everyday hatred, whether in the schoolyard or the criminal justice system. The moral centre of the film is located in the Aboriginal elders, whether in outback Western Australia, Vincent's traditional country, or in coastal Brooklyn Waters at the Mish. Early in the series, when Vincent returns home to make good the illness visited on his daughter by parental transgression of 'skin' laws, he learns that he still has a place in Aboriginal Law, even if he decides not to be further initiated. In the geographical location of the outback, on a working station run by the Aboriginal community who belong there, to country, the difference between the two laws is stark and, for Beth, incomprehensible.

The experience of incomprehension is dramatised as a conflict between Vincent's respect for Aboriginal Law as essential to his identity and Beth's insistence that traditional practices such as payback are barbaric, and that believing a child's sickness is brought on by being 'sung' is unenlightened superstition. The clash is resolved when Vincent refuses to do payback, handing over the responsibility for Law to his brother. However, the child recovers, confounding Beth's faith in secular enlightenment. A birth, followed by a ceremony of identity conferred on the newborn by the women, and a first kiss between Beth and Vincent, resolve the conflict in utopian ways, but it is crucial that Vincent's return to the coast, to work the difficult ground between two laws in Brooklyn Waters, is sanctioned by a male elder.

This sanction enables Vincent to move between 'our ways' and 'your ways' in future episodes, as the subplots unfold around contemporary social issues to do with unemployment, alcohol and community violence; white resentment against 'handouts' to Aboriginal students and community businesses; the return of a lost child removed from his Aboriginal mother by welfare; the danger of Ricky becoming another black death in custody; and the temptation of a career in the city for Beth and for Ricky's younger brother, a promising young footballer who wants to go to the city to develop his talent. Each of these issues dramatises what is happening, now, between Indigenous and settler communities, after the frontier wars. A subtext of habitual, entrenched racism, as the legacy of our colonial past, runs through the series, its virulence inexplicable from within the diegetic world of *Heartland*. One way to understand the enigma of this virulent undertow, most evident in the community of Brooklyn Waters, is to think of *Heartland* as a metaphor for what Australian identity might be if the nation defined itself in terms of Aboriginality, in Langton's sense, as an intersubjective reality which is the hidden foundation of the nation. This intersubjective concept of the nation as Aboriginal is precisely what is foregrounded in *Heartland*.

Each of the locations explored in the series involves different kinds of conflicts between two laws. In outback Western Australia, the remote Aboriginal community looks like a model of self-sufficient enterprise, with the beef industry underpinning the community's cultural self-determination. Yet the series makes much of the enigmatic and untranslatable aspects of the Law which sustain Aboriginal identity, even as the remote outback community embraces modernity. The enigmatic is coded in the music and sound effects which accompany Vincent's return home. The Aboriginal song which Vincent and Beth sing together as they arrive and depart in their four-wheel drive, and the tentative dance Beth performs with the women, appear to open a doorway between two cultures. Yet the threshold is impossible for Beth to cross. Her insistent questions and bewildered complaints, as she finds herself in incomprehensible situations, are often met with silence. In the end she has to learn by doing, by joining the crowd of children gathered around the new baby as they too learn the rituals and traditions open to them under the Law.

The situation is not reversed for Vincent when he finds himself in Sydney, staying with Beth and her former husband Garth in their harbourside house with champagne views. There is nothing untranslatable in Garth's competitive *bonhomie*, just as there is no enigma in the actions of the traffic police when they pull Vincent over for driving an expensive sports car up a one-way street. If Vincent's sense of identity, his origin, has been tested and made stronger by his return home, Beth's identity, without origin, has little to support it during her marriage crisis. There are no elders in her world, no place to which she belongs in relationship with the land and with others. In Sydney there are only transient friends, a mortgaged property, and a dog-eat-dog media hierarchy whose values, determined by ratings and the manipulations of talkback radio, no longer coincide with hers.

If Vincent and Beth represent different worlds, from which they are both in some sense alienated, the true historical drama of identity, of being caught between two worlds, is played out in Brooklyn Waters (that rural in-between place which is neither city nor outback) by Eddie/Ben, the lost boy taken from the Mish by the welfare. He has two names, two lives, two families to juggle, and no memory of ever being Eddie. His attempts to embrace an Aboriginal identity flounder as he is assailed by a series of untranslatable messages from his wife, his rediscovered community at the Mish, and from the white townspeople who say, 'makes no difference of course'. It does make a difference, of course, but the difference is enigmatic. He is told by Alf, the wise elder at the Mish, to feel his Aboriginality, his lost origins, in his heart and through the soles of his feet. Alf tells Eddie it doesn't matter that he can't remember his family: they remember him. But it does matter, and there is no resolution to Eddie/Ben's story.

All the ends do not tie up neatly in *Heartland*. The series ends in the bush where the rural town, with its history of embittered race relations, remains the site of daily struggles (exemplified by wise community elder Alf and liaison officer Vincent) to make a difference in the present. But the shift in perspective that the viewer is asked to make in *Heartland* involves thinking about what happened after the British colony pushed the frontier out from the first urban settlement, at Sydney Cove, to the bush, and to the outback. 'What happened' is perhaps best understood through Eddie's story: recovering his lost narrative as a stolen child (his origins repressed and layered over by a social policy of assimilation) points to the bigger story of how the nation might recover from repressing its origins in acts of dispossession of identity, language, land and culture, once guaranteed by Aboriginal Law. *Heartland* suggests that Indigenous Law itself, though still powerful, is now even more difficult to transmit to the next generation. As we discover through Eddie's thwarted efforts to assume his lost identity too quickly, and Beth's halting efforts to understand Vincent, reparation is a slow, gradual process of learning through contact, of not giving up on what is so difficult to translate. As Alf is always advising, 'Give it time'. However, as Eddie's exit from the series (after failing to save an Aboriginal enterprise because the equipment has been stolen by one of the white bureaucrats) demonstrates, the justifiable impatience of young men for rapid change works against the slow workings of moral authority vested in an untranslatable Law. The story of young Aboriginal women in terms of the Law is a mute point in the series. Their narrative function (as sacrificed victims of malevolent racism or as city lawyers making a dent in the justice system for young Aboriginal men) restores cultural transmission of the Law as men's business. Women's business is touched on but remains enigmatic, becoming a source of humour in the series, a shortcut for settling differences between Vincent and Beth.

The moral heartland of the series derives its authority from tradition, from the Law as it is practised in Vincent's outback country. This moral authority also survives, in a less powerful form, on the Mish, through male and female elders for whom 'our way' of doing things has evolved as each new policy era inaugurated new forms of survival and endurance in Aboriginal communities. *Heartland* imagines this history as a story of endurance through the repetition of everyday encounters between the survivors of the frontier wars. These encounters, which culminate in what the tabloid media might call 'a race riot' at the police station, bring into disrepute the law of the land imposed by British settlement. The main achievement of *Heartland* is that it requires the viewer to bear witness, emotionally, to the daily struggle of living under two laws of the land, whereby the dominant law is unable and unwilling to translate the extraneous messages coming from the original Law of this land. The main problem obstructing social justice and destroying bush communities, *Heartland* suggests, is the failure to recognise the ongoing effect of *terra nullius*. This founding myth created a history of denial that there is anything at all to be translated, that there are two laws shaping the reciprocal experience of Aboriginality in Australia. This is not to suggest that settler Australians should aspire to become Aboriginal, further appropriating a Law and a land which is not theirs for the taking. Rather,

Heartland, coming so soon after the *Mabo* decision through the large-scale conflicts of social melodrama, suggests the need not so much for a symbolic reconciliation of two laws as for a profound, imaginative recognition of the enigmatic messages coming from 'country'. This would include recognition of what is untranslatable in those messages. Beth, like Eddie, is always positioned as the one who doesn't understand. Unlike Eddie, she hangs around, learning as she goes that there are indeed things she might never understand. These things have a lot to do with the way history is embodied as a kind of unconscious to which Vincent himself does not have access. This unconscious imbues messages from the other with a strangeness or an enigma that is not easy to translate.[19] At times Vincent cannot explain to Beth what he knows or what he feels because the meaning is in his history rather than in his head. The difficulty of understanding different histories of race, gender and culture in the bush, the city and the outback is raised explicitly in the final episode of *Heartland* when Beth says to Phil that she doesn't think she'll ever understand Vincent. Phil's question to Beth lingers in the air, leaving Beth and the viewer to ponder the answer, 'Because he's black? Or just 'cause he's Vincent?' This enigma of social identity (blackness) versus the singularity of the other (Vincent) is precisely the territory that Dennis O'Rourke explores in *Cunnamulla*, a controversial montage of ten characters inhabiting an isolated rural town in outback Queensland.

Redeeming the Battler in *Cunnamulla*

Depending on where you come from, *Cunnamulla* can be seen as a depressing portrait of ten Australians locked into lives as dry and dusty as the cracked earth of the inland plains which, against the environmental odds, continue to support the district's pastoralists and their sheep runs. Or it can be seen as a 'symphonic' montage of moments in the short-lived cinematic lives of ten characters who are 'basically just living'.[20] The film opens to the sound of sheep dipping and closes to the sound of Chopin. If a rapprochement between redneck Australia, built on the sheep's back, and a cultured Australia, attuned to its European origins, is indicated by the soundtrack, then it is one that takes hold in the mind of the film's auteur, Dennis O'Rourke, rather than in the characters he creates through *mise-en-scène* and montage. For Paul, facing a prison sentence for a lifestyle built on break-and-enter, there is no culture in Cunnamulla. By 'culture' he means there is nothing in Cunnamulla to compare with the Aboriginal dancing and other things he learned during his stay in metropolitan Melbourne. If the outback stands for the sacred and for traditional Aboriginal culture in the social imaginary, this is not how Paul experiences Aboriginality in Cunnamulla. The same could be said for the other inhabitants of O'Rourke's observational documentary world. Unlike the social melodrama of *Heartland*, O'Rourke attaches no clearly coded set of universal meanings to his cast of characters.

Dispensing with a narrative structure, *Cunnamulla* has no time-frame of events to structure meaning for the viewer. Relying on observational techniques, O'Rourke's auteurist presence behind the camera corrupts the documentary ideal of detachment and distance between off-camera filmmaker and on-camera subject. This corruption of documentary distance is an essential part of what makes the film an auteurist project. What matters to O'Rourke is the transformative power of cinema, a power that requires an artist rather than a social activist behind the camera and at the editing bench. What interests O'Rourke is the transcendent possibility of the filmed moment, the 'pure cinematic power' of 'the landscape of the human face talking'. Whereas social melodrama edits for clear-cut political meaning as well as emotional affect, O'Rourke deploys affect, 'this emotional, sexual energy that drives us all', in the way he relates to his subjects through a conscious strategy of mutual vulnerability. For O'Rourke the power of the documentary lies in the tone or atmosphere captured by his 'recording angels', the cameras and microphones that do his bidding. They record sound and image, but they also do something else: they capture the moment, 'something that's in the air'.[21]

For O'Rourke, the characters in his film understand their role in this process. For him, it is this engagement between the apparatus of cinema, the eye of the filmmaker, and the screen presence of the characters that transforms observed reality into something meaningful. However, the intended meaning is not explicable. It happens symphonically, through formal variations on a theme. The first character introduced in the film is Neredah, married to Arthur, the town's taxidriver. The tone of the film is set by the static camera and microphone recording a corner of Neredah's kitchen, framing the landscape of her face, capturing the grain of her voice as she peers out through the louvres and tells O'Rourke the first of her stories, beginning with the one about throwing lollies out the window for the neighbouring kids. It's the repetition in her story of the *throwing* of the lollies that is arresting. It sets the tone for what is to come in Neredah's later scenes where she repeats the act of *spitting* as she tells another story of setting a young man straight by spitting on him in front of the crowd at a Bingo/Housie night. Neredah's storytelling style and something of her worldview is underlined again in another scene where she relishes and repeats the word *flogging* as she tells the story of encouraging a father to give his daughter a *flogging* with a fence paling, immediately after his release from gaol for child abuse. Neredah is confident of a sympathetic hearing and neither the camera nor the editing makes any judgement about her stories. Rather, O'Rourke edits for an 'ineffable' meaning, 'a meaning which I don't myself fully comprehend'.[22]

At its most successful, what happens in *Cunnamulla* is that the audience is forced to experience the enigma of each of its singular characters, of moments in their daily lives, shaped but not explained by social, economic and historical forces. The most forceful are the moments of stillness before the camera, moments in which the characters settle themselves in the frame and then proceed, in their own time, to fill the silence of being filmed with comments or stories or complaints which spring from the immediacy of their lives. Sometimes there is a conversation or argument with a friend, parent or neighbour, but mostly what happens is an act of composure, of self-possession, of self-disclosure before the camera. Whether this disclosure revives the shameful character of the ugly Australian or redeems the enduring character of the bush battler is a moot point. If the first view prevails, *Cunnamulla* becomes another far north badland in the national psyche. If the second view triumphs, *Cunnamulla* helps to solve an enigma in contemporary Australian politics. This enigma arises from the role of the battler in the politics of shame.

For John Grech, watching *Cunnamulla* with an international audience in Amsterdam at a documentary film festival, the film produced a familiar cringe of shame, translated into a warning about 'the real danger' of subjecting foreign audiences to 'the stereotypical structures of meaning that underlie this film'.[23] Grech's chief fear is that the film is 'maintaining the myth that Australia is (or can still be) characterized by an outback colonial town'.[24] Arguing against O'Rourke's claim that the film redeems the inhabitants of *Cunnamulla*, Grech laments the inability of anyone in the film (or 'Australians on the whole') 'to seek or give forgiveness' for the colonial legacy which continues to sap people's lives.[25] Declaring that '*Cunnamulla* reminded me of the things I ran away from in Australia', Grech does not pause to consider the rise of the battler as a much courted figure in Australian electoral politics since 1996.[26]

When One Nation won 23 per cent of the vote in the Queensland state election in June 1998, it signalled the return of the enduring figure of the battler under the banner of Pauline Hanson, whose popularity peaked after her maiden speech in federal parliament in September 1996. Through Hanson, the uncensored battler spoke out against the hegemony of an 'elite' cultural agenda supporting Aboriginal grants, Asian immigration, native title, and multiculturalism. Just as importantly to her supporters, Hanson also spoke out against bipartisan, neo-conservative economic policies and the sale of Australian assets, companies and jobs.[27] Although One Nation faded quickly from the political scene, the return of the battler as a proud rather than shameful character in national history owes much to Howard's fortuitous discovery, courtesy of One Nation rhetoric, of the electoral key to a central enigma in contemporary Australian politics. Robert Manne identifies this enigma as the problem of how to attract the battlers while keeping on board the winners of globalisation. Manne believes that Howard's post-*Tampa* policy on asylum-seekers 'provided the solution to the riddle that had vexed the major parties over the past 30 years'.[28] Howard's solution involved abandoning bipartisan support for a progressive cultural agenda, in place since the 1970s, by pursuing border protection policies which played on new anti-Muslim fears. Followed by September 11 and the war on terrorism, the *Tampa* incident took the heat off bipartisan economic consensus and enabled Howard to 'gazump One Nation and destabilise a Labor Party caught between its traditional working-class voters and its post-Whitlam professional middle-class support base'.[29]

The characters who disclose something of themselves to the camera in *Cunnamulla* are neither benign battlers in the Howard mould, nor shameful examples of the best and worst of Australia in Grech's reckoning. O'Rourke refuses to idealise the battler as the underdog in an international game stacked against the rural working class. Instead he exposes the battler to the steady gaze of his camera, inviting self-disclosure in the present moment of filming. These moments do not add up to an argument for redemption, as Grech might wish, or for political enfranchisement. Rather, what lingers is a contrast between the old inhabitants, set in their ways (there's nothing like a good flogging), and the young, still hopeful of a slightly better future (not going to prison, not getting pregnant at thirteen, not giving up on recording music). Grech argues that for this to be a palatable image of Australian identity for export, *Cunnamulla* needs to be contextualised by 'a hundred or so other films where people have managed to change their lives'.[30] O'Rourke's point is that his film is precisely about people 'basically just living' their lives.[31] If the shameless self-disclosure of these lives is intolerable for the viewer, that might be because the unconscious history buried in the message coming from *Cunnamulla* is that Aboriginality, in Langton's sense, as it is lived now by black and white Australians in this country town, is a potent space for a dynamic Australian identity, one that (as Hanson and One Nation demonstrated) cannot be relegated to a forgotten Queensland badland forever.[32] It remains to be seen whether this entangled, post-frontier identity can be harnessed for long to a xenophobic border protection mentality which does nothing to include the residents of Cunnamulla in the new borderless economy.[33]

Message from Moree

If *Cunnamulla* lacks sufficient context for some viewers, *Message from Moree*, broadcast nationally on ABC-TV on 28 May 2003, might be one of the films Grech would like to show to international audiences to counter O'Rourke's recidivist image of the ugly Australian. *Message from Moree* is easily understood as an inspiring story of social change in a New South Wales cotton town with an uglier reputation for entrenched racism than the badlands of Queensland. The message coming out of Moree constitutes a paradigm shift in the modern Australian social imaginary. For the first time since the end of the 19th century, the bush is portrayed as the cutting edge of social change, its cast of ordinary Australians achieving an extraordinary turnaround in a racially riven town after decades of 'all talk and no action' from visiting bureaucrats and politicians. The agent of change is portrayed as an unlikely, uneasy partnership between a white cocky, cotton farmer Dick Estens, and an Aboriginal woman, newly appointed chair of the Aboriginal Employment Service Cathy Duncan. The only thing they have in common is that they hate to fail, or at least that's how they put it as their difficult partnership begins to pay dividends for the black and white community of Moree, the community defined as those who want to move ahead together, regardless of the rednecks, the racists and the naysayers.

Message from Moree opens with a montage of images and sound bites from the recent past. Together the shock of these images helps support the film's claim that this is a documentary about a town coming back from the dead. It begins with Dick Estens and his idea that what was needed to save Moree was an Aboriginal Employment Service to 'get jobs and build leadership' in the Aboriginal community. The film ends with Cathy Duncan revealing that overcoming cultural ignorance on both sides is part of the solution, but the real learning curve is understanding business: more precisely, learning 'how to market what people don't want, an Aboriginal job-seeker'. The expansion of the Aboriginal Employment Service to other towns in the area is the measure of success of the strategy of community-building based on partnerships between those who have a stake in the outcome. Whether or not this is the face of John Howard's practical reconciliation model, the message from the film is that community-building works. What works in Moree is the hard slog of committee work, of board meetings and community-building awards nights, of mentors working as cultural translators so that white employers and black workers can find some common ground and be part of the change in Moree.[34] This change extends beyond the employment issue to community-building through education, sport, debutante balls, police liaison officers, the CROC festival and the girls' footy comp. What comes through for the viewer is not only the long history of acute suspicion between black and white communities, but the diversity within these communities, and the 'dynamic buzz' experienced by those who have taken the unthinkable step of walking forward in partnership across the cultural divide.

In a sense, the 'can-do' people of Moree have got together to overcome basic problems beyond the ken of city folk. When Cathy Duncan takes up her job as chair of the Aboriginal Employment Service, Estens is ever-present, with his boundless urgency for change impinging on Duncan's tentative assertion of her own authority. Yet somehow they persevere through the board meetings and awards nights and NAIDOC Week parade down a hostile main street until they finally pull together as an equal team on a trip to Canberra to lobby for support for their proposal to extend the Aboriginal Employment Service beyond Moree. One of the joyous moments in the film is when Duncan and another female member of the team dance inside the revolving doors of a Canberra public service building, celebrating the success of their proposal, but also perhaps their freedom from the very bureaucracy that trained Duncan in administration in Moree. The message from Moree might be that the benefits of privatisation of employment and other services might actually work in favour of initiatives that build communities, ameliorate long-standing inequalities, and promise a different future for Duncan's children and for towns like Moree. The message coming from the country in this documentary is that cosmopolitan Sydney or bureaucratic Canberra are not the only winners in the open market; that the divide between the winners and losers of globalisation is not simply a divide between highly skilled urban professionals and disenfranchised bush battlers; that the way to national recognition and self-possession for Indigenous and settler Australians is not going to be through One Nation or Howard's opportunistic backlash against the left-liberal cultural agenda of inclusion of the 1970s. And that the bush town, rendered abject by decades of unresolved historical conflict, is just as much a potential and actual site of canny social activism, on committees and in boardrooms, as the inner-city haunts of the left-liberal 'elite'. *Message from Moree* tells us that this is so, and that our mutual ignorance and perpetual puzzlement about each other form no impediment to social change and to the bigger picture of *social justice* (which, as a 1970s precedent, might serve us better than the more sullied 1990s term *reconciliation*).[35]

Notes

1 On the 'violent innocence' of emergent nation-states, see Marilyn Lake, 'History and the nation'. In Robert Manne (ed.), *Whitewash: On Keith Windschuttle's Fabrication of Aboriginal History*, Melbourne: Black Inc. Agenda, 2003, pp. 164–6.
2 ibid., p. 165.
3 On the restoration of the Koori name *Gariwerd* to a mountain range named by settlers as The Grampians, in Victoria in 1989, see Tony Birch, '"Nothing has changed": the making and unmaking of Koori culture'. In Michele Grossman (ed.), *Blacklines: Contemporary Critical Writing by Indigenous Australians*, Melbourne University Press, 2003, pp. 145–58.
4 On the different meanings of reconciliation in relation to Aboriginal sovereignty see Patrick Dodson, 'Lingiari: until the chains are broken'. In Michelle Grattan (ed.), *Reconcilation: Essays on Australian Reconciliation*, Melbourne: Black Inc, 2000, pp. 264–74.
5 On the role of 'the bush' in a national history written as the story of modern nation-building, see Russel Ward, *The Australian Legend*, Melbourne: Oxford University Press, 1958. On the bush as a key figure in Australian cinema, see John Tulloch, *Australian Cinema: Industry, Narrative and Meaning*, Sydney: Allen & Unwin, 1982, and Graeme Turner, *National Fictions: Literature, Film and the Construction of Australian Narrative*, Sydney: Allen & Unwin, 1993.
6 Mick Dodson, 'Indigenous Australians'. In Robert Manne (ed.), *The Howard Years*, Melbourne: Black Inc. Agenda, 2004, p. 139.
7 Tim Flannery, 'Beautiful lies', *Quarterly Essay*, no. 9, 2003, pp. 4–16.
8 Fabienne Bayet-Charlton, 'Overturning the doctrine: Indigenous people and wilderness – being Aboriginal in the environmental movement'. In Grossman, *Blacklines*, pp. 171–80.
9 See Germaine Greer, 'Whitefella Jump Up', *Quarterly Essay*, no. 11, 2003.
10 William D. Routt claims that the bush comedy or 'backblocks farce' of 1920–40, like the bushranger film, may well be one of Australia's few local genres. See W. D. Routt, 'Always already out of date: Australian bush comedy', paper presented at *Seriously Funny: 2004 National Screenwriters' Conference*, Melbourne, 2 April 2004.
11 See Mark McKenna, *Looking for Blackfellas Point: An Australian History of Place*, Sydney: UNSW Press, 2002.
12 On the politics of defining Aboriginality in non-essentialist terms, see Michael Dodson, 'The end in the beginning: re(de)finding Aboriginality'. In Grossman, *Blacklines*, pp. 25–42.
13 'Practical reconciliation' is a contentious term. Our use of it here is influenced by Noel Pearson on community initiatives and partnerships, rather than John Howard's assimilationist policies. See Noel Pearson, 'Aboriginal disadvantage', pp. 165–75, and John Howard, 'Practical reconciliation'. In Grattan, *Reconciliation*, 2000, pp. 88–96.
14 Cathy Caruth, 'An Interview with Jean Laplanche', *Postmodern Culture*, 11(2) 2001. <http://muse.jhu/edu/journals/postmodern_culture/vol11/11.2caruth.html>
15 ibid., para. 7.
16 ibid., paras 36–56.

17 Marcia Langton, *Well, I Heard It on the Radio and I Saw It on the Television: An Essay for the Australian Film Commission on the Politics and Aesthetics of Filmmaking by and about Aboriginal People and Things*, Sydney: Australian Film Commission, 1993, pp. 23–40.

18 See discussion of 'afterwardness' in Chapter 5.

19 See Cathy Caruth, 'An Inteview with Jean Laplanche', paras 25–33. Laplanche describes this 'extraneity, or strangeness' as foundational for the ego which is formed as an internal structure to process 'the reality of the other and his message'. For Laplanche messages from the other are always enigmatic because the other has an internal other, the unconscious.

20 Martha Ansara, 'On the poetry of madness: an encounter with Dennis O'Rourke', *Metro*, 126, 2001, p. 29.

21 O'Rourke quoted in Ansara, p. 31.

22 ibid., p. 30.

23 John Grech, 'Redeeming *Cunnamulla* or avoiding reality?' *Metro*, 126, 2001, p. 22.

24 ibid., p. 22.

25 ibid., p. 24.

26 ibid., p. 23.

27 On Hanson's maiden speech, see Robert Manne, 'The Howard years: a political interpretation'. In *The Howard Years*, pp. 14–17.

28 ibid., p. 43.

29 ibid., pp. 43–4.

30 Grech, 'Redeeming *Cunnamulla*', p. 24.

31 O'Rourke quoted in Ansara, 'On the poetry of madness', p. 29.

32 On the role of mythic badlands in preserving historical amnesia, see Ross Gibson, *Seven Versions of an Australian Badland*, Brisbane: University of Queensland Press, 2002, pp. 172–3.

33 Whether the Queensland battler in the sugar cane industry will vote for Howard in the wake of the 2004 bilateral trade agreement with the United States remains to be seen.

34 On mundane committee work as the principal form of effective left-liberal activism in Australian political culture, see Meaghan Morris, 'Lunching for the republic'. In *Too Soon Too Late: History in Popular Culture*, Bloomington IN: Indiana University Press, 1998, pp. 209–13.

35 From the point of view of 'backtracking' in Australian films, Cathy Duncan might be seen as reprising a role first played by Essie Coffey, from the rural town of Brewarrina, in collaboration with independent feminist filmmaker Martha Ansara, from Sydney, in the film *My Survival as an Aboriginal* (Essie Coffey, 1979).

7

Coming from the City in *The Castle, Vacant Possession, Strange Planet* and *Radiance*

To be asked 'where are you from?' in Australia today is to imply not only that there is geographic mobility within the nation's borders but that your family's origins, within living memory, are elsewhere. Cultural commentators have long pointed to the problem of being at home in Australia as a recurring theme, usually articulated in terms of Australia's lack of self-confidence, maturity and independence. The difficulty of asserting an independent nationhood, particularly in relation to Britain and the United States, but also within the region, has often been linked to a set of national character traits including defensive brashness, cultural cringe, cutting down of tall poppies and a self-deprecating sense of humour. This set of traits appears to contradict those depicted in the national archetypes of the independent bushman, the courageous Anzac and the egalitarian fraternity of the white working class. A further contrast emerges in contemporary Australian cultural studies, repudiating the 19th-century bush as the template for a British-derived national identity, turning instead to the cosmopolitan city, the multicultural suburbs, and the hedonistic holiday coast as templates for a dynamic, post-national, post-multicultural identity in the 21st century.[1] The problem of belonging, of being at home in Australia, of having a sense of identity, is evident in the afterwardness of the history wars that followed the *Mabo* decision, and the futureshock of globalisation across the new dividing line between 'elites' and 'battlers' in Australian society.[2]

Home as the place of belonging of white settlers in Australia was put to the torch by the shock reminder from the High Court in 1992 that *terra nullius* was achieved at the cost of dispossession of Indigenous people from their land, language and culture after 40 000 years of continuous possession. The purported threat of native title claims against suburban backyards was just one of the more extreme responses to the High Court's *Wik* decision in 1996.[3] This unfounded fear troubled a nation of property-owners who, for the most part, had spent their working lives materialising their democratic ideal of Australia as a working man's paradise through mortgages on quarter-acre suburban blocks, with a weekender (or caravan) at the beach as the ultimate Eden.

John Cameron divides Australians, most of whom are city-dwellers, into two groups in terms of different histories of attachment to place: 'Aboriginal and white non-immigrant Australians are struggling with the Wik decision and the stolen generation . . . Immigrant Australians are . . . coming to terms with the new land as it relates to their homeland experience.'[4] The first group of settlers can claim several generations of settler-ancestors going back as far as 1788, past the point of personal memory of a previous homeland. For most of us personal memory goes back to our grandparents. Everything before them becomes history or social memory. For long-term settlers, complacent pride in the achievements of a young nation over two centuries has been put to shame by the *Mabo* decision and the history wars that followed. The second group of settlers is identified with postwar migration, which occurred in waves, from Europe after the Second World War in the 1940s and 1950s, from Vietnam and Cambodia as Australia and the United States pulled out of that post-colonial conflict in the 1970s, and from refugee camps around the world as displaced people queue for visas or board boats to various destinations offering a future. This disparate group of recent settlers has a personal memory not only of grandparents but of the homeland they or their parents or grandparents left behind. These two groups have been described in terms of 'a real social experiment which could have gone awfully wrong'.[5] They are differently placed in relation to Australian national history and the iconic figures (bushmen, Anzacs, cricketers) that dominate the Anglo-Celtic social imaginary and underpin the national ethos of egalitarianism, mateship and fair play, an ethos that is still invoked on occasion.[6] The second group is more likely to be negotiating generational conflicts over maintaining a diaspora identity or blending the homeland identity into the melting pot of Euroamerican consumer culture in the Australian suburbs.[7] The first group is more likely to claim a longevity of attachment to specific places (if not to the nation) and a sense of belonging to those places. In the case of One Nation in the 1990s, this sense of belonging was transformed into an aggrieved sense of entitlement to the land, earned through hard work to pay off the mortgage and invest in the family's future. Both groups proved resistant to a left-liberal rhetoric characterising the nation's forebears as white invaders who stole the land and murdered, assimilated or incarcerated (on reserves or missions) the original inhabitants. For both kinds of settlers, forms of selective historical amnesia, supported by the modern nation's focus on progress and the future, have long sustained an image of Australia as an enviably harmonious place, the lucky country, where people have made sacrifices and undergone hardship in order to give their children a better life, a better future.

The displacement of national history into family history, and of national space into domestic space through suburban home-ownership, has enabled certain blind spots to be maintained as cornerstones of Australian politics. These blind spots are evident in the opinion polls and qualitative research conducted on reconciliation issues during the 1990s. The key contradiction identified by the 1999–2000 Newspoll commissioned by the Council for Aboriginal Reconciliation is that 'Australians want reconciliation but they are not anxious to do anything that could carry an imputation that they, or their generation, are to blame for what happened to Australia's first peoples'.[8] As a measure of success, perhaps, of the neo-conservative attack on 'black armband history', the Newspoll survey found that 'almost eight in ten agreed that, "Everyone should stop talking about the way Aboriginal people were treated in the past, and just get on with the future"'.[9] Research based on focus groups in 1999–2000 found universal agreement 'that the position of the Aborigines in Australia today is a tragedy'.[10] But the majority also held the opinion that past ill-treatment does not warrant special treatment today and that an apology to Indigenous people is not necessary – a view held particularly strongly by postwar non-British immigrants.[11]

Recent Australian films have taken a keen interest in the movement of urban characters between different locales, from city centres of commerce, romance and crime – *Risk* (Alan White, 2001), *The Bank* (Robert Connolly, 2001), *The Monkey's Mask* (Samantha Lang, 2001) – to suburban shops, bowling clubs and backyards as sites of community conflict and family strife – *The Wog Boy* (Alexsi Vellis, 2000), *Crackerjack* (Paul Maloney, 2002), *Fat Pizza* (Paul Fenech, 2003) – to the beach as a liminal space enabling a variety of encounters with the past and intimations of the future – *Mullet* (David Caesar, 2001), *Walking on Water* (Tony Ayres, 2002), *Blurred* (Evan Clarry, 2002). Urban films of the 1990s tend to rely on comedy, along with family melodrama or the crime thriller, to depict the experience of 'getting on with the future'. With some exceptions, the central characters in these films are urban or coastal dwellers with limited direct experience of the desert or the bush and even more limited experience of direct contact with Indigenous Australians. The generic audience addressed by these films might be imagined as mostly urban film-goers for whom the Anglo-Celtic core of the social imaginary, and the impact of the *Mabo* and *Wik* decisions on Australian politics, might be a common point of reference rather than identity.

The urban and coastal landscapes of Australia have yet to take on the iconic status of the desert and the bush in Australian cinema. In this sense feature films appear to lag behind Australian television, which has long embraced the urban location of much of its audience. Television takes the urban experience of its viewers and delivers it back to them as locations rather than landscapes: the suburbs in soapies (*Neighbours*) and sitcoms (*Kath and Kim*); the city in police series (*Homicide*); and the beach house in comedy-drama (*SeaChange*) and reality-TV (*Big Brother*). If, in the case of cinema, the desert has become the place for spiritual road journeys undertaken by unsettled Australians in the aftershock of *Mabo*, and the bush (or the country) is the frontline of reconciliation-in-practice, then the suburbs, the city and the beach might best be thought of as the future-oriented, amnesiac places in Australian settler identity, the places where the residues of traumatic histories take on surface, mimetic forms. The principal mimetic form of interest here is the cinematic image of the house and its approximation to the idea of home, whether it be a rundown suburban weatherboard, a negatively geared designer apartment, a solid-brick family bungalow, a fibro weekender, a caravan in the bush, or a Queenslander-on-stilts. These vernacular forms of domestic architecture (adapted by architects for Australian sites, and further imitated by set designers for cinema) have the capacity to evoke sense memories, to provoke a chain of involuntary associations for character and viewer alike of the urban lifestyle that has become recognisably Australian.[12] It is here perhaps, in phantasmagoric images from the coastal-urban heartland conjured by the mimetic machine of cinema, that the past becomes visible in the physiognomy of buildings and streets. This physiognomic presence of history and identity in local architecture, in the transnational modernity of urban landscapes, might suddenly be experienced in a momentary shudder of recognition, like a snapshot capturing an instant of time. Alternatively, the modernist focus on the future, on aspiration, opportunity and progress, is a strong current in urban genre films, particularly crime thrillers and romantic comedies. This chapter will compare two explicitly post-*Mabo* films set in working-class suburbs, *The Castle* (Rob Sitch, 1997) and *Vacant Possession* (Margot Nash, 1995) with two films that look beyond the city to the coast to imagine a post-suburban Australia and a post-national sense of belonging, *Strange Planet* (Emma-Kate Croghan, 1999) and *Radiance* (Rachel Perkins, 1998). Although they belong to different genres, each of these films features a particular kind of house, the weatherboard shack, as the place of memory which preserves the past (in *The Castle*) or stands in the way of a reconciled future (in *Vacant Possession* and *Radiance*) or simply enables a breather from the intensity of the present (in *Strange Planet*).

'Beginning to Understand How the Aborigines Feel' in *The Castle*

After the 10BA period of funding films through a tax write-off system, the new policy era of the Film Finance Corporation was marked by the popular success of three films, *The Adventures of Priscilla, Queen of the Desert* (Stephan Elliott, 1994), *Strictly Ballroom* (Baz Luhrmann, 1992) and *Muriel's Wedding* (Paul J. Hogan, 1994). These films instantly redefined Australian cinema as quirky suburban comedy. Breaking with the satiric anti-suburbanism of Australian literary and theatrical culture, quirky comedies applied a keen but not unkind eye to the daggy, grotesque and downright ugly aspects of the maligned suburban lifestyle.[13] Between them, *Priscilla, Muriel* and *Ballroom* mapped out a certain mindset linking the inner city, the suburbs, and the urban coastal sprawl in opposition to the interior, the desert, and the outback. The drag queens from the inner city in *Priscilla* had attitude, ambition and style in common with the rivalrous suburban preeners in *Strictly Ballroom*, and the 'dreadful' eponymous *Muriel* from the backwater sprawl of Porpoise Spit. If these drag queens, ballroom dancers and Abba fans revived film comedy in the 1990s by upstaging the ockers and larrikins of 1970s cinema, they did so with an edge of ambivalence about the much lampooned, much celebrated Australian Way of Life. This way of life, based on the affordable Australian dream of a lifetime mortgaged to the quarter-acre block, is a compromise between city and bush. The dream's origins go back to Governor Phillip's proposal for the layout of housing in Sydney in 1790.[14] Since the mid to late 19th century, the dream has become 'a central tenet of national life' for the majority of Australians who are reputed to enjoy the highest rate of home-ownership in the world.[15] What the suburban block seemed to guarantee was 'a marvellous compromise', a refuge from the frenetic pace of the nerve-racking modern city together with a taste of the freedom offered by the bush, encapsulated in the Australian backyard with its ubiquitous barbecue.[16] For those devoted suburban commuters who prospered during the postwar years and acquired a secure job in the city and a family sedan (either Ford or Holden), the freedom of the backyard might be supplemented by the weekender, a fibro shack somewhere down the coast, or a kit-home, inland, beside a river or lake. These denizens of the suburban dream, according to cultural pundits who bemoaned the mediocrity of the suburbs, were unabashed hedonists pursuing material goals and economic security to the overall detriment of the national culture, which suffered the consequences as generations of talented people left the country in pursuit of opportunities not available in the wasteland of

Australia. The signs of complacent insularity were said to be 'the censorious know-nothingness of Australian suburbanites and farmers' and the 'lack of a living critical milieu'.[17] The cost of an entrenched suburban lifestyle in environmental terms has been a slow-burning issue yet to be admitted to urban consciousness beyond concerns about expressways, wilderness areas and endangered species. Similarly, an uneasy historical consciousness, awakened in suburban homes by the Stolen Generations report in 1997, appears to have been placated since the nationally televised Sydney Harbour Bridge Walk for Reconciliation in May 2000 and the opening ceremony of the Sydney 2000 Olympics.[18] The sense that the past has been dealt with by the nation, politically and ceremonially, was reinforced by the Sea of Hands and the National Sorry Days. In the context of a pragmatic national ethos of 'getting on with the future', the extraordinary popular success of *The Castle* (Working Dog, 1997) deserves attention, given that the plot explicitly refers back to the High Court's 1992 *Mabo* decision.

The Castle is first and foremost a tongue-in-cheek comedy of suburban manners. Its comic strategies are twofold. The first relies on the comic disparity between what we see (*mise-en-scène*) and what we hear (direct narration by Dale, the youngest of Darryl Kerrigan's three sons). The voice-over is delivered in the guileless style of a school essay topic, along the lines of What I Did in the Holidays or A Day at the Beach with Mum and Dad. The key to the Kerrigans' world is the everyday repetition of family rituals (which become visual jokes for the viewer): Steve's esoteric bargains from the *Trading Post*, Dad's trophy room, Mum's gourmet home cooking. Through repetition the *mise-en-scène* opens up a comic distance between what the Kerrigans think about themselves and what the viewer might think of working-class life in a half-renovated weatherboard bungalow with jet planes coming in to land at the airport over the back fence. This comical gap in perception between viewer and character is reinforced by setting up a quizzical point of view within the film in two scenes. The first is when the property valuer comes to inspect the house. With great pride Darryl naively points out precisely those features (a fake chimney to make the house look cosy, toxic lead in the landfill in the backyard, proximity to the airport) guaranteed to devalue the property in a market based on 'location, location, location'. The second moment is in the High Court in Canberra when the land-grabbing corporation's high-powered legal defence team refers to the Kerrigans' suburban castle as an 'eyesore'. If we are invited to laugh at Darryl's ingenuousness in the first instance, the second instance invites us to empathise with Darryl's indignant response, 'They don't get it'. What the defence lawyers 'don't get' is the difference between land to be compulsorily acquired and a home made of people and love and memories. It is precisely this invitation to laugh at the Kerrigans' blind spots (their imperturbable knack of turning a negative into a positive), while empathising with their family values, that produces an ambivalent position of recognition and self-consciousness for the viewer.

The second comic strategy relies on a fish-out-of-water plotline which sees Darryl and his bumbling suburban solicitor, Dennis Denuto, take the 'big end of town' to court to stop a multinational corporation from acquiring Darryl's prized quarter-acre block, conveniently located next to an international airport. This turning point in the plot disrupts the cyclical repetition of contented scenes of suburban life, Kerrigan-style. It also produces another double-edged position for the viewer, whether to embrace the 'know nothing' insularity of the Kerrigans or to side with Laurie Hammill, the kindly, erudite QC who rescues them from the likely consequences of their ignorance. The film lets the viewer have it both ways, the innocence of insularity and the sophistication of experience. The insularity of the Kerrigans is social as well as geographical. Darryl's only daughter, Tracey, was the first to complete a tertiary education, at the local hairdressing college. The furthest any Kerrigan had travelled, before Trace and Con went to Thailand for their honeymoon, was Alice Springs. Darryl doesn't have to go far to find himself in unfamiliar waters. An appearance before the Administrative Appeals Tribunal sees him struggling for words, dumbfounded to find that 'It's just common sense' doesn't constitute a legal argument. The same thing happens when he persuades Dennis to represent him in the Federal Court. Dennis's assertion to the judge that 'It's the vibe of it' doesn't add up to a legal case for violation of Darryl's constitutional rights as a landowner. It's only when the avuncular QC steps in and saves the day by drawing on the *Mabo* and Tasmanian dams decisions of the High Court that Darryl's case is won. What is double-edged for the viewer is that, in court, as Dale tells us, Darryl and Dennis 'didn't get it. Often.' Although the case is won when the suburban battler joins forces with the educated elite to defeat the bully boys from the big end of town, the film suppresses any possibility that Darryl and Dennis could, between them, have the makings of a bush lawyer. In other words, the film denies the possibility that the ordinary, good-hearted suburban bloke could come to a workable understanding of the High Court's *Mabo* decision. The same could be said for the canny wife of the suburban bloke who asks, somewhat sceptically, 'Have you been drinking?' when Darryl declares, 'I'm beginning to understand how the Aborigines feel.'

In 1997, the year of the film's release, there was a fierce campaign by farmers, miners, pastoralists, conservative journalists, and the States to extinguish native title in the lead-up to Howard's Ten Point Plan to deal with the High Court's 1996 *Wik* decision.[19] The question arises, how far was *The Castle* prepared to take its audience with the *Mabo* case in the context of national

controversy over native title legislation? *The Castle* almost politicises suburban home-ownership when Darryl declares, 'The country's gotta stop stealing other people's land.' Almost, but not quite. The irony is that although
Darryl gets *his* day in court and wins his case on the strength of the *Mabo*
precedent, Eddie Mabo himself was never recognised by the High Court as
having a native title claim on his traditional land because he was adopted
into the Mabo family and was thereby disqualified as an authentic claimant[20]
(see Chapter 4).

The cruel ironies of the *Mabo* case cannot be accommodated within the
ingenuous worldview of the Kerrigans. The task of integrating courtroom
scenes into quirky suburban comedy is treated as a generic problem which
The Castle solves by casting Darryl as a fish out of water, an innocent abroad.
Dennis and Darryl literally become the court jesters, while veteran actor Bud
Tingwell as Laurie Hammill takes on the role of Queen's Counsel, putting
'common sense' and sentiment into legal discourse. As a retired expert in
Constitutional Law, Laurie saves the day by articulating to the High Court
the principle that, when it comes to acquiring property 'on just terms',
'competing rights cannot be weighed one against the other'. In the spirit of
wish-fulfilment characteristic of anti-authoritarian comedy, the High Court
rules in favour of fragile sentiment over heavy-handed profit. Unlike Eddie
Mabo, the Kerrigans prosper from that day forward. The audience is left
to ponder whatever might have been glossed over in the film's providential
ending where a happy neighbourhood (Anglocentric but inclusive) gathers
for a party. For the Kerrigans the pressing issues of the day are to do with
aspiration and opportunity. Their view is future-oriented and past differences are seen as no barrier to an inclusive future. Ethnic differences are
easily accommodated on screen as are class differences, signified by a little
blokey derring-do over a fancy set of Toorak gates. The violent solution to
territorial disputes is canvassed but deflated through humour. As Farouk
says to the corporate henchman, 'You have friend. I have friend who puts
bomb in car.' He doesn't of course, but Farouk enjoys playing with the Arab
stereotype, although it's hard to see the same joke being used in an Australian
commercial film after the terrorist attacks of 11 September 2001. Gender
roles in suburbia are also the target of humour. Darryl's fleet of Holdens (the
Camira, the Torana, the Commodore), his motor boat and his greyhounds
occupy outdoor space. Inside, the space belongs more to his industrious
wife, who 'should open a shop' with her arts and crafts hobbies. If Darryl
is the patriarch, his rule is benevolent and his foibles are tolerated by his
knowing family.

One way to look at the comedy of suburban manners in *The Castle* is
to measure the evident fondness the film has for its characters against their

'know-nothingness' when it comes to matters of colonial history, law and land rights. The film's happy ending comes at the cost of history. Darryl Kerrigan has been able to take up Keating's proposal (in his 1992 Redfern Park speech) that white settlers imagine what it must have felt like for Aboriginal Australians to be summarily dispossessed of their land and then their children.[21] What the film is unable to imagine is how the past is still present for Aboriginal people today, for whom the historical trauma of colonial dispossession is not over and done with. The *Mabo* and *Wik* decisions may have recognised that there are 'competing rights' to the land, but the issue of acquiring the land 'on just terms' has been bypassed by the native title legislation which favours pastoral, mining and other rights over the rights of those few Indigenous communities that can meet the stringent criteria defining those entitled to make land claims. Whether it is legitimate to ask these political questions of a famously low-budget, immensely popular screen comedy of the 1990s is another question. If ambivalence, or having it both ways, is part of the way *The Castle* positions the viewer, then it may be useful to think about quirky suburban comedy as a genial defence of an admittedly flawed Australian way of life.[22] This enables us to have it both ways. The nation's battler is brought in from the bush to struggle against adversity in the suburbs. From the security of his own backyard he can begin to imagine how the Aborigines might be feeling. However, he is under no threat from native title claims. Rather, the remorseless advance of the multinational corporation, with its smooth-talking teams of mobile executives, poses the more immediate threat to his contented way of life.

When Darryl Kerrigan takes the boat and the family up to Bonnie Doon, to his bargain-basement weekender with spectacular views of overhead power lines and a desolate lake, he sees not radiation and environmental degradation (even if the inedible carp are the only fish biting), but 'serenity.' When his amiable QC joins him for a spot of fishing it might appear that the divide between the battler and the cultural elite has been bridged. But it is the rapid rise of Darryl's hapless suburban solicitor, Dennis Denuto, that underlines the virtue of the suburban ethos of looking to the future rather than dwelling on the past. With no evident aptitude for the law, Dennis, at the very end of the film, is shown driving a flash car, operating a flash photocopier and admiring the brass plate on his new office building, on the strength of a class action against lead in landfill. These are visual and verbal jokes, but also material signs of Dennis's successful adaptation to the urban culture of upwardly mobile young professionals. The Kerrigans, with their rapidly multiplying fleet of trucks, represent the working man's other dream, a successful father-and-son business.

In comedy, the future is providential and it includes everyone in its happy ending. This is a generic convention that can be castigated for its exclusions or it can be understood as a utopian imagining of an open community based not on identity but on reconcilable differences. The film acknowledges this ideal as a wish, by opening and closing with the narrator's direct address to camera, emphasising that this is a story, and a bit of a tall one at that. For the Kerrigans, the High Court decision to recognise their affective ties to their 'eyesore' of a home breaks the circle of repetition which opens the film. The future after their *Mabo* decision will be different, as the coda quickly surmises. If we read this as a tongue-in-cheek allegory for the nation, the High Court's *Mabo* decision breaks the circle of denial of the past, thrusting everyone forward into a more prosperous future. In this view, pragmatic recognition of 'how the Aborigines feel about their land' is good for everyone, *if* it allows everyone the opportunity to prosper. Such a view simply cannot envisage a radical cultural difference which could not be accommodated within suburbia. In the period between *Mabo* and *Wik*, in the aftermath of Keating's Redfern Park speech and re-election in 1993, Macintyre argues that 'many longed for a more homely, less challenging national story'.[23] In 1997, the year after Howard's election victory and the return of the conservatives to government after thirteen years, *The Castle* provided precisely that: a 'homely, less challenging national story'.

Giving Back the Land in *Vacant Possession*

As Andreas Huyssen has pointed out, a resurgent politics of *memory* since the 1960s has been closely connected with the issue of *forgetting* in post-communist Eastern Europe and the Soviet, in post-apartheid South Africa, in post-dictatorship Latin America and in the debate about the Stolen Generations in Australia, 'raising fundamental questions about human rights violations, justice, and collective responsibility'.[24] *The Castle* references *Mabo* (along with the Tasmanian Dams case) while 'forgetting' the injustices of Eddie Mabo's non-recognition as a legitimate native title claimant. In this view, the past is over and done with. What matters is the future. An opposing view argues that the past is not over until collective responsibility is taken for the injustices of the past and their continuing effects in the present. The difficulties of guilt and responsibility for the past are explored in the first explicitly post-*Mabo* feature film, *Vacant Possession*, supported by the Australian Film Commission as a low-budget feature by an experimental, anarcho-surrealist-insurrectionary-feminist filmmaker, Margot Nash. In *Vacant Possession* the present (like the self) is represented as a multi-layered archive of scenes and memories from the past. As a surreal *mise-en-scène* of memories, dreams and flashbacks, what happened in the past is perceived as an integral part of what's happening now. The film is set under the flight path close to Sydney Airport. After years in exile, making her living as a gambler, Tessa, whose social memory stretches back to the arrival in Botany Bay of the first fleet of convicts, arrives home on one of the planes flying in and out of Australia, offloading their human cargo into the industrial landscape around Botany Bay, forgotten 'birthplace of a nation'. Tessa's young neighbour, Milly (a member of the local Aboriginal community whose social memory goes back 40 000 years or more), has a white cat named Captain Cook – not because he's white, says Milly, but because he came to stay, even though no one wanted him, and he wouldn't go away. Tessa returns to Australia to claim her inheritance after her mother's death. Instead, it is Tessa herself who is reclaimed by the past.

Part of what haunts Tessa is an archive of memories stored in the sand dunes, in the mangroves, and in the windows, doorways and ceiling of her mother's abandoned weatherboard house. The semi-industrial landscape of one of the city's older working-class areas is possessed by hidden histories, familial and national. Tessa's teenage love affair with Milly's uncle, Mitch, is part of what could not be reconciled in family or national histories founded on the amnesia of *terra nullius*, the social Darwinism of racial assimilation, and the White Australia policy. The coastal Sydney landscape, imbued with these histories, differs from the Melbourne quarter-acre block defended from corporate takeover in *The Castle*. The flat, featureless expanse of cleared land around Melbourne Airport is laid bare. It is there for everyone to take in at a glance, at worst a functional 'eyesore', at best a noisy but convenient location. The landscape around Tessa's mother's house in *Vacant Possession* is a different matter. Not everything can be taken in at a glance. The place, like memory, reveals itself in image-fragments, from the mysterious mangrove roots below the waterline, to Mitch's snake dreaming in the sand dunes, to Milly's map of Mabo Australia hanging on her bedroom wall.

The Kerrigans' home is said to hold their memories, but the suburban landscape in *The Castle* seems curiously incapable of inciting a flow of memory, a chain of associations to reveal the past in the present. Although Tessa's home (with its living memories) is finally blown away in a symbolic storm, clearing a path into the future, the business of reconciling with the nation's past is not so readily achieved. When Tessa wants to give her mother's cherished suburban block of land back to Milly's family as compensation (for Mitch, for the child Tessa miscarried, for the uncompensated history between settler and Indigenous Australians), Milly's response highlights how far Tessa is from understanding why 'we don't want your house'. Although

Tessa turns her face to the future, 'for the first time', at the end of the film, indicating that her work of mourning the past is complete, the outline of this future is harder to see than the aspirational, suburban one summed up in Dale Kerrigan's final voice-over in *The Castle*. Tessa has much to learn from Milly, and also from her own sister, about taking responsibility for the burden of the past in a series of daily, mundane, nurturing acts, rather than a cathartic storm of homecoming emotions.[25]

Strands of Space in *Strange Planet*

In contrast to *The Castle*'s integration of the Mabo decision into its ethos of suburban prosperity, the inner-city film locates its upwardly mobile characters in a corporate landscape that no one seems to have a claim on. This cityscape, to which no one belongs in a meaningful way and which is therefore open to all comers, is a useful setting for films contemplating two aspects of 21st-century experience. The first is the *uneventful* experience of time as boredom, of everyday life as duration and repetition rather than change.[26] In this sense, a historic *event* is belated, in so far as constructing something as an 'event' in history occurs afterwards, rather than at the time it happens. The second is the experience of simultaneous happenings, unfolding and entwining fortuitously, like strands in space. Both are aspects of urban experience of time and space in late modernity, but they are played out quite differently in films of different genres. *Strange Planet* (Emma-Kate Croghan, 1999) is an urbane Sydney film which looks to the future millennium, constructing the present in terms of a multi-strand narrative which engages with the history of romantic comedy as a genre of social integration.[27] *Strange Planet*, like *The Castle*, has a providential ending. Its many strands briefly entwine at a festive gathering of three newly formed couples around the breakfast table at a secluded beach house. By contrast, *Radiance* (Rachel Perkins, 1998) is a Queensland coastal film. Its provisional ending involves three sisters burning down the family's house, secluded in the Queensland canefields, then heading for the open road.

The location of *Strange Planet*'s unfolding and entwining stories is provided by Sydney, filmed as a post-national cityscape rather than a familiar tourist attraction. The city's famously abundant sunlight is exploited to heighten the sensuousness of its suburban streets, while at night its multi-lane roads, designer interiors and neon facades are transformed into modern, abstract surfaces of colour, speed, and movement. In keeping with the genre's sophisticated comedy, Sydney is filmed as a seductive, international cityscape, not unlike the intense visual abstraction of Tokyo in *Lost in Translation* (Sofia Coppola, 2003). In this city of surfaces, Ewan, Joel and Neil are partners in a young, upmarket law firm. Their designer apartments and postmodern offices are as far from Dennis Denuto's ramshackle suburban shopfront in *The Castle* as you can get. The trendy bars and party venues they frequent match their workplace and homes. The one exception to designer living for these male professionals is the local pub. When the perfect marriage, the one-night stand or the dating service land them in trouble, they retreat to the front bar of the local pub in search of the consolations of mateship. Judy, Alice and Sally work in the post-industrial service sector, in radio, a café and a bookshop, respectively. Their shared house in a tree-lined street has had a make-over, eliminating all traces of the inner-city working class, long since despatched to the outer suburbs by gentrification. When their lives hit rock bottom, the women seek comfort in the confectionery aisles of a Bi-Lo supermarket, or in the intimacy of their bedrooms.

As one month gives way to the next in this tightly structured narrative, these two sets of characters cross paths in the city, but they don't meet until the year has completed its full cycle, bringing them together by chance on New Year's Eve at a perfect hideaway, a remote, shabby-chic beach house. At the beach, *Strange Planet* pays homage to the genre of romantic comedy, in both its classic and retro modes, by citing the final conjugal scene from *The Awful Truth* (Leo McCarey, 1937), and by naming Cary Grant movies as Sally's touchstone for understanding the chance meeting of couples 'fated to be mated'. Romantic comedy is a fairly neglected genre in Australian cinema, perhaps because its convention of subjecting its characters to a steep learning curve requires them to attain a deeper knowledge of their own erotic desires in order to be able to recognise their heart's desire in another. Romantic comedy's discourse on fate and erotic attraction demands a sexually sophisticated city as its setting (New York, London, Sydney). Even the rare screwball comedy *Paperback Hero* (Anthony J. Bowman, 1999) which begins and ends in the Australian outback develops its erotic themes in Sydney. Increasingly, (from *Four Weddings and a Funeral*, Mike Newell, 1994 to *Love Actually*, Richard Curtis, 2003), contemporary romantic comedy also demands a multi-strand narrative, weaving together the full range of characters created by the genre in its classical Hollywood phase, from the wise-cracking divorcees (Cary Grant and Irene Dunne), to the mismatched virgin and playboy (Doris Day and Rock Hudson), to New Hollywood's nervous neurotics (Woody Allen and Diane Keaton), to the new romantics (Meg Ryan and Tom Hanks) of Nora Ephron's comedies.[28] With her first and second features dedicated to the genre, Emma-Kate Croghan declares herself a post-national filmmaker by taking Hollywood, British and French cinema as her reference points. At the same time, her films have a specific local flavour:

the student cafés, film culture and shared houses of Melbourne in *Love and Other Catastrophes* (1996) and the urbane, postmodern physiognomy of Sydney (the city of the libertarian Push since the 1930s and of Mardi Gras since the 1970s) in *Strange Planet*.

Although its six main characters are juggling their respective futures (of work and love), *Strange Planet* has a cyclical temporal structure rather than a forward trajectory. Its action takes place month by month, from one New Year's Eve to the next, creating a temporal pattern of repetition and renewal which promises to bring things full circle. There is a notion of change in this cyclical temporal structure which is different from the historic *event* (such as the High Court decision in *The Castle* which brings a central conflict to a climax and resolution). The multi-strand narrative is concerned with the non-eventful duration of modern life where nothing much seems to happen, but sooner or later things do change. Rather than a central conflict reaching a crisis point, multi-strand narratives tease out the moments of understanding which come *after* the event; for instance, the three male characters are forced to ponder the enigmatic nature of erotic feelings: *after* Joel's wife suddenly leaves him; *after* Ewan's casual affair results in an abortion for Bridget; *after* the disaster of Neil's 98.7 per cent perfect match made by computer. For the female characters, the moment of understanding of the event is truly belated.[29] For hard-bitten Judy, understanding her cynical affairs with older, married men comes years after the trauma of her mother's early death and her father's disappearance into drugs and rock'n'roll. For suburban-bred Alice, a flash of understanding that she has been stuck for too long in the aftermath of a failed love affair segues into a revitalising encounter with a punching bag, and time in the therapy chair reviewing the past. For flighty Sally, it's a cumulative montage of indiscriminate erotic events, and a sleepless night, that brings the dawn of understanding. Rather than begin to imagine how the enigmatic other feels (as Darryl Kerrigan does in *The Castle*), the characters in *Strange Planet* begin to understand where their own enigmatic feelings are coming from. Invariably this involves coming to terms with the repetition of the past and letting a new cycle begin. The final sequence of *Strange Planet*, where the characters meet fortuitously at the beach, epitomises the film's postmodern sense of time as cyclical and layered, and of space as multi-stranded.

The festive ending at the beach is entirely conventional in terms of the genre of romantic comedy. The characters, like many before them indebted to Shakespeare's romantic comedies, leave behind the cares of the city and travel to a green space where magical things happen, false identities are discarded and recognition of one's true desire is pre-ordained. The film's final resonant image of belonging to a providential and festive community in a post-national, post-multicultural Australia expands the genre beyond the conventional marriage of young lovers to right partners. To achieve this utopian ending *Strange Planet* transforms the traditional Australian weekender into a shabby-chic shack with million-dollar views across rolling green lawn and rippling water, to blue hills silhouetted against an iridescent morning sky. The final scene of enchanted lovers gathering around the laden breakfast table to celebrate the New Year is an aspirational image as well as a providential one. It is a corporate image of modernity as the good life, globally marketed by the transnational infotainment industry that drives the new economy in which randomly linked characters seek to prosper, to love, and to belong to a community based on mutual affection. This is a sensuous image of the designer lifestyle offered by 21st-century modernity.

What's interesting finally about *Strange Planet* is that when the credits roll and the final lyrics fade, there is silence, followed by the cavernous sound of waves building and crashing, accompanied by the squawking of seagulls. This dissonant reprise of the forgotten sound of a childhood holiday, at the end of an urban-dwelling, post-national comedy, takes us back to nature, back to the beach. This aural return to an idyllic place of belonging is double-edged: it holds out the promise of an affective community, drawn together on the strength of enigmatic longings, momentarily fulfilled; yet this idyllic moment of connection occurs in a 'green space', a landscape protected by nostalgia from the aftershock of colonial history and the futureshock of globalisation. The multiple strands of stories which entwine for a magical moment at the beach enable *Strange Planet* to pose a question about the 'weightlessness' of home and belonging in a post-suburban world of young professionals on the move. This question, arising from late modernity's 'shifting locations' and 'short-term bonds', has been articulated by Margaret Morse: 'How then, does one manage the investment of sympathy without deep anchors?'[30] This question is at the heart of post-colonial narratives of home and identity which loosen the moorings of an increasingly cosmopolitan social imaginary in post-*Mabo* Australia.

Cutting Through the Canefields in *Radiance*

In his reading of the unique poetics of land in six preambles to the Constitution devised since 1998 by Australian writers for the Australian Republican Movement, Mark McKenna was struck by 'the depth' of each writer's 'attachment to Australia as country'.[31] McKenna suggests that 'the centrality of the land' to these preambles expresses a wish 'to end the sense of alienation and exile that is embedded in [non-Aboriginal Australians'] colonial experience'.[32] This growing sense of settlers belonging to the land is clearly derived from an acknowledgment of the spiritual tie between Aboriginal people and the land. However, *Radiance* (Rachel Perkins, 1998) insists on a less reverent attitude to the meaning of land and home in the lives of young Aboriginal women who have few reasons to believe in family values or the republican's quest for a renewed sense of national identity. The return home of three sisters for their mother's funeral in *Radiance* tests the possibility of unanchored, post-Indigenous identity by placing three daughters of an Aboriginal mother centre stage to sort out the lies and fantasies about their shared past.

Radiance is a family melodrama, leavened by naturalistic comedy and a theatrical *mise-en-scène* which treats the house, the car and the beach as sets for expressive performances by each of the three 'sisters', Nona, Cressy and Mae. Based on a stage-play by Louis Nowra, *Radiance* was adapted by Nowra and Perkins for the screen. They claim their film is about any three sisters reuniting for their mother's funeral, where the past is an issue but the women's Aboriginal identity is not.[33] As Marcia Langton has insisted, Aboriginality 'is a *social* thing': arising from 'intercultural dialogue', either face to face or mediated by television, music, books or films, Aboriginality 'is created from our histories'.[34] Although *Radiance* grants Aboriginality the status of an unmarked identity (a status usually confined to white masculinity in Australian cinema), it is an explicitly post-*Mabo* film in that it deals with the original act of dispossession of Indigenous land and identity, signified by Nona's desire to return her mother's ashes to the island of her grandparents. The island, now a Japanese tourist resort, is revealed in a number of cutaway shots from the verandah of the mother's house. *Radiance* also deals with assimilation policies as the second act of dispossession: of Nona hidden from the authorities after Mae and Cressy are taken from their mother, one educated to become a nurse, the other to become an opera singer. And the film ends with a dramatic act of reverse dispossession, the burning down of the mother's beach house, an unrenovated Queenslander-on-stilts, hidden between the sea and the canefields. As it turns out, the disputed house, a 'gift' from the faithless Harry (who lives with his socially recognised family in a suburban bungalow), never legally belonged to the mother.

This particular beach house is a far cry from the suburban dream of a fibro weekender, updated in *Strange Planet* to match an aspirational lifestyle. A shack in the canefields, rather than a haven at the beach, the mother's house is a piece of evidence in a long history of perfidy. It is also, like the mother's house in *Vacant Possession*, alive with unreconciled memories. However, unlike the workings of memory to reveal the past in Nash's film, *Radiance* establishes the unreliability of memory in the way that Nona's fiercely defended memory of her father, the Black Prince, is a screen for unspoken histories, unspeakable traumas. Further, Perkins shows that there can be no final moment of truth about the past. Each of the daughters tells a different story. The mother is represented in the film in three ways: through a glamorous photograph establishing her youthful beauty; through her empty armchair which conjures discordant memories for Nona, Cressy and Mae; and through conflicting tales of love, hate and abandonment recounted by each of the daughters. By performing for each other, individual identity is released from a false family genealogy as each daughter takes on an aspect of the mother and the sisters. Nona puts on a kimono and wig to perform Cressy's aria as the abandoned woman who loses her child in *Madama Butterfly*. Mae dons the mother's unworn wedding dress and veil, signifying the blighting of her own sexual hopes by the shame of her mother's promiscuity and descent into madness. Cressy discards her tailored grey outfit in stages, changing into one of Nona's stretchy sheaths to tell Nona the truth about the Black Prince and to help Mae burn the house to the ground.

At the end of *Radiance*, the three daughters don sunglasses and wigs to escape the scene of the crime in Mae's high-powered, violet Ford. Until now, Mae has used her car as a machine to cut through the canefields, burning rubber and blasting the humid silence with rock music.[35] But the roads always bring her back to the tarnished delusions given form by her mother's house. The ignominy of non-recognition of the mother's ownership of the house is the final shame which Mae has added to a lifetime of bearing the hurt and anger of her mother's ambiguous status under the law. Mae cannot escape her mother's house until the sisters' improvised rites of storytelling bring the past out into the open. When the house is doused in petrol and left to burn, the past is no longer hidden, but it remains unforgiven. The shame of being the daughters of the anonymous men who visited that hidden house in the canefields is gone forever, but the differences between the sisters/daughters remain. However, as they depart the scene of their post-colonial origins, their genealogy is clearer : they are all daughters of bastards. This leaves the future open to invention. As Nona climbs into the back seat of the car, she says to Cressy, 'No way am I calling you Mum.' The open road stretches out before them. They'll make it up as they go along. However, the coastal landscape traversed by this long road already has a history. Unlike the desert, the coast does not lend itself to the fantasy of *terra nullius*. The coastal stretch of open country, farmland, tourist towns, suburbs and city centres is invested with local histories, with stories of what it feels like to be at home, to belong to these places before and after *Mabo*. These disparate stories are more like a multi-strand narrative than a coherent national history, contingent and floating, rather than omnisciently anchored in a unifying truth. It could well be that modernity's anchorless mode of belonging, lightly, to a montage of places, to a bastard of a national history, is what defines a post-national cinema.

Notes

1 S. L. Goldberg and F. B. Smith, *Australian Cultural History*, Cambridge University Press, 1988. A Bicentennial anthology whose idea of culture as 'writing, painting, ballet, music or scholarship' (p. 3) ties in with ideas of Australia as insular, second-rate and far removed from the centres of European, British and American excellence.

2 Robert Manne, 'The Howard years: a political interpretation'. In Robert Manne (ed.), *The Howard Years*, Melbourne: Black Inc. Agenda, 2004, p. 27.

3 Newspoll, Saulwick & Muller and Hugh Mackay, 'Public opinion on reconciliation: snap shot, close focus, long lens'. In Michelle Grattan (ed.), *Reconciliation: Essays on Australian Reconciliation*, Melbourne: Black Inc., 2000, p. 49.

4 John Cameron, 'Introduction: articulating Australian senses of place'. In John Cameron (ed.), *Changing Places: Re-imagining Australia*, Sydney: Longueville Books, 2003, p. 9.

5 Martin Krygier quoted in ibid., p. 8.

6 See Sir William Deane, 'Australia Day message 2000'. In Grattan, *Reconciliation*, 2000, pp. 9–11.

7 On Australian cinema and multiple constructions of nationhood as European-derived, diasporic, multicultural-Indigenous, or melting pot, see Tom O'Regan, *Australian National Cinema*, London: Routledge, 1996, pp. 306–30.

8 Newspoll, p. 33.

9 ibid., p. 34.

10 ibid., p. 37.

11 ibid., p. 38.

12 On vernacular forms of modernism in fashion, design, architecture as well as photography and cinema see Miriam Hansen, 'The mass production of the senses: classical cinema as vernacular modernism', *Modernism/Modernity*, 6(2) 1999, p. 60.

13 For a discussion of this love-hate relation to the suburbs see Alan Gilbert, 'The roots of Australian anti-suburbanism'. In S. L. Goldberg and F. B. Smith (eds), *Australian Cultural History*, Cambridge University Press, 1988, pp. 33–49.

14 ibid., p. 33.

15 Jim Forbes and Peter Spearitt, 'Rum corps to white-shoe brigade'. In Julianne Schultz (ed.), *Dreams of Land: Griffith Review*, Summer 2003–2004, p. 32.

16 Gilbert, 'The roots of Australian anti-suburbanism', p. 35.

17 Goldberg & Smith, *Australian Cultural History*, p. 4.

18 Linnell Secomb, 'Interrupting mythic community', *Affective Communities: Cultural Studies Review*, 9(1) 2003, pp. 85–100. Compares historical forgetting in the Olympic 2000 Opening Ceremony with Messianic moments of the past in the present in Kim Scott's novel, *Benang: From the Heart*, 2000.

19 Stuart Macintyre, 'Frontier conflict'. In *The History Wars*, Melbourne University Press, 2003, pp. 149–153. Discusses conservative resistance to land rights and native

title legislation, and the Hindmarsh Island dispute over the status of secret testimony from Ngarrindjeri women.

20 We discuss the injustices and anomalies of the *Mabo* case for Eddie Mabo and his family in Chapter 4.

21 Paul Keating, 'The Redfern Park speech'. In Michelle Grattan (ed.), *Reconciliation*, 2000, pp. 60–4.

22 On the question of ambivalence and the class positioning of the critic in relation to *The Castle* see Lorraine Mortimer, '*The Castle*, the garbage bin and the high-voltage tower: home truths in the suburban grotesque', *Meanjin*, 57(1) 1998, pp. 116–24.

23 Macintyre, 'Frontier conflict', p. 128.

24 Andreas Huyssen, 'Present pasts: media, politics, amnesia'. In Arjun Appadurai (ed.), *Globalization*, Durham & London: Duke University Press, 2001, p. 63.

25 For a more extensive analysis of the house, history and family in *Vacant Possession* and *Radiance* see Felicity Collins, 'Bringing the ancestors home: dislocating white masculinity'. In D. Verhoeven (ed.), *Twin Peeks: Australian and New Zealand Feature Films*, Melbourne: Damned Publishing, 1999, pp. 107–16.

26 Patrice Petro, 'After shock/between boredom and history'. In P. Petro (ed.), *Fugitive Images: From Photography to Video*, Bloomington IN: Indiana University Press, 1995, pp. 275–6. See Chapter 5.

27 On *Strange Planet* as part of a brief cycle of romantic comedies see Felicity Collins, 'Brazen brides, grotesque daughters, treacherous mothers: women's funny business in Australian cinema from *Sweetie* to *Holy Smoke*'. In Lisa French (ed.), *Womenvision: Women and the Moving Image in Australia*, Melbourne: Damned Publishing, 2003, pp. 167–82.

28 On the genre's four main phases and key conventions see Steve Neale, 'The big romance or something wild? Romantic comedy today', *Screen*, 33(3) 1992, pp. 284–99.

29 See Chapters 5 and 6 on Jean Laplanche's understanding of the temporal structure of belatedness or afterwardness.

30 Margaret Morse, 'Home: smell, taste, posture, gleam'. In Hamid Naficy (ed.), *Home, Exile, Homeland: Film, Media, and the Politics of Place*, New York and London: Routledge, 1999, pp. 68–9.

31 Mark McKenna, 'Poetics of place', *Dreams of Land: Griffith Review*, ed. Julianne Schultz, Summer 2003–2004, p. 188.

32 ibid., p. 192.

33 Louis Nowra and Rachel Perkins, '"Let the turtle live!" a discussion on adapting "Radiance" for the screen', *Metro*, 135, 2003, pp. 34–41.

34 Marcia Langton, *"Well, I Heard It On The Radio And I Saw It On The Television": An Essay for the Australian Film Commission on the Politics and Aesthetics of Filmmaking by and about Aboriginal People and Things*, Sydney: Australian Film Commission, 1993, p. 31.

35 On Mae's car see Catherine Simpson, 'Notes on the significance of Home and the Past in *Radiance*', *Metro*, 120, 1999, pp. 28–31.

Trauma, Grief and Coming of Age

8

Lost, Stolen and Found
in *Rabbit-Proof Fence*

The feature film *Rabbit-Proof Fence* (Phillip Noyce, 2002) was prompted by and responds to *Bringing them Home* (1997), the controversial national inquiry into the thousands of Aboriginal children forcibly taken from their families by Australian state authorities from 1900 to 1970, an inquiry that changed the face of Australia's self-understanding.[1] While not the first film to deal with this subject, *Rabbit-Proof Fence* is a 'breakthrough film'. It earned more than AUS$1.2 million in its first week of screening, reversing the historical lack of interest by Australian audiences in films about Aboriginal people.[2] More than this, it became *the* film of the Stolen Generations, providing a set of powerful images that captured the popular imagination of both young and older Australians.

Set in outback Australia in 1931, the film takes its name from the wire fence that once ran from the south coast of Western Australia through to the north, acting as a barrier to rabbit hordes migrating from the east to the west. For the three Aboriginal girls at the centre of this true story – Molly (Everlyn Sampi), Daisy (Tianna Sainsbury) and Gracie (Laura Monaghan) – the fence is a lifeline. After escaping from the isolated Moore River Native Settlement where they were taken to be trained as domestic servants, the girls use the rabbit-proof fence to navigate their way across more than 2000 kilometres of some of the world's harshest terrain to their home in Jigalong, a small government outpost located at the far north end of the fence. By bringing this story of the girls' epic journey to light, the film, like its namesake, is a vehicle for retracing the past – that is, a means for recovering what director Phillip Noyce calls 'stolen histories': the experiences of Indigenous Australians that, until recently, non-Indigenous Australia largely refused to recognise. As we show in this chapter, the film does this partly by drawing on narrative techniques and visual devices from Hollywood genres to create a compelling adventure story. This film about returning home also performs some backtracking of its own by reworking a number of key elements of the lost child mythology from classic Australian films such as *The Back of Beyond* (John Heyer, 1954), *Walkabout* (Nicholas Roeg, 1971) and *Picnic at Hanging Rock*

(Peter Weir, 1975). And finally, as we discuss in the last section of this chapter, the film's rhetorical elements of testimony and witnessing are best understood in terms of international screen studies debates about memory, history, trauma and film.

From Hollywood to Jigalong

It is a long time since Australian director Noyce made a film outside America, where he is best known for directing Hollywood action blockbusters such as *Clear and Present Danger* (1994) and *Patriot Games* (1992). So what exactly attracted Noyce at this point in his career to make the low-budget film *Rabbit-Proof Fence*? Noyce claims he was initially attracted to what he calls the film's 'universal elements' as a story of escape.[3] This revelation takes on deeper significance when we learn that Noyce's decision to produce and direct *Rabbit-Proof Fence* was precipitated by a personal crisis. As he tells it, he was in New York working with the actor Harrison Ford on the storyline of the proposed adaptation of Tom Clancy's novel *The Sum of All Fears*. Ford was uncertain about being involved. Every other day Noyce would go up town to Ford's apartment on Central Park West and present him with new improved versions of the storyline. After ten days, Ford was still unhappy and wanted to change the ending completely. So Noyce called the head of Paramount studios who told him he should make all the changes Ford requested because the film already had a release date and time was running out. At that point Noyce claims he exploded. Or, as he puts it in one interview:

> I suddenly thought, I'm not really making a film, I'm making sausages and I felt like a sausage maker . . . Almost on the spur of the moment I decided 'Fuck this, I've spent enough time as a migrant worker in this Hollywood system. It's time to make something for myself and something that I'm more connected to.'[4]

Noyce's decision to make this film about a young girl's determination to return home after being forcibly taken from her Aboriginal mother and community is also then his own act of 'returning home'. Indeed, the film provided an opportunity for Noyce to overcome the peculiar alienation of the expatriate: the experience of feeling like an outsider in a host country – 'a migrant worker in Hollywood' – and, at the same time, an outsider at home. As Noyce puts it, 'About four years ago . . . I had reached the stage where I thought I would no longer be able to return to Australia and make films, because every time I came back to Australia I felt more and more of an outsider, cut off from the issues, from Australian preoccupations.'[5]

Surveying popular and critical reviews of *Rabbit-Proof Fence*, we find that most Australian critics welcomed Noyce's decision to return home and reconnect, as he suggests, with Australian issues. The film is consistently praised for being both profoundly moving and politically astute. Many critics also comment on the film's timeliness – 'long overdue', as one critic wrote.[6] The film is based on a non-fiction book written by Molly Craig's daughter, Doris Pilkington-Garimara, and many of the reviews and commentaries address the film's claim to historical truth.[7] For critic Evan Williams, for example, '*Rabbit-Proof Fence* has been made with such transparent humanity and idealism it scarcely seems to matter whether the story is true or not'.[8] For others, however, it matters a great deal. Upon its release in 2002, *Rabbit-Proof Fence* became a target in the neo-conservative anti-Stolen Generations campaign and the history wars debate (see Chapter 1). In a scathing commentary in the *Daily Telegraph*, one of the campaign's leading players, columnist Piers Akerman, attacked the film's depiction of historical events and figures, claiming they were misleading to audiences.[9] He also used a sustained assault on the film's depiction of this episode in Australian history to take several swipes at the public intellectual Robert Manne, who a week earlier had published a feature article on the Stolen Generations in the *Sydney Morning Herald* in which he describes *Rabbit-Proof Fence* as 'the first important feature film on the subject'.[10]

Akerman's attack on *Rabbit-Proof Fence* and its admirers rehearses the arguments and rhetorical stance of the wider ongoing campaign against *Bringing Them Home*. As Manne notes, *Bringing Them Home*, which is based on the testimonies of more than 500 witnesses, had a profound impact on national identity. In the days following the report's tabling in parliament, politicians openly wept as they acknowledged the report's findings that a minimum of 10 per cent and perhaps as many as 30 per cent of all Aboriginal children born between 1900 and 1970 were forcibly removed or 'stolen', as Indigenous people put it, from their mothers and communities.[11] Public response followed suit, mediated by a national media that by and large accepted both the findings and the emotional tone of the report. It was an intense moment of national shame and collective remorse that crystallised around the question of a national apology to Indigenous Australians. In fierce opposition to this general mood of shame and call for an apology, neo-conservative politicians, academics and journalists began a series of public attacks on the report, claiming, among other things, that it damaged Australia's 'good name'. For Manne, retired Liberal politician Peter Howson goes as far as to suggest that the report's findings about the racist and genocidal dimensions of the state-sanctioned policies of removal are an act of treachery.[12] Akerman's commentary takes a similar view, directly disputing as racist and genocidal the way the film represents the policies and administrative practices of Western Australia's then Chief Protector of Aborigines, A. O. Neville. Here and elsewhere, Akerman argues that Aboriginal protectors like Neville did not 'steal' children from their families but rather 'rescued' them from hostile tribal Aborigines who refused to recognise children of mixed descent. Noyce's public refutation of Akerman's claims refers to a wealth of historical and anthropological evidence to the contrary.[13]

But there is something else at stake in Akerman's attack on *Rabbit-Proof Fence*. His commentary also displays an age-old cultural prejudice that emerged as a peculiar by-product of the anti-*Bringing Them Home* campaign, namely the Platonic suspicion of the image. Campaigners against the report argue that the document is fundamentally flawed because it is based on the testimonies of witnesses, which are, in their view, 'distorted memories' of the past, instead of what they call 'official' history: government documents, statistics, legislation, and the like.[14] In his analysis of the campaign, Manne explains that despite the fact that left-wing intellectuals and historians have provided a great deal of 'official history' to support witnesses' claims, neo-conservatives have continued to pursue this line of thinking, culminating in a national conference on the subject titled 'Truth and Sentimentality' and organised by the right-wing journal *Quadrant*.[15] Here, participants argued in one way or another that they were dealing with historical truth based on empirical evidence while the left or new intelligentsia, which includes at least one of the authors of *Bringing Them Home*, infect the public spheres of politics and media with a dangerous sentimentality about the so-called 'Aboriginal problem' which, they claim, encourages an anti-Australian ethos.[16]

Returning to Akerman's commentary we find a similar line of thought when he dismisses the film's contribution to national culture and history on the grounds of an effect Ross Gibson calls 'international contamination' (discussed in Chapter 5).[17] For Akerman, *Rabbit-Proof Fence* cannot be regarded as 'one of Australia's best films' because it is culturally inauthentic, or, to use his words, 'a Tinseltown version of an Australian story'.[18] Here, Akerman accuses the filmmakers of taking licence in their representation of historical reality, suggesting that the film fails as a work of history because its primary aim is to elicit emotion. 'The film *Rabbit-Proof Fence*', he writes, 'is not about facts; it's about sentiments'.[19] In other words, while Noyce sees *Rabbit-Proof Fence* as a form of escape from 'the sausage factory' that he believes the Hollywood studio system is, Akerman perceives the film as nothing more than an imported sausage: a distasteful, overblown product that is positively 'un-Australian' in its appeal to the emotions.

It is interesting to note that while Noyce's response to Akerman in the *Sunday Telegraph* pays careful attention to questions of historical accuracy, it sidesteps Akerman's attack on the melodramatic style of the film and the question of cultural contamination. Elsewhere, however, Noyce is more than happy to defend the film's Hollywood elements, especially its appeal to the senses. At a Q and A session following a screening in Newcastle, Noyce told the audience that from the very start his aim had been to make 'a mainstream film'.[20] He did not, he said, want to make 'an art-house film seen only by the converted'. On the contrary, as he admits in an interview with Jane Mills: 'Hollywood knows how to reach audiences. I've learned the lessons in marketing and casting that Hollywood teaches. Now I have to use these skills to sell an Indigenous story to the mainstream. It's not overtly political but covertly. Hollywood can do this and do this well.'[21]

The marketing of *Rabbit-Proof Fence* indicates that Noyce has learnt Hollywood lessons well, for it was the most widely publicised Australian film in recent years. In the weeks leading up to the film's national release, Noyce and others involved in the project, including scriptwriter Christine Olsen, author of *Doris Garimara Pilkington*, as well as the surviving real-life subjects of the film, Molly Kelly (née Craig) and Daisy Burungu, appeared on numerous current affairs and talk shows on both commercial and state television networks. At the same time, promos comprised of visually striking images of the young girls crossing the desert, accompanied by Peter Gabriel's highly percussive score were broadcast at regular intervals in prime-time television. Noyce also applied his lessons in star-making. Print and screen media ran special features on the film's new and 'old' stars, making the film's release a notable media event. The popular magazine for teenage girls, *Dolly*, for example, ran a four-page spread on thirteen-year-old newcomer Everlyn Sampi, who plays Molly. We also saw a spate of features on the revival of David Gulpilil's career, enabled by his supporting role in *Rabbit-Proof Fence* as the tracker, Moodoo, as well as his then forthcoming lead role in *The Tracker* (Rolf de Heer, 2002). Judging from the questions asked at the Q and A in Newcastle, many people who went to see *Rabbit-Proof Fence* had also first seen Darlene Johnson's documentary on the making of the film, *Follow the Rabbit-Proof Fence*, produced by the Nine network. More intimate and frank than most behind-the-scenes promotional films, this film documents Noyce's search for three young girls to play the lead roles (more on this documentary below).

In addition to the Hollywood-style promotional campaign, the film itself bears testimony to Noyce's mastery of Hollywood genres, in particular the action film. The narrative structure of *Rabbit-Proof Fence* is the chase film, a structure that dates back to silent American classics such as Buster Keaton's *The General,* through to classical Westerns such as John Ford's *The Searchers.* The first third of this chase film shows the three girls being taken away from their home in northern Western Australia to the Moore River Native Settlement, south of Perth, while the remaining two-thirds show their escape and the subsequent chase to recapture them as they make their way north. The first section of the film also allows for the introduction of A. O. Neville (Kenneth Branagh), the Western Australian Chief Protector of Aborigines from 1915 to 1936, who has complete power over all Aboriginal people in the state, including Molly, Gracie and Daisy. When Neville learns that the girls have escaped from Moore River, he organises the full-fledged search that sets off classic chase elements, including physical tests and narrow escapes as the pursuers close in on the girls only to lose them again. The film's cinematographer, Chris Doyle, aptly describes the film as 'a road movie on foot'.[22]

The chase element of the film also allows for the development of an unspoken relationship between Molly and Moodoo (David Gulpilil), the black tracker Neville sends to recapture the girls. Knowing she will be followed by Moodoo, Molly cleverly devises a number of strategies to cover their tracks and thus evade capture. As the chase intensifies, Moodoo develops a deep admiration for Molly's cleverness and her determination to return home. For viewers, this helps to generate a greater level of anticipation, as well as a more intense form of identification with the characters, thus contributing to the film's overall entertainment value. The fictionalisation of the relationship between Molly and her adversary is also typical of the many small departures the film makes from the non-fiction book version of the story based on Molly and Daisy's oral histories, that is, techniques of dramatisation. Overall, however, the film is at pains to remain faithful to this specific story of Aboriginal child removal. As Noyce explains: 'Christine [Olsen, scriptwriter and co-producer] and I felt that there was an acceptable point towards which we could push the story of the movie and that there was this fence we couldn't cross, even though it would make it a more dramatic journey and more conventional film.'[23]

The self-imposed restraint on the part of the filmmakers regarding the historical facts of the story results in an interesting mix of the political history genre, maternal melodrama and the romance-quest. This is not a smooth hybrid form. Rather, it might be best described as a grafting of one genre onto another, with the joints being especially noticeable in the film's somewhat clunky cutting back and forth between the girls' journey home and scenes of Neville at work. In the 1930s, Neville was an influential figure in national debates and conferences about Aboriginal affairs.[24] Along with Cecil Cook, Chief Protector in the Northern Territory, he was one of the nation's most enthusiastic proponents of eugenicist strategies for 'breeding out the colour', such as the removal of 'half-caste' children from their families, as well as the prohibition of marriages between 'half-castes' and 'full-bloods' and the active encouragement of marriages between 'half-caste' women and European men. In 1937, he led a Commonwealth meeting on this issue, asking: 'Are we going to have a population of 1 million blacks in the Commonwealth or are we going to merge them into our white community and eventually forget that there ever were any Aborigines in Australia?'[25] The film dramatises this aspect of Neville's thinking in his delivery of a lecture on his policies of child removal to a group of women from a local ladies benevolent society. The scene contributes nothing to the plot; indeed, as Noyce suggests, scenes like this one *distract* from the drama of the journey. Rather, the function of this particular scene is to show the political, legal and administrative context for the girls' situation, fulfilling the film's political aim of communicating the findings of *Bringing Them Home*, including the racist, genocidal thinking that underpinned policies of Aboriginal child removal.

It should be noted, however, that while this visible tension between realistic historical detail on the one hand and a highly conventional plot on the other takes a specific form in *Rabbit-Proof Fence*, it is by no means unique to this film. Nor is it, as Akerman suggests, foreign to Australian cinema. On the contrary, this visible tension is characteristic of a subgenre of Australian action-adventure films known as lost in the bush or lost children films. So already we can see how *Rabbit-Proof Fence* looks outward to global cinema through its use of elements from Hollywood genres while at the same time backtracking across well-worn ground in Australian national cinema.

The Lost Child Found

The lost child is a recurrent theme in the Australian cultural tradition. Narratives of lost children date as far back as the colonial period, where this figure characterised the hardship of life in the bush for new settlers. As Peter Pierce's comprehensive study of the subgenre shows, by the end of the 19th century the regular newspaper reports and stock illustrations of lost children that had well and truly captured the popular imagination had become the basis of literary works by many well-known Australian writers, including Henry Kingsley, Marcus Clarke, Henry Lawson, Joseph Furphy and Ethel Pedley, as well as visual renderings of the theme by well-known artists such as the

Heidelberg school painter Frederick McCubbin.[26] In cinema, lost children narratives date back to the 1930s with Charles Chauvel's mythic *Uncivilized* (1936). They are also prevalent in the so-called New Australian cinema with features such as *Walkabout* (1971), *Lost in the Bush* (Peter Dodds, 1970), *Barney* (David Waddington, 1976), *Picnic at Hanging Rock* (1975), and *Manganninie* (John Honey, 1980), as well as contemporary cinema in *The Missing* (1998) and *One Night the Moon* (2001). *Rabbit-Proof Fence* backtracks over and reworks many of the elements of this cultural tradition.

In her survey of Australian action-adventure films, Susan Dermody argues that lost in the bush or lost children films are in the romance-quest mode: 'a form that organises meaning in stories as diverse as Homer's *Ulysses*, the biblical story of Moses, nearly every fairytale, and Shakespearean romances, such as *The Winter's Tale*.'[27] What is interesting about Dermody's study of the Australian action film in terms of the conventions of the romance-quest is that she emphasises two main elements: first, the quest is fulfilled through a series of physical challenges in *unfamiliar territory*, and second, the motivation of the hero is *idealist* rather than comic-tragic or satiric and pessimistic.[28] Moreover, Dermody argues that these films depict their respective searches or struggles to fulfil an ideal against a background of *real anxieties*.[29]

Working with Dermody's somewhat idiosyncratic, we could say 'Australianised', definition of the romance-quest, we can ask what exactly is the real, or social, anxiety behind the Australian tradition of lost children films. In a recent in-depth study, Pierce convincingly argues that the recurring motif of the lost child in Australian painting, literature and film amounts to 'a peculiarly Australian anxiety', namely European settler anxiety about belonging.[30] Pierce shows how on one level these stories and images function as warnings of the very real dangers posed by life in the bush and the outback. But they also have a much deeper cultural significance. For Pierce, the image of the forlorn lost child that haunts both popular culture and canonical works by Australian writers and artists stands for an older generation of European settlers: 'Symbolically, the lost child represents the anxieties of European settlers because of their ties with home which they have cut in coming to Australia . . . The child stands for the apprehension of adults about having to settle in a place where they might never be at peace.'[31]

As Pierce observes, one of the best known images of the lost child is the stock 19th-century magazine illustration of a group of two or three children entwined in an exhausted sleep at the foot of a tree.[32] Originating from true stories, such as the famous colonial story of the three Duff children lost in the bush in the Wimmera area of Victoria in 1864, this image is routinely rehearsed in melodramatic narratives of the lost child, for example *Picnic at*

Hanging Rock, where it sparks an uncanny remembrance, contributing to the film's blurring of the lines between fact and fiction, fantasy and reality. In *Rabbit-Proof Fence* this highly recognisable composition of lost children appears early in the chase when Molly, Gracie and Daisy collapse in a huddle after an exhausting day of being on the run with little water and no food. But while *Rabbit-Proof Fence* invokes iconic images of the lost child in the melodramatic mode, it also inverts their meaning in quite significant ways. As mentioned above, the image of the exhausted, sleeping lost children has come to symbolise the European settler's vulnerability in a hostile and indifferent landscape, hence reinforcing long-standing settler anxieties about belonging. Here, the image of the three young Aboriginal girls overwhelmed by the unfamiliar landscape serves an entirely different purpose by helping to establish a major theme of the story: Molly is compelled to return home not only because she desperately wants to be reunited with her mother but also because the land in and around the Moore River settlement is, quite literally, making her ill.

This idea of Molly being out of sorts with the landscape is visually expressed in the film's striking use of colour and camera angles. Speaking of his technique, cinematographer Chris Doyle explains: 'I was looking for something that suggested the torment, the cruelty of the journey, the loneliness, the isolation and the expanse.'[33] Working against the rich palette and lighting techniques of the pastoral tradition in Australian period films such as *Picnic at Hanging Rock*, the girls' journey across unfamiliar territory is dominated by the use of desaturated colour. As Doyle suggests, this bleaching effect highlights the bleakness of the journey. It also stands in stark contrast to the oasis-like qualities of the scenes at home in Jigalong. This new post-*Mabo* approach to the Australian landscape is central to the film's radical inversion of the meaning of lost child films. Here, the image of a hostile, indifferent landscape actively allows for an Indigenous notion of 'country', that is, the idea that Aboriginal people belong to a particular area of land, have customary obligations to that land and are physically and emotionally affected when they are taken from their 'country'.

In addition to redefining the meaning of land in lost child stories, *Rabbit-Proof Fence* opens the way for a post-*Mabo* interpretation of the peculiar affect of the lost child story. More than just a symbol of ties cut, as Pierce suggests, lost child narratives are shot through with a peculiar sense of loss generated by their dramatisation of the impossibility of returning home. In many narratives this loss is played out through Aboriginal characters. As Pierce notes, historically, lost children stories are one of the few subgenres in Australian literature and film that acknowledge relations between Aboriginal and non-Aboriginal Australians, for many involve a black tracker who is often summoned 'too late'.[34] This idea of too lateness is foregrounded in the musical *One Night the Moon*. Based on the experiences of a well-known black tracker, Sergeant Alex Riley, the film tells the story of a racist father who flatly refuses to allow an Aboriginal tracker onto his land to help search for his lost daughter.[35] When the search party fails to find the child, the tracker is summoned by the mother. The tracker quickly locates the child, but by then it is too late, for the girl is dead. For Pierce, the role of Aboriginal people in lost children narratives from the colonial period constitutes a terrible irony: 'Often they [lost children] were saved by Aboriginal men who had been dispossessed of this same land.'[36] He goes on to suggest that the tracker is potentially 'a most potent image of reconciliation between black and white Australia'.[37]

There is little evidence to assess the effect of colonial images of Aboriginal rescues of lost children as images of reconciliation, and they were, according to Pierce, soon forgotten.[38] What interests us more about the role of the Aboriginal tracker in this narrative tradition is the analogy between the ill-fated lost child of the bush and the fate of Aboriginal people, reinforcing the colonial notion of Aboriginal people as the 'dying race'. According to Pierce, the first lost child story in Australian literature was a poem by Charles Thompson titled 'Blacktown' (1826), which reflects on the fate of Aboriginal 'possessors' after they abandoned an Aboriginal settlement established for them by Governor Macquarie.[39] This popular colonial/colonising image of Aboriginal people's tragic failure to integrate into modern life is the basis of *Jedda* (Charles Chauvel, 1955), a story reworked in Tracey Moffatt's post-colonial experimental film *Night Cries* (1990). This image is also reproduced in *Walkabout*, Nicholas Roeg's film about two British children – the Girl (Jenny Agutter) and the Boy (Lucas Roeg), as they are known – who are abandoned by their father in the outback only to be rescued by a young Aborigine (David Gulpilil).

Made in 1971, *Walkabout* is known for its stunning images of the Australian landscape or what Susan Dermody describes as its 'shocking beauty'.[40] In an interview in which he discusses the making of the film, Roeg admits he was attracted to the project because it provided the opportunity to work somewhere 'that had hardly been surveyed', 'a big, empty backcloth', a place where it is possible to project the kinds of primal fantasies explored in this film.[41] More problematically, Roeg extends this conception of the Australian landscape as a blank canvas, a landscape that 'hasn't been tampered with', to its Indigenous inhabitants.[42] Reminiscing on his selection of the then unknown, inexperienced Gulpilil to play the role of Aboriginal boy, Roeg describes Gulpilil as 'not stained by anything, except life'.[43] This Rousseauesque idea of Gulpilil the actor concurs with the film's representation of the Aboriginal boy as a 'noble savage'.[44] It also emphasises the provocative ending in which the Aboriginal boy directs the children to an abandoned settlement on the fringe of a mining settlement, only to take his own life by hanging himself from a tree. The film suggests that the boy is overwhelmed by grief after witnessing a buffalo culling. His grief is later exacerbated by the Girl's rejection of his 'marriage proposal' communicated through a spectacular and highly primitivised dance sequence. His death is emblematic of the girl's refusal to submit to her primal urges, to stay lost in the bush. This idea of Aboriginality is further emphasised in the epilogue where the girl is shown some years later in her ultra-modern urban kitchen daydreaming of idyllic moments shared with the Aboriginal boy. As others, including Pierce and Dermody, suggest, the Aboriginal boy is the true lost child of this film. For in the logic of this narrative, there is no place for Aboriginal people in modernity other than as the subject of a European romantic longing for an ideal primitive past.

Rabbit-Proof Fence succeeds not only in avoiding the kind of primitivism at work in *Walkabout* but in countering its image of Aboriginal people as *the* lost children by telling a story of Aboriginal survival and resistance. Despite Neville's efforts to have Molly and the others recaptured, she and Daisy finally return home. 'She will not submit', as Neville puts it. The triumph of their return is encapsulated in the image of Molly emerging from the desert carrying her younger sister in her arms. In this way, again, *Rabbit-Proof Fence* invokes the lost child films of the past while at the same time bringing something new to the genre. Unlike the tragic ending of *Walkabout*, where the Aboriginal boy rescues the girl and boy only to take his own life in despair, *Rabbit-Proof Fence* offers a powerful image of Aboriginal survival of colonial violence and subjugation. In doing so, it inverts two centuries of the representation of Aboriginal people as a doomed or dying race, a group of people who have no place in modernity. More specifically, it reorients the peculiar sense of loss and belatedness associated with the lost child narrative away from settler anxieties of belonging to the post-*Mabo* issue of how the nation can best face up to the shame of the Stolen Generations.

According to Pierce, stories of lost children have always served as a form of 'communal remembrance', uniting communities in their collective mourning.[45] One of the most famous cinematic representations of the lost child is a dramatic re-enactment of a true story in John Heyer's award-winning documentary *The Back of Beyond* (1955), a poetic exploration of life in the outback seen by large cinema audiences here and overseas. In this re-enactment, two young blonde-haired, fair-skinned sisters set off from their homestead into the blinding heat of the desert to seek help after their mother unexpectedly dies. The most poignant moment in this depiction of their story is when the girls cross their own tracks. At this point, the older girl, like us, realises that they have been travelling in circles. Not wanting to panic her younger sister, the older girl keeps on walking. Their tiny figures trace a line across the desert dunes before they disappear into the distance. The image of Molly emerging from the desert carrying her sister Daisy is a mirror reversal of the former image. As such, it *recovers* – in both senses of the word – a trace of cinematic history for contemporary audiences. And just as in the past stories of lost children, such as Heyer's, encouraged collective public memory, *Rabbit-Proof Fence* is a powerful invitation to all Australians to remember publicly the Stolen Generations, to 'bring them home'.

Returning Home

On 13 January 2004, Molly Kelly died in her sleep at Jigalong. *The Age* report on her death named Kelly as 'the heroine of the film *Rabbit-Proof Fence*', validating the important role the film played in bringing the largely 'hidden' story of Kelly's epic journey to public attention. Here, Molly's journey is described as one that 'ranks as one of the most remarkable feats of endurance, cleverness and courage in Australian history'.[46] In this way, we can say that the film has achieved the director/producer's aim of 'recovering stolen histories'. But in an important way the report also draws attention to what is not recoverable, or what we would call the 'unspeakable' aspects of this remarkable story. In the first paragraph we learn that despite all Molly's incredible strengths, including her cleverness and outstanding ability to endure physical pain and deprivation, indeed despite the film's phenomenal success both at home and internationally, which has made Molly Kelly a national heroine, 'she died with one regret: she was never re-united with the daughter taken from her 60 years ago'. It is precisely this aspect of Molly Kelly's life that brings us to the traumatic dimensions of *Rabbit-Proof Fence*.

So far we have shown how *Rabbit-Proof Fence* grafts the political-historical drama genre onto the romance-quest to create a compelling story that invokes and at the same time reworks many of the themes, conventions and melodramatic aspects of the Australian cultural tradition of the lost child or lost in the bush narratives. This mix of historical realism and the romance-quest works exceptionally well in the final act where it is integrated with Indigenous aspects of the narrative. On the precipice of death from starvation and physical exhaustion, Molly, the heroine, summons the strength to pull herself back and make the final leg of the journey home to her mother and community. The film suggests that this strength derives from the mother's and grandmother's traditional 'singing', the two women camped on the outskirts of their country beside the fence. The heroine is also awakened and revitalised by the sound of a bird call – her traditional totem. This call opens her eyes to the sight of her country on the horizon, or 'Home', as she sighs to herself. To the sounds of soaring music, Molly lifts her exhausted younger sister in her arms and carries her towards home. Meanwhile, we cut to Neville's office where he receives news that his patrol officer has reached Jigalong. Neville replies, instructing the officer to recapture the girls. But the patrol officer is spooked. Heading out into the bush in the dead of night, he is unnerved by the women's singing. When he encounters Maude, a face-off ensues and he quickly retreats. This leaves the women free to greet the returning girls. Seeing their mother and grandmother in the distance, the girls begin to run, puffing and giggling; they cannot contain their joy. In this moment of reunification, all the women sob loudly. Molly's joy is tainted by her concern for the lost Gracie. 'I lost one', she confesses, referring to Gracie's recapture by patrol officers. On one level, this image of the reunification of three generations of Aboriginal women offers a satisfying resolution to the story, effectively assuaging social anxieties about past race relations, in particular the issue of the Stolen Generations. Certainly, if the film ended on this moment of triumph we could all have left the theatre assured that, as with most romance-quests, the hero's return resolves all the problems raised in the course of the story. But this is not where the film ends.

In a vein similar to *Schindler's List* (Steven Spielberg 1991), *Rabbit-Proof Fence* ends with an epilogue: a flash-forward to the real-life subjects of the film, shot in the documentary mode. Here, the real-life Molly's narration resumes in Aboriginal language, subtitled in English. It serves to remind us that all along this has been Molly's story, a story which began the film in the Aboriginal tradition of contact narratives: 'This is a true story of me and my sisters . . . My mother told me about how the white men first came to Jigalong . . .' Now, over a sequence of aerial shots of the vast expansiveness of the Australian outback, Molly's voice returns to control the story's ending: 'We walked for nine weeks, a long way, all the way home. Then we went straightaway and hid in the desert. I got married. I had two baby girls . . .' As a recount of events following her return home, the epilogue reinforces the film's claim to historical truth: the existence of the real-life subjects validates the authenticity of the story. But more than this, as with 'Schindler's Jews', who appear at the end of *Schindler's List*, Molly speaks as a *survivor* of the specific historical trauma the film refers to – the Stolen Generations. In this way, the film is much more than a historical drama or romance-quest narrative or even a maternal melodrama. It is an instance of trauma cinema in which spectators are addressed as witnesses.

The growing interest in film studies in trauma cinema directly relates to the emergence of trauma theory as a new paradigm in the humanities for thinking about memory and history. Based on Freud's notion of psychic trauma, this new body of theory concerns itself with the processes of remembering and transmitting memory of catastrophic, overwhelming events, in particular political historical events, such as the Holocaust, race crimes, rape in war. A traumatic memory is distinguished from other modes of memory by its peculiar temporality: a memory that unexpectedly emerges only some time *after* the traumatising event or episode in the form of a flashback or nightmare. For this reason, trauma theory is crucial to the post-WWII politics of victimhood and blame, which involves the recognition of the delayed memories of victims of catastrophic events. One of the key questions for trauma theorists is how trauma is signified. For Cathy Caruth, a leading figure in trauma theory, traumatic memory is understood by a kind of hermeneutics that focuses on gaps and absences.[47] By this she means that instead of using methods of cultural analysis that dig deep into the minds of survivors in the hope of uncovering buried memories, we need to apply Freud's concepts of traumatic latency and belatedness to think about the ways in which traumatic experience emerges as an unconscious delayed response. For Caruth, literature is a privileged site for such responses. In her close analysis of Freud's *Moses and Monotheism* she shows that while individual authors or collective producers may not be aware that their narratives are delayed responses to trauma, the texts themselves always bear signs of the trauma in their gaps and absences.[48] The role of the cultural critic is to use trauma theory to identify such instances. For screen theorists, this means analysing how trauma is transmitted in the relations between a text and its spectators – that is, identifying instances when cinema enables the transmission of traumatic events in indirect ways, through *what is not said and shown*.

To consider how cinema might do this involves moving beyond questions of representation, beyond film as a way of representing specific traumatic events and episodes, as in genres such as the war movie or political historical dramas.[49] As we have seen, this application of trauma is riddled with the problems of referentiality: problems of historical accuracy, competing interpretations of events and claims to truth. In a critical move designed to take us beyond these problems of referentiality, film critic Thomas Elsaesser rethinks trauma cinema as instances in film where the notion of referral is put into crisis, prompting spectators to consider, without foreclosing, the problem of cinematic referral to the past.[50] This can occur in non-realist films, such as *Hiroshima Mon Amour* (Resnais, 1959), where techniques such as non-linearity, fragmentation, non-synchronous sound and repetition mimic the delayed, fragmented nature of traumatic memory. It can also occur in isolated instances in realist narratives, which Janet Walker describes as 'intrusive moments': flashbacks, sudden changes in camera angles, fragmentation.[51] These new critical approaches to trauma and cinema are helpful for thinking through the different critical interpretations of the taking-the-children-away scene in *Rabbit-Proof Fence*.

Approaching the film as a political-historical drama – which it is – the neo-conservative Akerman took offence at this particular scene from *Rabbit-Proof Fence*, claiming that because it departs from Pilkington's written account of the event it 'misleads' viewers about the historical truth of the story.[52] In response, Noyce argues that the scene is a 'typical' representation. In her comments on the scene, Jane Mills takes a different approach. For her, the problem lies not with questions of representation and historical accuracy but with processes of identification.[53] She argues that the scene is not as effective as it might have been because it occurs too early in the film. She writes that because we have not yet had time to identify with the girls we cannot feel the full effect of the event.[54] Mills is right to suggest that in terms of classical narrative structure the scene comes too early. It begins as a typical ration-day at the small isolated government outpost. Molly's mother, Maude (Ningali Lawford), is there to collect her ration of flour. She jokes with the European government officer, while the girls chat with other European men, employed by the government to maintain the fence. Suddenly the mood changes. A car approaches and as Maude realises that the driver is here to take the girls away she begins to scream out to the girls, telling them to run. We would argue, however, that it is precisely the scene's too-soonness, its intrusive quality that allows for something other than character identification.

As Mills suggests, this scene marks a different visual and aural register: life at Jigalong is suddenly all movement and commotion. The hand-held mobile camerawork creates a skewed perspective on events. A lot of the scene is shot from an extremely low angle, positioning us as spectators at the centre of the physical struggle between the officer, Maude and Molly. The soundtrack is also sped up in a cacophony of harsh, percussive sounds combined with the girls' piercing screams. These skewed, low-angle, mobile shots are juxtaposed in a series of rapid edits with extreme close-ups of Daisy and Gracie's stunned faces as they watch through the car windows, the action circling them *and us*. The film then cuts back to a wide-shot, the car receding into the distance to the sound of the girls' grandmother wailing. In this way, the scene allows for two kinds of spectatorship. The sudden intrusion of non-realist techniques draws us into the action of the scene, involving us in the violence of the separation. But the scene then quickly repositions us at a distance. In the logic of identification, it may have worked better for us to have stayed with the girls. By repositioning us back with the mothers, to one side, the film insists that we *witness* the aftermath of the trauma: the mother collapsed under the weight of shock and grief, the old woman hitting her head with a sharp stone in a traditional grieving ritual. In its intrusiveness, the scene takes us out of the historical time of the film's narrative, transporting us into the now. As a cultural response to *Bringing Them Home*, the film rehearses recognisable public symbols and images of the Stolen Generations, effectively making the film another forum for the 'public hearing' of the trauma of child separation.[55] Darlene Johnson's remarkable documentary, *Follow the Rabbit-Proof Fence*, supports this interpretation of the scene as public hearing or re-enactment.[56] Here, we discover just how difficult it was for the actors to perform this scene, which is in effect a re-enactment of a trauma that continues to affect all of the Aboriginal participants in the film in more or less direct ways. For Everlyn Sampi, who plays Molly, performing this scene was especially traumatising, for she found herself re-enacting her real-life mother's experience. For this reason alone, Johnson's documentary is crucial viewing.

Traumatic intrusion in *Rabbit-Proof Fence* is not, however, limited to these direct scenes of taking the children away. Returning to the epilogue mentioned earlier, we find what is for us the most shocking revelation of the film. In her account of what followed her return home, Molly Kelly explains how she was forced to *repeat* the horrendous trek from Moore River to Jigalong:

> We went straightaway and hid in the desert. I got married. I had two baby girls. Then they took me and my two girls back to that place – Moore River. And I walked all the way . . . back to Jigalong again, carrying Annabelle, the little one. When she was three, that Mr Neville took her away. I've never seen her again.

In the space of a few seconds the comforting effect of the triumphal journey home is completely undercut as we try to comprehend the full meaning of Molly's recapture, her second undertaking of this incredible trek, only to have her youngest child forcibly removed from her by the same man who removed her from her mother – a child whom we know from the media report of Molly's death mentioned earlier was never 'found', that is, never reunited with Molly.

On a visual level, Molly's narration bridges the film's slippage from narrative film, through a series of landscape shots, to the final documentary sequence in which the real-life subjects Molly Kelly and Daisy Burungu seemingly emerge out of the desert, indeed, out of the past into the present.

What we see are two strong, proud older Indigenous women, striding out across their country, their home. They are two 'found' members of the Stolen Generations, with Molly once again leading the way. As we review this footage now in the wake of news of Molly Kelly's death, we reflect on Noyce's stated aim of wanting to use film to recover 'stolen histories'. What we know is that the thousands of untold, 'buried' stories of Aboriginal child removal cannot be fully recovered for the public record. We cannot use film to magically reconstruct lost or, to use Caruth's term, unclaimed experience in the same way that film designers and set builders reconstructed the rabbit-proof fence. This film has, however, allowed for a better understanding of the truly traumatic nature of the forced removal of Aboriginal children from their families, that is, child separation as an event that is repeated in various forms of loss, like a nightmare, long after the original injury. A willingness by audiences to be witnesses to this public testimony of child separation is evident in the film's success. As a film that was prompted by and quickly responded to a large public outcry about the findings of *Bringing Them Home*, the film's success also confirms that, as in the past, present-day Australians are perhaps more willing to acknowledge and take responsibility for the trauma of child separation than other shameful episodes in our colonial history, suggesting that at some level of the Australian social imaginary 'the Aborigine' may still be seen as *the* 'lost child'. If this is so, then the image of Molly emerging from the desert, both as a child and later as a grown woman, is an iconic image of Aboriginal survival that shatters that particular myth by demanding recognition of Aboriginal people as being *at home* in their country.

Notes

1 See Human Rights and Equal Opportunity Commission, *Bringing Them Home: Report on the national inquiry into the separation of Aboriginal and Torres Strait Islander children from their families*, Canberra, 1997. Robert Manne argues that 'No inquiry in recent Australian history has had a more overwhelming reception nor, at least in the short term, a more culturally transforming impact.' He shows how within a short period of *Bringing Them Home* being tabled in parliament in 1997, the issue of the Stolen Generations and the associated question of a national apology 'moved from the margin to the centre of Australian self-understanding and contemporary political debate': 'In denial: the stolen generations and the right', *Quarterly Essay*, no. 1, 2001, pp. 5–6.

2 *Rabbit-Proof Fence* opened nationwide on 21 February 2002 on a hundred screens. It grossed AU$1.2 million in its first week, increasing to approximately AUS$7.5 million by the end of the year, making it the second highest grossing film in Australia in 2002. (It was pipped by well-known comedian Mick Molloy's *Crackerjack*, released in November 2002 on 203 screens, which earned AUS$7.7 million.) It has also performed

reasonably well internationally: New Zealand (NZ$1.3 million); UK (£1.6 million), USA (US$4.3 million). It has been picked up by distributors in Germany, France and Mexico. Source: *Inside Film*, April 2003, p. 59.

3 ibid., p. 128.
4 Hunter Cordaiy, 'The truth of the matter: an interview with Phillip Noyce', *Metro*, 131–42, pp. 128–9.
5 ibid., p. 128.
6 Becker Entertainment, *Rabbit-Proof Fence Media Kit*, p. 11.
7 Doris Pilkington-Garimara, *Follow the Rabbit-Proof Fence*, Brisbane: University of Queensland Press, 1996.
8 Evan Williams, *Australian*, 23 February 2002.
9 Piers Akerman, 'Artistic licence spoils this saga', *Sunday Telegraph*, 3 March 2002, p. 89.
10 Robert Manne, 'The colour of prejudice', *Sydney Morning Herald Weekend Edition*, 23–4 February 2002, Spectrum, pp. 4–7.
11 ibid., pp. 24–8.
12 ibid., pp. 51–7.
13 Phillip Noyce, 'Rabbit-proof defence', *Sunday Telegraph*, 10 March 2002, p. 99.
14 On Ron Brunton's accusation of 'false memories', see Manne, 'The colour of prejudice', pp. 31–42.
15 On the *Quadrant* weekend seminar 'Truth and Sentimentality', see ibid., pp. 86–93.
16 ibid.
17 Ross Gibson, *South of the West: Postcolonialism and the Narrative Construction of Australia*, Bloomington and Indianapolis IN: Indiana University Press, 1992.
18 Akerman, p. 89.
19 ibid., p. 89.
20 Q&A Session, Tower Cinema (Greater Union), 30 March 2002.
21 Mills, 'Truth and the rabbit-proof fence', *Real Time*, 48, April–May 2002, p. 15.
22 Becker Entertainment, *Rabbit-Proof Fence Media Kit*, p. 17.
23 Cordaiy, 'The truth of the matter', p. 130.
24 See *Bringing Them Home*, p. 30.
25 Extracts from Neville's writing and interviews are reprinted in *Bringing Them Home*, 1997.
26 See Peter Pierce, *The Country of Lost Children: An Australian Anxiety*, Cambridge University Press, 1999.
27 Susan Dermody, 'Action and adventure'. In Scott Murray (ed.), *The New Australian Cinema*, Melbourne: Nelson, 1980, p. 81.
28 ibid., p. 82
29 ibid.
30 Pierce, p. xii.
31 ibid.
32 For detailed analysis of 19th-century representations of the lost child, including illustrated magazines, see Pierce, *The Country of Lost Children*, pp. 3–94.
33 Becker Entertainment, p. 17.
34 Pierce, *The Country of Lost Children*, p. xii.
35 The idea for this fictional film was prompted by an SBS documentary, *Black Tracker* (Michael Riley, 1997) about Sergeant Alexander (Alex) Riley.
36 Pierce, *The Country of Lost Children*, p. xii.

37 ibid., pp. xii–xiii.

38 ibid., p. xiii.

39 ibid., p. 3.

40 Dermody, 'Action and adventure', p. 83.

41 Richard Combs, 'Not god's sunflowers: Nicholas Roeg on *Walkabout*'. In Raffaele Caputo and Geoff Burton (eds), *Second Take: Australian Filmmakers Talk*, Sydney: Allen & Unwin, 1999, p. 165.

42 ibid., p. 170.

43 ibid., p. 168.

44 On representations of Aboriginality in film, see Marcia Langton, '*Well, I heard it on the radio and I saw it on the television': an essay for the Australian Film Commission on the politics and aesthetics of filmmaking by and about Aboriginal people and things*, Sydney: Australian Film Commission, 1993.

45 Pierce, *The Country of Lost Children*, p. xii.

46 Tony Squires, 'Remarkable life by "the fence" ends for Molly , 87', *The Age*, 15 January 2004.

47 Cathy Caruth, 'Unclaimed experience: trauma and the possibility of history', *Yale French Studies*, 79, Literature and the Ethical Question, 1991, pp. 181–92.

48 ibid., p. 182.

49 Susannah Radstone, Introduction, 'Special debate: trauma and screen studies: opening the debate', *Screen*, 42(2) 2001, pp. 188–93.

50 Thomas Elsaesser, 'Postmodernism as mourning work', *Screen*, 42(2) 2001, p. 194.

51 Janet Walker, 'Trauma cinema: false memories and true experience', *Screen*, 42(2) 2001, p. 194.

52 Akerman, 'Artistic licence spoils this saga', p. 89.

53 Jane Mills, 'Truth and the rabbit-proof fence', *Real Time*, 48, April–May 2002, p. 15.

54 ibid.

55 Here, we are thinking of resonances between the close-ups of the children's and mother's hands flattened against the impenetrable barrier of the glass window and the nationwide Sorry Day's 'sea of hands' that uses the Aboriginal rock painting motif of the hand to symbolise the nation's apology, an image of reaching out to bring stolen children home, literally and metaphorically.

56 Johnson's documentary is included as a special feature on the collector's edition *Rabbit-Proof Fence* DVD, distributed by Magna Pacific and Becker Entertainment.

9

Escaping History and Shame in *Looking for Alibrandi, Head On* and *Beneath Clouds*

Australian film critics often claim that one new film or another marks the coming of age of the Australian film industry. In the 1980s, *Gallipoli* (Peter Weir, 1981) achieved this by telling the story of the Allies' World War I invasion of Turkey from an Australian perspective. In the 1990s, the term was no longer applied to nationalist narratives but to 'outward-looking' genre films, such as the thriller *Lantana* (Ray Lawrence, 2001) and the musical *Moulin Rouge* (Baz Luhrmann, 2001), as discussed in Chapter 2. In addition, each era of the Australian cinema has its share of coming-of-age narratives. In a reappraisal of the genre, Raffaele Caputo argues that the coming-of-age film serves as a 'mirror' of the nation's development.[1] Stories of personal maturity are often set against the background of a major turning point in a nation's past: the Vietnam War in *American Graffiti* (George Lucas, 1973), World War II in *Summer of 42* (Robert Mulligan, 1971) and *Racing the Moon* (Richard Benjamin, 1984). The subgenre routinely uses first-person narration – an adult looking back at a key turning point in his or her adolescence, a socialising moment in which he or she crosses the threshold into the world of adulthood. As Caputo and others have argued, this characteristic nostalgic view leads to a depiction of the past as a more innocent and secure place than the present, even when set against a background of large-scale historical turning points.

This tendency in the coming-of-age film to depict the past as an innocent and secure place is part of what Charles Acland identifies as 'the adult gaze' – the coming-of-age film's attribution of adult values and significance to events involving adolescents.[2] Take *Stand By Me* (Rob Rainer, 1986), for example. Using a retrospective first-person narration, the film tells the story of a young adolescent, Gordie, who is having difficulties coming to terms with the death of his brother. The film focuses on a group adventure in which Gordie and his mates set out to find the dead body of a missing boy. As the adult narrator tells it, this adventure marks a profound turning point in his life, for the shocking sight of the immobile body releases a newfound inner strength, allowing Gordie not only to accept his brother's death but to courageously challenge a group of older local boys who were also interested in claiming the body. Gordie's friends recognise him as the hero of the day. But for the narrator, this struggle over the dead body, this coming to grips with death, represents his coming of age, the moment when he crosses the threshold into the adult world, putting him at a distance from his boyhood friends.

Several problems arise when stories about teen experience are told from the perspective of an adult. In her work on the teen genre, Lesley Speed convincingly argues that the nostalgic adult perspective serves to contain adolescent experience.[3] Drawing on Lawrence Grossberg's sociological studies of contemporary youth culture, Speed shows how the nostalgic coming-of-age film contains 'the mobility and immediacy' of youth experience.[4] In modern consumer societies adolescence marks a period of transition in which teenagers discover powers of mobility that allow them to inhabit spaces in between the private sphere of the home and the public sphere: shopping malls, cars, dances, sporting events, and so on. It is also a period in which experience is paramount, leading to the popular notion of living for the moment. Speed interprets the coming-of-age film's quest to contain this mobility and immediacy as an adult desire for 'moral and ideological certainty'.[5] Caputo makes a similar case in his analysis of late 1980s to early 1990s Australian coming-of-age films. Caputo recalls that in Australia 'in the 1980s the notion of coming-of-age had its use, politically, with the sparks of an economic turn-a-round (or was it a sporting triumph?), as both a description of the nation's character, and a promise of better things to come for the whole nation'.[6] For Caputo, this promise of better things to come for all rests on Australia's development as a multicultural society. In his analysis of a group of multicultural coming-of-age films, Caputo interprets the development of characters such as Marthe and Ermanno in *Devil in the Flesh* (Scott Murray, 1989), 'away from Anglo-Celtic notions of puritanism and patriarchy to a more European equality, openness and warmth' as a mirror reflection of social changes that have taken place in Australia since the early 1960s.[7] In other words, in the uncertain times of the 1980s, nostalgic coming-of-age films including *Devil in the Flesh*, as well as Australia's most highly acclaimed coming-of-age film, *The Year My Voice Broke* (John Duigan, 1987), may have been of little interest to younger audiences but nevertheless serve a useful purpose by reassuring baby-boomer audiences that the nation's future is in good hands.[8]

However, if we turn to coming-of-age films in Australia in the 1990s, especially those centred on youth experience, we find a very different story about where we are as a nation. Here, nostalgia is displaced by an emphasis on the immediacy of the moment. And yet, as we show in the following analyses, this group of films invites us to consider the relation between the past and the present. In *Looking for Alibrandi* (Kate Woods, 2000), *Head On* (Ana Kokkinos, 1998) and *Beneath Clouds* (Ivan Sen, 2002) stories of coming of age reveal a picture of young Australians as the inheritors of a nation divided on issues of race relations, land politics, national security, and how best to deal with shameful episodes from our colonial past. These films are very different in style and content. What they have in common, however, is the expression of a form of teen mobility fuelled by the desire to 'escape history'. Our aim is to show that while this desire should not be taken as equivalent to the forms of denial of history and amnesia discussed in previous chapters, it is symptomatic of the specific difficulties of coming of age in post-*Mabo* Australia. We also want to show how this desire, which is articulated differently across various social divisions and identity categories such as gender, ethnicity, race, sexuality and location, can lead to a new way of thinking about the politics of shame.

'You Can't Let the Past Run Your Life': *Looking For Alibrandi*

Looking For Alibrandi is directed by Kate Woods, one of a new generation of Australian film directors who move easily between the film and television industries. The film is based on the novel of the same name by Melena Marchetta, who also wrote the screenplay. The award-winning novel was first published by Penguin in 1992 and is an all-time favourite book for thousands of Australian teenagers. On the book's impact on teenagers of the 1990s, director Woods is quoted in media releases as saying that when actors were auditioning for parts in the film they all lined up for Marchetta to sign their copies of *Looking for Alibrandi*.[9] She also says they wanted to meet the writer because everyone could identify with the book so much. It is, she says, 'universally loved', as indicated by its success here in Australia, as well as in Denmark, Italy, Germany, Spain, Norway and Canada. But as the director insists, the story is distinctly Australian. For Woods, it was important that the film bring out this Australianness without recourse to what she describes as 'the overly self-conscious or parodying approach of contemporary Australian cinema', that is, so-called quirky films such as *Muriel's Wedding* (P. J. Hogan, 1994) and *The Castle* (Rob Sitch, 1997). She also aimed for a certain visual quality that she describes as 'authentic urban': 'I wanted to have an urban Australia, but I wanted working urban Australia.

I really didn't want pretty picture postcards.'[10] This aim is achieved by the film's use of locations and non-professional actors. It is shot in over forty locations in inner western and eastern Sydney, with many scenes involving non-professional 'locals', such as the use of hundreds of secondary school students in the interschool speech day scene at the Sydney Opera House, as well as the inclusion of many members of Marchetta's family in scenes depicting community and family celebrations.

With its emphasis on questions of identity and belonging, *Looking for Alibrandi* is a multicultural narrative in a vein similar to classic films of the early 1990s, such as *The Heartbreak Kid* (Michael Jenkins, 1993) and *Strictly Ballroom* (Baz Luhrmann, 1992). The main character and narrator, Josie Alibrandi, is an Italo-Australian teenage girl. She is one of a small minority of scholarship girls or 'wogs on handout' as her nemesis, the very rich Anglo-Celtic Carly, calls them, at an exclusive Catholic girls' school in Sydney's eastern suburbs. As with all multicultural narratives, the story foregrounds questions of cultural difference, beginning with Josie's confession of her desire to escape from her life in the Italian community of inner western Sydney – 'Little Italy', as she calls it. As the illegitimate daughter of the once socially shunned Christina Alibrandi and granddaughter of the very traditional and highly superstitious grandmother, Cartia, Josie desperately aspires to make a future for herself in the world of the wealthy Anglocentric middle classes of eastern Sydney.

The first third of the film depicts Josie as a feisty, independent girl trapped between two opposing forces. On one side of the city, Josie is subjected to the repressive gaze of the close-knit Italo-Australian community. Her experience of the constrictions of tradition is beautifully realised in a fantasy sequence depicting the community as a well-organised spy-ring. On the other side of town, at school, the forms of racial prejudice that reduce her to 'an ethnic' limit Josie's potential. As with many multicultural narratives, issues of racial and ethnic conflict are raised in the staging of an intercultural romance. There are two Anglo boys of interest to Josie: John Barton and Jacob Coote. John is the idealised image of Josie's fantasies of escape into the middle to upper-class Anglo world. He comes from a long line of wealthy conservative politicians. In a scene that must invoke vivid memories for any spectator who attended a single-sex school, John and a group of other boys arrive at Josie's school for an interschool debate. Leading the others, John is luminous: blonde-haired, fine-featured, confident and yet at the same time graceful. For Josie, John is one of those chosen few who knows exactly who he is and where he belongs. What Josie fails to see is that beneath John's outward confidence and good manners lies a deep sense of despair, for he is equally burdened by the constrictions of family traditions and expectations.

Meanwhile, Josie also crosses paths with the rough-mannered but nevertheless charming Jacob Coote. At the interschool speech day, Josie gives a predictably safe, well-written 'aspirational' speech about individual success and social responsibility. But it is Jacob's speech that captures the teenage audience's imagination. Jacob is the captain of the local state school, Cook High, and speaks as a member of a globalised youth culture. Using explicit references to media culture and mass violence, he expresses his disgust at the world his generation has inherited in direct, humorous and colloquial terms. This direct, down-to-earth intelligence catches Josie's attention. But on her first date with Jacob, this working-class 'Anglo' proves to be none too subtle on the issue of cultural difference, causing Josie to stomp off from what she describes as 'the shortest date in history'.

We would be mistaken, however, to see this film only in terms of multiculturalism. On one level, the opposition between John and Jacob reproduces the stereotypical class distinction that characterises Australian cultural traditions of Anglo-Celtic masculinity: the serious, intellectual, gentrified John versus the self-mocking, lovable working man Jacob. But their differences turn out to be more complex than this. Jacob has a warm and loving relationship with his widowed father, while John is burdened by the weight of tradition and family expectations. This attention to family relations in the boys' back-stories is just one of the many ways that the film allows for teen identification across cultural borders such as gender and class. As the story unfolds, we see that Josie's quest to discover who she is and where she belongs is also shaped by factors other than cultural difference. The film realistically depicts the Higher School Certificate as a make or break event in her life. And as with Jacob, Josie has to deal with a wide range of challenges that situate her as a member of an increasingly globalised youth culture. Throughout, Josie struggles with the gap between media projections of teenage experience and her lived reality. In an early scene, she rescues herself from a teacher's reprimand by providing a cutting, on-the-spot critique of the ways in which girls' magazines can be patronising and demeaning. The impact of these projected images of youth culture on teen self-image is also realised in fantasy sequences. In one instance, Josie imagines the exclusive world of a model's photo-shoot, starring 'the perfect' Carly. On another occasion she projects herself as 'the star' of a media conference: here she is married to her 'crush' John Barton, who is now the youngest ever conservative Prime Minister of Australia while Josie is leader of the opposition. This depiction of Josie as a strong-willed, media-savvy girl takes the appeal of Looking for Alibrandi beyond the terms of national cinema, situating the film in an international post-feminist, post-multicultural subgenre of coming-of-age films that feature articulate, independent and at times extremely stroppy 'kick-ass' girls: *Girlfight* (Karyn Kusama, 2000), *10 Things I Hate About You* (Gil Junger, 1999), *Bend It Like Beckham* (Gurinder Chanda, 2002), *Real Women Have Curves* (Patricia Cardoso, 2002). And as with all of these films, *Looking for Alibrandi* also draws on aspects of American teen film and television, especially in its use of music.[11]

But while *Looking for Alibrandi* is both international and outward-looking in its approach to issues of teen identity and culture, it is also very much a film of its time. Its foregrounding of questions of personal history and shame resonates strongly with a wider post-*Mabo* politics of shame. As the story goes, Josie's lack of knowledge about her paternity is an obstacle to her development of a sense of self, a sense of belonging. Indeed, her family's shame about Josie's illegitimacy is one of the main reasons she desperately wants to escape from the family and community. In the repressive traditional world of 'Little Italy' Josie will always be a marginalised, shamed subject, not knowing who her father is. That is, until the day that Michael Andretti, former neighbour of the Alibrandis, returns to the community. The film's brilliant casting allows for a powerful shock of recognition when the dark-haired, olive-skinned Josie opens the door to greet Michael Andretti, instantly recognising the family resemblance. Her father's face is a mirror-image of her own. For Josie, this shock of recognition is traumatic. Her initial response to the truth of his identity is to refuse to acknowledge him. She doesn't want to be an Andretti, her father's daughter. But as one might expect, the uncovering of this secret of her origin leads to the revelation of others. Putting two and two together, Josie learns that her mother is not who she appears to be, that is, an Alibrandi. Rather, she is the child of her grandmother's extramarital lover: an attractive Anglo bushman by the name of Sandford. In a highly pitched emotional scene played in both English and Italian, Josie confronts her grandmother with her suspicion. Josie's courage in challenging her Nonna, exposing the false basis of her religious and moral traditions, as well as her superstitious beliefs in curses, frees three generations of women from the 'chains of the past', allowing them to move forward as a family and as proud, independent women.

As with many second-generation multicultural narratives, *Looking for Alibrandi* eschews the nostalgia and melancholic longing for the past that characterises first-generation multicultural narratives in favour of an unsentimental view.[12] It also manages to sidestep the problematic binary structure of good Ethnic/bad Anglo or what Tom O'Regan calls 'othering the Australian' in films such as *They're A Weird Mob* (Michael Powell, 1966) and *Strictly Ballroom*.[13] Instead, this film about 'Josephine Andretti who was never an Alibrandi who should have been a Sandford and may never be a Coote' speaks in a direct and honest way about the burden of history to a generation of teenagers who have inherited a nation divided on the issue of how best to deal with shameful episodes from the past. Hence this is not a mirror reflection of the nation's coming of age but of the traumas preventing maturity. In the end, *Looking For Alibrandi* conforms to the multicultural narrative's tradition of a final scene of intercultural, inter-generational integration. Here, Jacob Coote joins Josie's family and their Italian neighbours in the work and festivities of 'Tomato Day', an annual community activity. But despite this celebration of plurality, things are not entirely resolved. Josie is not sure if she has a future with Jacob Coote. Her father is here today, but may well return to Adelaide. Her mother seems to have forgiven her grandmother, but we cannot be sure. What is of interest, however, is that Josie's coming of age, which as we have seen involves facing her past and accepting the complex nature of her identity, forces the older generations to reveal and take responsibility for their secrets. In this way, Josie is an enabling figure, which is something new in this genre. Unlike the classic teen films in which the adult gaze prevails and the primary function is to reassure, Josie is insistent in her childlike refusal to follow her family's traditions, to become a subject of shame as her mother was made to be. In doing so, her courage opens a way forward for all, showing how the flexi-bility associated with the mobility and immediacy of youth allows for the possibility of facing shameful episodes from our past without recourse to either guilt or denial.

'He Ran to Escape History. That's His Story': *Head On*

Like *Looking for Alibrandi*, *Head On* is a coming-of age film that allows us to consider the mobility and immediacy of contemporary teen experience. But unlike *Alibrandi*'s sweet, effervescent approach to these aspects of teen experience, *Head On* is a high-velocity assault on the senses. Techniques such as hand-held camera, tight, claustrophobic framing and rapid editing emphasise the visceral nature of the experiences the film depicts: sex, drug-taking, music, dancing and violence. This kinetic style divided Australian critics. Many of the older, mainstream critics found the film's aesthetic unrelenting, concluding that it was a bleak and depressing piece. Other critics, however, were dazzled by the film's energy, claiming it marked a coming of age of the film industry. Paul Fischer wrote, 'It would be true to say that with first-time director Ana Kokkinos' audacious work [*Head On*] Australian cinema has come of age,'[14] while FILMINK describes *Head On* as 'a shot of adrenalin straight to the heart of Australian cinema'.[15] The film also went on to become a mainstream breakthrough, which is quite astounding considering its 'R' rating and non-mainstream subject: a queer/ethnic coming-of-age story. It was perhaps this success that contributed to the film's support by AFI voters. At the 1998 AFI awards *Head On* won five awards, including Best Film for its highly respected, experienced producer, Jane Scott, and Best Achievement in Directing for relative newcomer Ana Kokkinos. The film has also gone on to win numerous international awards in both mainstream and Gay and Queer film festivals. Yet despite this acclaim the film is somewhat of a misfit in the canon of Australian cinema, often overlooked in favour of quirky films such *The Castle* and *The Adventures of Priscilla, Queen of the Desert* (Stephan Elliot, 1994) on film courses and other lists.[16] There has also been surprisingly little academic writing on it, leading us to conclude that it is in many ways not only a film about a troubled teen but is itself the troubled teen of 1990s Australian cinema.

This description of *Head On* as a troubled teen is indebted to Chris Berry's critique, one of the few academic reviews of the film.[17] Berry argues that *Head On* has been too easily pigeonholed as either an 'ethnic' or a 'gay' film. It is, he says, both of these things. But he also insists that its breakthrough in mainstream Australian cinemas suggests there is something else going on. For Berry, this something else relates to its coming-of-age narrative. Just as we suggested that *Looking for Alibrandi* draws on techniques and popular themes in the contemporary American teen film, in particular the kick-ass girl films, Berry argues that *Head On* has a lot in common with a new crop of American coming-of-age films such as *The Opposite of Sex* (Don Roos, 1998), *Buffalo 66* (Vincent Gallo, 1998) and *The Ice Storm* (Ang Lee, 1997). In these films teenagers 'struggle to cope with self-absorbed parents'.[18] Like the teens in *The Breakfast Club* (John Hughes, 1985), the young protagonists in this new crop of films are the children of baby-boomers, that is, the sons and daughters of the generation of teens depicted in classic nostalgic teen films such as *American Graffiti* or *Stand By Me*. In earlier American teen films, such as *Rebel Without a Cause* (Nicholas Ray, 1955), teen rebels are misunderstood, troubled youth crying out to be understood, indeed pleading to be rescued by their parents and other adults. By the 1980s young disgruntled protagonists, like those in *The Breakfast Club*, no longer plead with adults but forthrightly demand their attention: 'Don't You Forget About Me'. In the 1990s, however, troubled teens are long past believing that the baby-boomer generation has any workable solutions to offer, let alone the ability to rescue teens. Ari, as Berry suggests, belongs to this latter group of rebels.

The kind of alienation expressed by Ari in *Head On* and, more importantly, *embodied* in the film's aesthetic of speed, takes us beyond the available terms of identity politics. Unlike Josie, who desperately wants to discover who she is and where she belongs, Ari knows he is a Greek Australian who likes to have sex with men. His dilemma takes the form of a double bind: he simultaneously belongs to and is rejected by his patriarchal Greek community. As a result, Ari lives a double life. And as the film shows in its numerous scenes of Ari's self-destructive behaviour, this duplicity is tearing him apart. He lashes out at people he despises. He lashes out at people he loves. And he pushes his body to its physical limits in an all-night drug, sex and alcohol binge.

The film also registers other, global forces that impact on Ari's experience. The film's aesthetic speaks suggestively to the speed of changes in perception and experience of time and space that cultural theorist Andreas Huyssen describes as 'an ever-shrinking present'.[19] The great paradox of our globalised era is that while the world is expanding through the opening up of borders, such as those of nation-states and trade zones, on another level we experience the world as one of ever-narrowing horizons through issues such as border protection. Temporal experience has also been transformed. The distance between the past and the present is increasingly diminished through multiple forms of 'musealization': that is, 'an expansive historicism of our contemporary culture, a cultural present gripped with an unprecedented obsession with the past' (discussed in Chapter 1).[20] At the same time, Huyssen and others make a convincing case for significant 'entropy' of our sense of future possibilities. But in this description of global anxieties about the speed of change and ever-shrinking horizons of time and space, Huyssen takes care to note that such anxieties are also always experienced in local registers, that is, tied to histories of specific nations and states.[21] *Head On* is a simultaneous articulation of these two registers – global and local. As Berry notes in his article, Ari is a child of global mobility. In a series of flashbacks we see Ari with his young radical parents. In one episode, they are demonstrating against the military dictatorship of Greece in the 1970s. Another episode evokes post-WWII immigrant arrival scenes. The film's inclusion of these flashbacks does not, however, invite a nostalgic view of the past. Rather, we are invited to see Ari's parents through his eyes, recognising a certain despair and disappointment that leads the unemployed Ari and, surely, so many others of his generation to distrust political rhetoric, to scoff at politicians' promises of 'better things to come for all'. Or as Ari says, 'They tell you that God is dead, but, man, they still want you to have a purpose.'

So if, as we suggest, Ari represents a new kind of troubled teen, then it is one that is neither convinced nor consoled by the rhetoric of identity politics. Asked whether he is proud to be Greek, Ari responds: 'Proud to be

Greek? I had nothing to do with it!' Similarly, the discourse of Gay Liberation is of little relevance to him. For as Berry points out, Ari's relationship with Toula/Johnny (Paul Capsis) 'has shown Ari what it means to be publicly visible as a man who has sex with other men and continues to live in the Greek community'.[22] For this teen there are only two possible options to escape the constrictions of his double bind, the 'ever-shrinking present'. At first, Ari dreams of returning to Greece, fleeing the country, just as his parents once fled the repressive regime of their homeland. But Ari's mother quickly points out to him the futility of this dream. Better than most, Ari's mother knows from her own experience as a low-paid migrant factory worker that there is no 'space' outside the globalised economy that we can magically escape to. Ari's only other option is to 'escape history'. Unlike Josie in *Looking for Alibrandi*, who escapes the repressive forces of tradition by exposing secret episodes of shame from the past, Ari chooses to hide his 'shame' – living as a self-appointed abject outcast in a permanent state of disconnection or, as it is put by Christos Tsiolkas in his novel *Loaded* (on which the film is based), in a permanent state of 'fast forward':

> Fast forward past birth, early childhood, school . . . Fast forward to an old man, a drunk putting his hands between my legs. I enjoy it . . . Press play. Peter and me share a bong . . . Fast forward past movies. Sneaking into *Caligula* . . . Fast Forward through more instructions. This is how you fuck, this is how you drink, this is how you take drugs . . . I aint ever going to connect. Stop tape. Press Play . . . He ran to escape history. That's his story. Press Stop. Tape is terminated.[23]

Head On is a powerful mimetic realisation of Ari's desire to live in fast-forward mode. In its high-velocity account of twenty-four hours in Ari's life, it bears testimony to the incredible speed of change that Australia has experienced at both a global and national level in the past ten years or more: the new post-*Mabo* politics of race including the Pauline Hanson phenomenon, the rapid switch in focus from Keating's 'big picture', to Howard's narrowed horizons, the ever-improving economy that has led to an ever-expanding gap between rich and poor, and so on. The film is also an interesting indicator of the different levels of where we're at as a nation in terms of queer issues. On one level the film's mainstream breakthrough in its theatrical release indicates a considerable interest in queer issues. At the same time, the film is in itself a vivid display of what Fran Martin describes as the centrality of shame to forms of gay and queer identification (more on this below).[24] In reviews of *Head On*, much has been made of the final visually striking image and its audacious voice-over. Here, Ari rallies against a world he refuses to take in, a world that he speeds through in fast-forward mode. In a Jean Genet-like gesture of homosexual abjection he cries:

> I'm a whore, a dog, and a cunt.
> My father's insults make me strong.
> I accept them all.
> I'm sliding toward the sewer, I'm not struggling.
> I can smell the shit, but I'm still breathing.
> I'm gonna live my life.
> I'm not going to make a difference
> I'm not going to change a thing
> No one is going to remember me when I'm dead
> I'm a sailor and whore,
> and I will be until the end of the world.

As a coming-of-age moment this is a wonderfully perverse image. Ari's words are both powerful and expansive. He is not a 'rebel without a cause' but rather the embodiment of anti-rebellion, a lived form of a powerful refusal to engage, to be subjugated. But as Ari dances in circles on an empty wharf at Port Melbourne there is also something alarming about this image. Ari's words express his determination to escape time, space and the socialising forces of history by immersing himself in the speed and immediacy of the present, exposing the wounds of his shaming in a form of homosexual abjection. As such, the film itself refuses to submit to the genre's tendency to look back, to reassure its audience, to satisfy the patriarchal, heterosexist fantasy of familial unity. The question is, however, what does Ari's decision to disengage say about the nation's maturity and possibilities for moving forward in such a way that we might recognise the injurious wounds of shame inflicted on Ari and others excluded from the social imaginary.

Before It's Too Late: *Beneath Clouds*

Beneath Clouds is also underscored by a strong desire to escape history. But unlike other coming-of-age films discussed in this chapter, it is not set in urban Australia. Rather, the film's story takes place on the back roads of rural New South Wales, somewhere between Moree and Sydney. The director, Ivan Sen, is currently the Australian film industry's *wunderkind*: a multi-talented graduate of the Australian Film, Television and Radio School who writes, directs and composes film scores. The quality of his work was recognised at the 2002 AFI awards, where he pipped Phillip Noyce (*Rabbit-Proof Fence*) for the award of Best Achievement in Directing for *Beneath Clouds*. To date, all Sen's Australian films are set in rural Australia and feature young black protagonists. All reports indicate, however, that the director 'bristles' when his films are labelled 'Aboriginal'.[25] This is not because Sen has a problem identifying as an Indigenous Australian. Rather, as with many contemporary Aboriginal artists, including filmmaker Tracey Moffatt, Sen fears the problems that may arise when his work is pigeonholed this way. These problems include Australian audiences' historical lack of interest in stories about Aboriginal people and their culture, the assumption that because his films feature Aboriginal characters they will be worthy, 'message'-type films, and, most problematically, perhaps, that Sen 'speaks' as a representative of all Aboriginal people.

Beneath Clouds is none of the above. This may be a generational thing. His films are about young people and address a younger, globalised audience of Australians that Marcia Langton argues have grown up with a different set of images of Aboriginality from previous generations. As Langton sees it, this younger generation of Australians is empowered by their access to a global world, 'at once cosmopolitan and networked'.[26] As such, they are, she writes,

> able to relate to the Aboriginal world in a less troubled way than their parents and they are almost oblivious to Australia's blinding colonial legacy of white supremacy and race hatred. Their images of the Aboriginal world are not the images of monochromatic misery that their parents see, but a heady mix of politics, sport and culture.[27]

They are a generation of younger viewers many of whom see Aboriginal art as the most significant marker of Australian modernity. They welcomed the strong Aboriginal presence in the opening and closing ceremonies of the 2000 Olympics, cheered Cathy Freeman in her historic Olympic win, were loyal viewers of the *Bush Mechanics* (ABC-TV) series and *The Mary G. Show* (SBS TV), and so on. But this viewing experience does not, as Langton argues, necessarily make younger Australians more tolerant of forms of Aboriginal disadvantage. They are, she thinks, 'less niggardly than their parents' generation ... true advocates of the "fair go", because their sense of fairness tells them that everyone should take responsibility for their own fate to the extent that they can'.[28] *Beneath Clouds* takes a similar line on questions of individual responsibility. Unlike most narrative films about Aboriginal people, this is not straightforward social realism. Rather, it is a highly stylised film in the art-house tradition that explores complex and difficult questions about Aboriginal diversity and difference.

Beneath Clouds tells the story of Lena, a young, fair-skinned Aboriginal girl who leaves her home in what appears to be a small, deprived rural town in search of her long-gone Irish father. Throughout, Lena's Aboriginality is ambiguous. She is perceived by most people she meets on her journey as white. In a study of assimilation experience that combines critical and subjective perspectives, Ian Anderson explains how in the postwar assimilationist era, children of mixed descent, like Lena, were categorised as 'mixed blood', 'urban', 'non-traditional' or 'hybrid' Aborigines.[29] Moreover, the 'hybrid' Aborigine was 'constructed as ambiguous', perceived therefore as belonging to neither race.[30] This perceived lack of racial background in turn led to a construction of the 'hybrid' Aborigine as 'belonging nowhere' and, most significantly, 'having *no history*'.[31] Although this story is set in the present, Lena bears the history of this imposed construction of the 'hybrid Aborigine' on Aboriginal people of mixed descent as an internalised shame. She wears her in-betweenness on/in her skin, on her perpetually unsmiling face. Unlike Josie in *Looking for Alibrandi* who is searching for her identity, Lena's story is one of a *retreat* from Aboriginality, or more specifically, an attempt to escape from an imposed shamed subjectivity that leaves her in a state that Anderson describes as grieving for a lost history, 'a grieving over a tremendous loss which is in itself then denied as being yours'.[32] In this state, Lena sets out to find a history that can include her.

Lena's desire to escape her in-betweenness is expressed as a deep ambivalence towards forms of contemporary Aboriginal and rural experience examined in documentaries such as *Cunnamulla* (Dennis O'Rourke, 2001). Her decision to leave home in search of her Irish father follows two events in her life: news of her young girlfriend's pregnancy to a local boy and her brother's arrest by the police for petty theft. It is her mother's reaction to her brother's arrest, however, that is the real catalyst for her flight. In a fairly wooden, social realist moment, we are introduced to Lena's mother and stepfather as stereotypical alcoholics: uncaring and abusive. The mother's lack of concern about her young son's arrest casts her as the abandoning mother. In her lack of regard for her child's future the mother is made to bear the full weight of the social problems that destabilise many Aboriginal communities: alcoholism, domestic abuse, child neglect. Lena leaves her home and her mother in the belief that reunification with her Anglo-Celtic father will provide her with the sense of belonging and pride that she longs for.

Along the way, Lena crosses paths with Vaughn, who is also Aboriginal. Vaughn is on the run, having just escaped from a juvenile detention centre. Like Lena, he is searching for a lost parent, in this case his dying mother. But Vaughn is deeply ambivalent in his feelings for his mother. He resents that she hasn't been to visit him in years, yet he still desperately wants to return home before she dies. However, unlike Lena who actively retreats from her Aboriginality, Vaughn is very much determined by his Aboriginality, and proudly so. Being a dark-skinned Aborigine, Vaughn's identity is constructed in and through a different set of historical racialising images, in particular the stereotype of the angry young black delinquent. In scene after scene, Lena is either warmly welcomed or at worst politely ignored by European Australians, while Vaughn is at best regarded with suspicion and in the worst cases verbally and physically attacked. Only one episode – a lift from a quietly spoken grazier – offers Vaughn any respite from racial prejudice.

But this is not just a story about race and identity. It is also about experience of place and historical memory. As a road movie, *Beneath Clouds* is structurally and stylistically very different from *Head On*, which, as we argued earlier, mimics the speed of changes in urban experience of time and space. Here, a sparse visual style combined with minimalist performances by the two leading first-time actors serves to express a certain melancholy in contemporary youth experience: a state of boredom that easily gives way to depression and despair. This is achieved through the film's structural opposition of mobility and stasis. Long exterior sequences of Lena and Vaughn on foot on the back roads of country New South Wales with cars speeding past them at 120 kilometres an hour are juxtaposed with claustrophobic interior scenes in the various cars that stop to pick them up along the way. In this way, *Beneath Clouds* is a new take on the car icon in Australian cinema. In her analysis of 1970s and 1980s Australian cinema, Meaghan Morris argues that that the car offers 'a utopian space to escape or "reconstitute" sexual and family relations': 'In a country with huge distances *and* isolated centres of sparse population, cars promise a rabid freedom, a manic subjectivity. They offer danger *and* safety, violence *and* protection, sociability *and* privacy, liberation *and* confinement, power *and* imprisonment, mobility *and* stasis.'[33] But as the film shows, for Indigenous Australians these oppositions apply in different ways. In this sense, *Beneath Clouds* has lot in common with *Backroads* (Phillip Noyce, 1977).

Backroads was directed by Noyce in collaboration with Aboriginal activist Gary Foley. It was made on a low budget at the height of the Aboriginal Land Rights movement. Although it had an extremely limited theatrical release it has gone on to be recognised as one of the most interesting films of its time.[34] It tells the story of a dead-end journey on the back roads of New South Wales by Gary (a young rural Aborigine) and Jack (a red-necked Anglo bloke) in a stolen beat-up car. Along the way, a French tourist, one of Gary's male relatives, and Anna, a directionless young woman, join them. Stephen Muecke rightly argues that the significance of the film lies not in the journey itself – they never do make it to Sydney – but in what he calls 'intervals between events', which allow for 'the release of new possibilities'.[35] These intervals are, Muecke suggests, moments of exchange: 'In the intervals the characters gain and lose identities, transferring and transforming cultural understandings.'[36] Invoking Bachelard's phenomenology of space, Muecke suggests that a poetic logic of interval in this film allows for a new perception of landscape that takes us beyond the old imperial view of land 'as something to be possessed and built on towards understanding it as *the cultural transformation of country*. Moving images, including those framed by car windows, give us the possibility of seeing landscape as variable rather than fixed, as in landscape paintings. In the intervals between sites stories can emerge.'[37]

In this regard, *Beneath Clouds* backtracks across the route taken in *Backroads*, both literally and in its poetic of space. Both films begin on the back roads and highways of western New South Wales. As with the non-Aboriginal characters in *Backroads*, Lena begins her journey with a fixed idea of the relationship between identity, landscape and history. She desperately wants to belong to her father's homeland, Ireland, fetishising images of misty rolling hills she carries with her in a photo album. Vaughn opens her eyes to the beauty of her/their own country. And more than this, he teaches her how to read the landscape as 'country', in the Aboriginal sense of this term, that is, in terms of sacred and cultural knowledge. Here, however, exchange of knowledge, exchanges of ways of knowing, is not cross-cultural, as it is in *Backroads*. Rather it is an intra-cultural exchange *staged* as cross-cultural: a series of exchanges and plays in/with identities between Lena, posing as white, and Vaughn, who thinks Lena is white (or does he?). As moments of what Laleen Jayamanne calls 'cross-cultural mimesis', the intervals in *Beneath Clouds* allow for even more possibilities of transforming identity positions than *Backroads*.[38]

The most significant of these intervals occurs on a roadside on the outskirts of Vaughn's home town. As they turn a corner the two teenagers are confronted by a looming ridge in the mountain ranges of this area. 'Pretty, hey', says Vaughn. Lena nods. 'My pop', Vaughn continues, 'used to tell me about that place. The farmers chased all the blackfellas up there a long time ago. They just shot them and pushed them off.' The film cuts to a wide-shot of a European-looking family pulled over to one side of the road, oblivious to the ridge towering above them, their heads buried in a road map. Vaughn continues: 'Now, no one gives a shit. Suppose they've got their own shit to worry about.' Lena's gaze is fixed on the ridge, recognising, as if for the first time, the history embedded *in* the land. As she stares up, Vaughn's thoughts unexpectedly turn to his mother in a strange non sequitur: 'No wonder she left me. She must have known how I was going to turn out – fuckin' criminal for a son.' Lena turns her gaze away from the ridge towards him. But there are no words of comfort, simply an admission of her own. 'My dad left me, you know. Mum blames me. Says he wanted his life and all that.' Vaughn responds with puzzlement. 'Never knew any whitefella before. Not like you, anyway.'

This moment of shared histories of violence and abandonment, colonial and other, is interrupted by the screech of a car. In the front seat is a group of young Aboriginal men, Vaughn's 'cuzes', as he refers to them. Lena reluctantly accepts a lift, squeezing into the back seat between Vaughn and an older Aboriginal woman. The car circles around the bend to the other side of the ridge, which now fills the frame of the car window. The two women raise their lowered eyes to watch this moving, slowly de-forming image only to then lower them again, as if in remembrance of the dead. The cuzes in the front seat are playing at being 'Black Gangstas', one toying with a seriously large gun. In the back seat, Lena feels the old woman's gaze upon her and turns to face her: 'Where are your people from, girl?' she asks. Shamed by the woman's recognition of her Aboriginality, Lena turns towards Vaughn to gauge his reaction. He turns away, looking confused. Perhaps he is feeling betrayed. Or he may be disappointed that Lena is not a 'whitefella' and therefore not the first and only white person to befriend him. But the 'truth' of Lena's identity is not of primary concern here. Rather, what is of the utmost importance is her answer. For Lena to continue to hide her Aboriginality, that is, to play with the possibility of not being Aboriginal, at this point would be not only to deny the history she has learned to recognise *in* the land but also to take responsibility for a history that is not her own. That is, to take responsibility for, or at the very least be implicated in, a history of violence against Aboriginal people, including the injuries of shame that have produced her feelings of being without history, belonging nowhere.

As a coming-of-age film, *Beneath Clouds* might have ended, as many do, with 'a return home'. But this is not an option for either Vaughn or Lena. Escaping from a violent conflict with police that occurs after the interval described above, the two teenagers race to Vaughn's mother's house. It is, however, too late. The only sign of Vaughn's mother is a pool of blood on her bed, and an abandoned oxygen mask. Lena reaches out to comfort Vaughn. But he forcefully rejects her advance. With the sounds of police sirens approaching closer, Lena quickly assesses her choices. She can stay behind and repeat her mother's history, watching Vaughn be hunted down by police, as with Gary in *Backroads* or Jimmie in *The Chant of Jimmie Black-smith* (Fred Schepisi, 1978), 'going down' herself, perhaps. Alternatively, she can leap onto a train headed for Sydney. Lena chooses the latter, refusing to submit to a certain macho suicidal tendency that historically characterises stories of Aboriginal resistance. Her decision to leave Vaughn is thus unpredictable and uncompromising in its anti-heroic stance. 'Harsh', as a teenager might say. But Lena is determined in her decision to move forward no matter how uncertain her future may be, to escape a history of violence, colonial and other.

Subjects of Shame

Each of these three coming-of-age stories expresses a desire to escape history. What we have also seen is that at the base of this desire is a self-understanding as a subject of shame: 'the bastard', 'the wog', 'the queer', 'the half-caste', 'the black'. These subjects are historical in the sense that they are the unrecognised subjects and/or the actively excluded subjects of Australian Federation and its cornerstone the White Australia policy. The Australian character cannot be foreign, female, queer or black. While each of the teen characters explores different tactics for dealing with these historically imposed forms of shame, collectively their stories bear testimony to what Fran Martin calls the fundamental injury of the shamed, or what we call in the context of this study post-*Mabo* trauma. In her culturally sensitive analysis of the politics of shame in Taiwanese *tongzhi* (Queer) cultural production, Martin considers options for self-representation for subjects of shame, in particular, ways that might allow us to 'linger . . . on the "negative" elements of shame, pain, depression and alienation'.[39] In doing so, Martin draws our attention to crucial cultural differences between North American and Taiwanese identity politics. Engaging Wendy Brown's work on a politics of recognition in North America that involves self-exposure as the injured, or what Brown calls modes of 'social injury or marking', Martin makes a convincing case for how this mode of identification can be productive in the Taiwanese context. Martin makes a crucial point about how it is possible for a political demand for recognition to be premised on reparation rather than revenge and *ressentiment*. That is, she distinguishes between self-exposure of a foundational injury of shame (whose purpose is to revenge or overthrow the perpetrator) and a self-exposure that aims to heal both the injured and the witness.[40] This reparation is possible because in the act of making his or her injury visible – 'acts of public hearing' – the subject of shame assumes that the hostile spectator is capable of love.[41] This plea for empathy thus constitutes a different form of social recognition, one premised on ideas of love and empathy. This distinction is suggestive for our analysis of the ways in which Australian coming-of-age films in the post-*Mabo* era open up a new way for thinking about the politics of shame, one that takes us beyond legalistic and moral understandings of shame.[42]

As we have discussed in previous chapters, Howard and his government actively resist public discussion of shame. They also actively defend the Australian character, advocating pride in the past. But what Martin shows in her analysis of *tongzhi* cultural production, and what we see here in this group of very different coming-of-age stories, is that in many instances the exposure of the pain and injury of shame can be enabling. Just as Martin suggests the reparative impulse can repair both the *tongxinglia* and the hostile collective spectator, each of these coming-of-age films resists the nostalgic tendency in the coming-of-age story to reassure its audience and insists that they acknowledge the injuries of historical forms of shame as they are lived in the present. And surely this is something cinema is good at – the creation of an intimate sphere in which it is possible to expose the vicissitudes of pain and shame, a place where such pleas for empathy can be recognised as demands for reparation of historical trauma.

Notes

1 Raffaele Caputo, 'Coming of age: notes toward a re-appraisal', *Cinema Papers*, 94, 1993, p. 13.
2 Charles Acland, *Youth, Murder, Spectacle: The Cultural Politics of 'Youth in Crisis'*, Boulder CO: Waterview Press, 1995, pp. 118–22.
3 Lesley Speed, 'Tuesday's gone: the nostalgic teen film', *Journal of Popular Film and Television*, 26(1) 1998, p. 25.
4 ibid., pp. 27–8.
5 ibid., p. 25.
6 Caputo, 'Coming of Age', p. 16.
7 ibid.
8 On the teen film's purpose to reassure adults, see John Lewis, *The Road to Romance and Ruin: Teen Films and Youth Culture*, New York and London: Routledge, 1992, p. 151. For an interesting commentary on the Australian teen film and its audiences, see Mark Freeman 'The Australian Teen Film', 2001, <http://home.vicnet.au/~freeman/articles/ozteenfilm.hyml>
9 Kate Woods, quoted in Special Features, 'Biographies', *Looking For Alibrandi*, DVD, distributed by Roadshow Entertainment.
10 ibid., 2002.
11 In the DVD audio commentary, producer Robyn Kershaw says that in the post-production stage the production team made a decision to replace the original 'retro' music with contemporary Australian, independent music. This served to do two things. It contributed to the film's aim of situating the story in contemporary working, urban Sydney. We would also add that it contributes to the film's strong sense of immediacy and its anti-sentimental view.
12 For an introduction to multiculturalism and the arts in Australia, see Sneja Gunew and Fazel Rizvi (eds), *Culture, Difference and the Arts*, Sydney: Allen & Unwin, 1994.

13 Tom O'Regan, *Australian National Cinema*, London and New York: Routledge, 1996, pp. 250–6.

14 Paul Fischer, 'The World of Film in Australia: Urban Cinefile', <http://www.urbancinefile.com.au>

15 As quoted in VHS videotape cover notes, distributed by Village Roadshow.

16 This observation is indebted to discussions with Jodi Brooks. It is also based on personal experience of problems encountered when teaching this film. When Therese Davis used the film as a set text in an undergraduate Australian Cultural Studies course at the University of Newcastle complaints by self-identified Christian students led to an unprecedented boycott by a small number of students, as well as formal written complaints to the Vice Chancellor.

17 Chris Berry, 'The importance of being Ari', *Metro*, 118, pp. 34–7.

18 ibid., p. 36.

19 Andreas Huyssen, 'Present pasts: media, politics, amnesia'. In Arjun Appadurai (ed.), *Globalization*, Duke University Press, Durham and London, 2001, p. 68.

20 ibid., p. 70.

21 ibid., p. 63.

22 Berry, 'The importance of being Ari', p. 37.

23 Christos Tsiolkas, *Loaded*, Sydney and New York: Vintage, 1995, pp. 146–50.

24 Fran Martin, *Situating Sexualities: Queer Representation in Taiwanese Fiction, Film and Public Culture*, Hong Kong University Press, 2003.

25 See Stephanie Bunbury, 'Beyond black and white', *Age*, 19 May 2002, republished <http://www.theage.com.au/articles/2002/05/18/1021544084403.html>; Daniel Browning, 'Ivan Sen interview', *Message Stick*, ABC Radio, published 24 May 2002, <http://www.abc.net.au/message/blackarts/film/s720711.html>.

26 Marcia Langton, 'Correspondence: whitefella jump up', *Quarterly Essay*, no. 12, 2003, p. 80.

27 ibid., p. 80.

28 ibid., pp. 80–1.

29 Ian Anderson, 'Black bit, white bit'. In Michele Grossman (coordinating ed.), *Blacklines: Contemporary Critical Writing by Indigenous Australians*, Melbourne University Press, 2003, p. 46.

30 N. J. B. Plomley, 1977, as cited in ibid., p. 46.

31 Anderson, 'Black bit, white bit', p. 46.

32 ibid., p. 47.

33 Meaghan Morris, 'Fate and the family sedan'. In *Senses of Cinema*, 19, 2002, p. 9. This essay was originally published in *East-West Film Journal*, (4)1, 1989, pp. 113–34.

34 Susan Dermody and Elizabeth Jacka, *The Screening of Australia*, vol. 1, Sydney: Currency Press, 1987, p. 188.

35 Stephen Muecke, '*Backroads*: from identity to interval', *Senses of Cinema*, 17, 2001, p. 3.

36 ibid., p. 3.

37 ibid., p. 6.

38 See Laleen Jayamanne, *Toward Cinema and Its Double: Cross-cultural Mimesis*, Bloomington and Indianapolis IN: Indiana University Press, 2001. On the transformational qualities of mimesis, also see Michael Taussig, *Mimesis and Alterity: A Particular History of the Senses*, New York and London: Routledge, 1993.

39 Martin, *Situating Sexualities*, p. 244.

40 ibid., pp. 246–8.

41 ibid., p. 246.

42 As Manne explains, while the idea of collective guilt makes no sense because legally guilt for a wrongdoing is always a matter of individual responsibility, it is possible for the peoples of a nation to share feelings of shame about episodes from the past just as they share feelings of pride. See Robert Manne, *The Way We Live Now: The Controversies of the Nineties*, Melbourne: Text Publishing, 1998, pp. 12–14.

10

Sustaining Grief in *Japanese Story* and *Dreaming in Motion*

Throughout this book we have proposed that the post-*Mabo* era in Australian cinema can be read through the metaphor of backtracking. This intermittent activity of reviewing, mulling over and renewing icons, landscapes, characters and stories defines contemporary Australian national cinema. In our conclusion we want to propose that, in the post-*Mabo* context, this brooding passion for raking over the national repertoire of icons serves as a vernacular mode of collective mourning, a process involving both grief-work and testimony. If this is the case, then Australian national cinema, since the *Mabo* decision, has been an occasional participant in creating and corroborating national recognition of *terra nullius* as the nation's troubling, founding myth. This raises the question of whether a national cinema is in the business of confirming the nation's consoling myths or contesting the nation's historical memories. As Ross Gibson says at the end of his book on the badlands of central Queensland, 'Myths help us live with contradictions, whereas histories help us analyse persistent contradictions so that we might avoid being lulled and ruled by the myths that we use to console and enable ourselves.'[1] Gibson's eloquent piece of literary backtracking ends with an exemplary call to mourn the failures and losses of the past in order to overcome the denial of the violence that founded the nation. In this view, mourning is a way to achieve national maturity by 'recognising the issues that we wish we could deny, ignore or forget'.[2] In various ways, the two kinds of film projects discussed in this chapter explore the badlands of our social imaginary, asking us to bear witness to traumatic traces of a history we can no longer deny, ignore or forget. To give up the consoling and enabling myth of *terra nullius* is to displace white settler Australia as the core of national identity and national history. For Australian national cinema, thinking beyond the founding myth is a perplexing task, one which requires backtracking over familiar ground, whether that be the desert, the bush, the suburbs or the beach, in order to reconcile current knowledge about the past with present experience of the history wars, and to imagine a more accommodating sense of national identity for the future.

In the cycle of films discussed in Chapter 1, the shift in identity occasioned by the *Mabo* decision is made explicit. These films are clearly part of the resurgent 'memory industry'[3] which has become so prolific in Western societies since the early 1980s, exemplifying a paradigm shift from modernity's focus on 'present futures' to postmodernity's preoccupation with 'present pasts'.[4] In this concluding chapter we will look at two kinds of film projects, each recognisable as part of Australian national cinema's engagement with history, memory and identity. The films belonging to these two projects are less explicit than *The Tracker* or *Rabbit-Proof Fence* in their post-*Mabo* historical consciousness, but their preoccupation with 'present pasts' is intimately tied to the work of memory and mourning. This work, of backtracking through consoling myths about the colonial past, is seen as a prerequisite for mature nationhood by many post-*Mabo* pundits engaged in the history wars described in Chapter 1.

The first project belongs to the art-house circuit of international films, often launched at the Cannes Film Festival before being released to local audiences. The most recent Australian film to succeed at Cannes is *Japanese Story* (Sue Brooks, 2003). The film's marketing team used the premiere at Cannes to launch an international campaign before returning home to scoop the pool with eight wins at the 2003 AFI Awards. Set in the Pilbara iron ore region, the film reprises the sweeping landscape tradition of the 1970s period film along with the contemporary off-road, cross-cultural movie imbued with the sensibility of the post-*Mabo* period. The second project is a package of five short films supported by Film Australia and the Indigenous Unit of the Australian Film Commission, *Dreaming in Motion* (2003). Unlike the high-profile cycle of feature films around the Indigenous–settler theme released in 2000–02, *Dreaming in Motion* brings together a mosaic of Indigenous Australian perspectives on the present. The films range in genre from the road movie to the urban comedy. The ethic and aesthetic of this kind of project is indebted to the 1970s independent cinema. Thomas Elsaesser, writing about New German Cinema, defines this kind of filmmaking in terms of *erfahrung*. This term is broader than its English translation as 'experience'. It implies a direct relation between the filmmakers and their audiences, both of whom 'rediscovered the cinema as a new public space, promising very personal experiences, but which through discussions and debates could be verbalised or rationalised in a political discourse'.[5]

Grief-work, *Erfahrung* and *Amae*

Part of what was politicised in New German Cinema of the 1960s and 1970s was the historical amnesia which had prevented postwar Germany from acknowledging and mourning the nation's role in perpetrating the Holocaust. In this chapter we approach *Japanese Story* and *Dreaming in Motion* as two recent projects which bring grief-work into the public sphere of Australian cinema as a way of overcoming historical amnesia.[6] Grief-work in filmmaking extends the debate about the post-*Mabo* state of Australian nationhood by exploiting cinema's capacity for *affective* experience. It is this capacity for *affect* (defined as feeling or emotion, often leading to action) that makes grief-work a possibility in a cinema of *erfahrung*.

In order to understand the connection between history and affect in *Japanese Story* and *Dreaming in Motion*, we want to establish how a cinema of *erfahrung* asks the spectator to bear witness to the traumatic presence of the past by approaching film itself as a kind of grief-work. In her research into grief-work as a contemporary cultural phenomenon, Kathleen Woodward takes up Freud's well-known distinction between mourning and melancholia. Citing Barthes' *Camera Lucida* as an example of literary grief-work, Woodward distinguishes grief-work from both mourning and melancholia. She does this in order to defend a non-pathological (and politically useful) will to *sustain* mourning by lingering over images of the dead, 'a response to loss that situates itself between mourning and melancholia'.[7] Woodward rejects Freud's insistence that mourning must either come to a healthy end or become pathologically melancholic: rather than 'sever the bonds of love' (the healthy outcome of mourning) or maintain the 'open wound' (the melancholic option), grief-work enables us to respond to loss in creative ways that sustain memory rather than deny the pain of loss.[8]

Woodward defines grief-work as a constellation of cultural texts which 'sanction a discourse of grief' by shifting the emphasis of mourning from 'a gradual giving up of those lost' to 'remembering them in a sustainable grief'.[9] If the issue of historical amnesia has defined modernity since the Holocaust, then *Japanese Story* might be considered an international film which explores sustainable grief as an aspect of surviving the aftershock of *Mabo*. In this sense the numbness or amnesia of aftershock can only be overcome through the ongoing process of *afterwardness*, or deferred revision of the past, discussed in Chapter 5. In this respect the grief-work undertaken in *Japanese Story* is a departure from the long-standing trope of male melancholia as the key characteristic of the Australian outback film.

In her second essay on the cultural uses of grief, Woodward turns from Freud and Barthes to Klein and Kristeva: 'In *Studies on Hysteria* Freud articulated a theory of affect which resonates with the dominant tradition in Western culture of the emotions as negative: the emotions are associated with woman – and with death – and they are something to be gotten rid of.'[10] Here, Woodward draws on Klein's theory of mourning as a process of self-integration which depends on fully experiencing the 'emphatic emotions – including hatred, guilt, distrust, elation, revenge, anxiety, despair, triumph, jealousy, sorrow, and fear'.[11] Rather than get rid of the emotions, Kleinian analysis 'affirms the value of a rich if volatile emotional life' achieved through mourning.[12] In contrast with Freud's hysteric, Woodward sees the prototypical analysand (post-Holocaust) as the numbed woman: for Klein (and Kristeva)[13] it is the absence of grief, the 'lack of affect' which is pathological (and historical).[14] In Woodward's view, grief-work responds to Kristeva's contention that, since the Holocaust, 'to live in our grief . . . is our emotional testament to and heritage of our time'.[15] *Japanese Story* is centrally concerned with the 'numbed' figure of the modern career woman whose journey charts a Kleinian passage of the emotions whereby 'triumph yields to guilt, and guilt to love, which accompanies the desire for reparation'.[16]

Although there is considerable distance between *Japanese Story* and *Dreaming in Motion*, each of these projects is committed to remembering the past in sustainable grief. *Dreaming in Motion* testifies not only to communal suffering but also to the desire of Indigenous Australians to be seen and heard in national cinema on their own terms. This entails overcoming what has been censored in the melancholic cinema of settler Australia, a cinema noted for the longevity of its white, fraternal gaze. If the issue of unacknowledged loss and suffering defines Indigenous experience in the aftershock of colonialism, then the five short films which comprise *Dreaming in Motion* bear witness to a post-colonial politics of overcoming shamed subjectivity, discussed in Chapter 9. The films made under the banner of *Dreaming in Motion* might be considered forms of traumatic cinema in that they ask the spectator to acknowledge the shame and injury inflicted on Aboriginal subjectivity in the aftershock of 200 years of colonisation. As post-colonial grief-works, these five short films demand that the spectator be prepared to extend a type of tolerance called *amae* (the word was coined by Japanese psychoanalyst Takeo Doi).[17] This involves, in Chris Berry's words, 'a kind of attention to the needs of those perceived as having suffered, as having an unresolved grievance that demands indulgence'.[18] Berry makes the point that, although making space for *amae* is frowned upon as narcissistic regression in Freudian psychoanalysis, in Japan '*amae* is seen as a positive quality'.[19] Australian films are not noted for their capacity to indulge the emotions associated with historical grievance, traumatic experience and loss. *Japanese Story* and *Dreaming in Motion* ask the viewer to participate in a new kind of spectatorship based on the social acknowledgment of cinema as a space where the experience of suffering can be indulged, performed and recognised.

Guilt, Grief and Reparation in *Japanese Story*

Building on its international debut at Cannes, *Japanese Story* (Sue Brooks, 2003) uses three forms of backtracking to build an audience locally and to sell in overseas territories.[20] The first backtrack reprises the desert landscape as a timeless template of national character. The story is set in the spectacular Pilbara region of Western Australia, its vast natural scale matched by the gargantuan mechanical scale of the iron ore mining industry, courtesy of BHP-Billiton. The second backtrack involves a journey to the desert: two miniature urban figures arrive at an unexpected moment of intimacy in the vast, 'unmapped' outback. The third backtrack entails Toni Collette's return to screen in a quintessential Australian role, a role honed into national recognition through a series of iconic, laconic performances of Australian masculinity by the likes of Chips Rafferty, Ray Barrett, Bill Hunter, Bryan Brown, Jack Thompson and Russell Crowe. Together, these three backtracking movements in *Japanese Story* expand a restricted national palette of laconic emotions to include guilt, grief and the desire for reparation.

Japanese Story had its origins in a proposal from Film Australia's Sharon Connolly to scriptwriter Alison Tilson in the mid-1990s, a period dominated by One Nation's populist stance against Asian immigration and debates about whether the Prime Minister should apologise to the Stolen Generations and those who continue to suffer as a result of colonisation. Connolly was interested in commissioning a film that would explore the cross-cultural tensions ignited by a relationship between an Australian woman and a Japanese man. Film Australia commissioned two script drafts before its charter changed, preventing it from further investment in feature films. Inspired by Connolly's vision of a Japanese man driving alone through the Australian desert, Tilson (together with producer Sue Maslin and director Sue Brooks) scripted a cross-cultural road movie, based loosely on romantic comedy's battle of the sexes, involving an Australian geologist, Sandy (Toni Collette), and a Japanese businessman, Hiromitsu (Gotaro Tsunashima). The backdrop to this encounter was relocated, before the shoot, from the Whyalla industrial area of South Australia (where Tilson grew up) to the more remote Pilbara iron ore region in Western Australia.

Although Collette's performance as Sandy, the Perth-based geologist, opens the American cut by the film's distributor (Samuel Goldwyn), the Australian cut of the film begins with Gotaro Tsunashima as the somewhat enigmatic Hiromitsu, alone in the desert, neither tourist nor businessman, though he goes through the motions as both. The film's post-*Mabo* consciousness is marked by Hiromitsu's sampling of Australian music on CD, with Yothu Yindi's 'Treaty' playing in the hire car as Hiromitsu photographs his own estranged presence in the emptiness of the Australian outback. The narrative then shifts to Sandy in Perth (at work, at home, at her mother's place) before she is thrown together with Hiromitsu at Port Hedland regional airport. Their initial encounter turns into a wry comedy of cross-cultural misunderstanding as they make their way, somewhat haphazardly, by four-wheel drive into iron ore country. Here the film takes on a documentary tone as Sandy and Hiromitsu experience a Lilliputian shift in scale at the BHP-Billiton mine. It is this shift in scale, this diminution of mundane worries (as much as an unscheduled night bogged in the desert) which takes Sandy and Hiromitsu out of themselves and leads to mutual recognition and an idyllic cessation of conflict as they embark on a serendipitous detour together, 'off the map'.

In the first act of *Japanese Story*, broadly recognisable cultural differences are mapped onto (slightly bent takes on) gender and sexuality, producing low-key comic moments typical of the misrecognitions of romantic comedy. Broad differences are played out on the road as Sandy and Hiromitsu warily assess each other according to gender as well as cultural stereotypes. In the second act, cultural differences become a point of reciprocal exchange between Sandy and Hiromitsu, rather than sources of mutual misreading. In due course, the ironies of gender are put aside in favour of the more subtle tensions of sexuality and desire. As initial prejudices give way to sexual intimacy, Sandy dons Hiromitsu's black trousers in a slightly surreal expression of the enigma of antagonistic desire central to romantic comedy.

Although the first two acts of the film are structured by a familiar plot device of mutual antagonism followed by sexual *rapprochement*, a disturbing undercurrent of buried feeling makes itself felt early in the film through Sandy's emotional obtuseness towards her colleagues, her sexual partners and her best friend. The film establishes early, through her mother's collection of obituaries, that Sandy is habitually careless with her own feelings and insensitive to how others see her. When she is forced to go on the road with Hiromitsu, she glimpses herself through his eyes, and feels what it's like to be in his clothes. This recognition leads to a stolen moment, a breathing space, desired by both characters, from family, work, and self. Together, Sandy and

Hiromitsu find a waterhole, a rocky oasis, somewhere out there, beyond the iron ore mines, off the map. And there the idyll comes to a shocking end. By taking its characters on a final detour, off the map, the film loosens the cultural moorings of identity for a moment of freedom before shock releases a deluge of *affect* for Sandy, and for the tolerant spectator willing to indulge Collette's sustained performance of shock, loss and grief.

Breaking with the melancholic, defeated endings typical of Australian landscape cinema, *Japanese Story* uses the third act to deliver a sudden shock, contravening narrative expectations set up in the first two acts of the film. The dramatic turning point is based on a deeply embedded, culturally specific foreboding, to which Hiromitsu, as an outsider to Australian bush lore, is not privy. This turning point hangs on a single moment of horrified recognition when Sandy, and the knowing spectator, realise that Hiromitsu is about to *dive* into the waterhole. Generations of Australian childhoods are captured in the suspended moment of impending catastrophe. For the audience that grew up on dire warnings of holiday drownings, shark attacks, snake bites, tourists perishing in the desert, and children lost in the bush, Hiromitsu's dive embodies the dangers lurking everywhere in the foreignness of the Australian landscape.

Japanese Story invokes this cultural habit of dread in order to break with the early comic tone established in the first act and to extend the film's initial premise of cultural and gender difference. Against expectations, the resolution to cultural difference is worked out in terms of guilt, grief and reparation, rather than sexual intimacy. The fatal snag beneath the serene surface of the waterhole suggests that whatever lurks below the surface of Sandy's becalmed life cannot be appeased by an idyllic moment of escape to the desert. The strength of *Japanese Story* lies in its belief that the audience will change gears and let go of the love story to arrive with Sandy at a deeper, though no less intimate, form of self-recognition through the eyes of another. It is here that the film speaks most forcefully to contemporary Australia, suggesting, through Sandy's hidebound character, that a profound shock, a sudden moment of realisation, can break through habitual barriers of cultural insularity and emotional numbness.

Japanese Story delivers much more than we have come to expect from Australian films in the way it resolves its premise by opening up a space for *amae*. If we follow Berry's argument that in Japan (among other places) there is a positive acceptance of the social need to indulge the public performance of grief, then the title, *Japanese Story*, takes on an unexpected meaning.[21] In this sense the film's Japanese story is to be found in the sustained attention to the problem of how to turn Sandy's grief and guilt into an act of reparation. This process of taking on responsibility for the dead is performed through the slow accretion of finely observed details. A distinctive view of life is expressed in the film's shifting of gears back and forth between the closely observed minutiae of Sandy and Hiromitsu's encounter with each other's difference, and the aftermath of a sudden, devastating moment of clarity about our common fate, writ large. This contingent view of life is evident in earlier films by the Gecko creative team (Brooks, Maslin and Tilson).[22] It is manifest in their acute observation of the accidental details which make up a life, and the sudden rupture of the everyday by fate or accident. It is this moment of rupture which carries the denouement of the film into relatively unexplored territory in Australian landscape cinema.

While *Japanese Story* was in development during the late 1990s, a road trip into the Australian outback became the leitmotiv of two other feature films involving a romance between Australian and Japanese characters in lead roles, *Heaven's Burning* (Craig Lahiff, 1997) and *The Goddess of 1967* (Clara Law, 2001). Unlike these two post-national films, *Japanese Story* reprises an unmarked, Anglo-Celtic rather than cosmopolitan or multicultural concept of Australianness. The film emphasises the difficulties of cultural translation in terms of *national* differences (even in the iron ore industry where doing business with Japan is part of the daily routine). This emphasis harks back to a core sense of Australianness honed into the landscape and the body from one generation (of films, of screen actors) to the next.

In *Japanese Story* the territory of grief and guilt is connected directly to the landscape and the body in a way that suggests culturally imbued habits are enigmatic but not untranslatable. Rather, cultural difference can be translated and understood through the body. Sandy, as her mother's daughter, and Hiromitsu, as the son of a powerful off-screen father, embody certain culturally recognisable emotions and gestures inculcated from one generation to the next. The task of the final act of the film is to show how Sandy's embodiment of grief opens up the possibility of reparation between antagonistic cultures, beyond the sexual and linguistic exchanges of the first two acts of the film.[23] This attempt at translation takes place in the context of an inward-looking, post-*Mabo* sense of Australian nationhood.

The landscape tradition has, over several decades, distilled a repertoire of national gestures, embodied and honed by icons of Australian masculinity. The longevity of the outback landscape in Australian cinema has perpetuated the idea that the national character, forged in the bush, will be defeated by the desert. There's a certain melancholy at the heart of this tradition, yet in *Japanese Story* grief breaks through the toughened emotional exterior of settler Australians. For perhaps the first time in landscape cinema, this melancholic settler is embodied as female by the emotionally inarticulate Sandy. By contrast, Hiromitsu and and his wife Yukiko, through the emphatic formality and precision of their gestures, seem capable of expressing with great self-possession and cultural ease a subtle, ethical response to the emotions aroused by betrayal, guilt and loss.

Ultimately, the film insists that cultural difference can be translated and understood in ways that go deeper than the exchange of business cards or even the erotic encounter of bodies. As the film draws to a close, an exchange of objects takes place between Sandy and her mother, and Sandy and Yukiko, suggesting an ethical alternative to the business economy and the sexual economy explored earlier in the film. The reciprocity between Sandy and Yukiko is grounded in Sandy's identity as her mother's daughter, affirmed at a moment in the film when Sandy needs to make a new move.

Sandy's return home from the desert takes her to a rare moment of cultural translation near the end of the film during a formal reception with Yukiko and her Japanese attendants. Resting on the arm of a chair, Sandy takes on the embodied composure, presence and stillness we have come to associate first with Hiromitsu and then with Yukiko. There's something in the way that Collette's performance of grief reaches this moment of composure, by taking on cultural difference, that is deeply tied to the post-*Mabo* era. This era demands that Eurocentric Australians do the work of mourning entailed in giving up a form of emotional insularity which turns a blind eye to our history and place in the Asia-Pacific region.

This national habit of insularity is registered in Collette's lean, taut body, her laconic distance, and unadorned face. Collette's bony embodiment of Sandy contrasts with the full-bodied Muriel, the female grotesque of *Muriel's Wedding* (Paul J. Hogan, 1994), who launched Collette's career and made her an icon of early 1990s quirky comedies. Since then, Collette's international career, and her various nominations for supporting roles, have put some distance between her screen persona and Muriel. Thus it is intriguing to see Collette return, a decade later, to the Australian screen in a reprise of an awkward, laconic masculinity whose lineage stretches from Chips Rafferty to Russell Crowe. Some may object that Collette in fact reprises the resourceful and independent bush woman, renowned in Australian film and literature since the 1920s. An argument could be made for that position. However, a post-*Mabo* reading might prefer to align Sandy (and Collette's face in the film) with Ross Gibson's description of 'the generic Central Queensland face that takes shape in every generation of settler-descendants'.[24]

A landscape unto itself, this face can still be seen today in pubs and diners, in the cabs of trucks. The mouth is a serrated horizon-line. Furrows mark a neck and jaw-line champed to the rigours of adversity. Eyes are tarped with forebearance. When one encounters the face in bus stations and roadhouses, it is usually not reading or talking. It is persisting, wasting no vigour, wisely, and keeping to itself whatever it knows.[25]

In this face Gibson sees 'a regional "affliction" . . . Or . . . history'.[26] It is this historically afflicted character that is feminised in Collette's face, eyes widened, lips filled out, yet stripped to the bone, honed to an abiding grief which the film, in its final movement back to Perth, wishes the spectator to indulge.

Without setting aside the film's interest in the cross-cultural encounters opened up by late modernity's global flows of people and capital, it is the post-*Mabo* 'opening of the heart' to grief which we take to be the unexpected, unpredictable move that connects *Japanese Story* to the recent set of backtracking movements we have seen in the revival of the desert landscape tradition in a series of films from *Tracker* and *Rabbit-Proof Fence* to *One Night the Moon*. Although *Japanese Story* does not directly confront the abiding issue of white–settler misrecognition of Indigenous land rights based on *terra nullius*, the film does connect grief and guilt to the landscape tradition and its investment in a laconic, masculine national identity. This connection has become more overt in Australian films of the post-*Mabo* era and need not be mistaken for a reprise of earlier forms of national insularity. Rather it is an invitation to the audience to indulge the public performance of grief and guilt in a national cinema that tends to shy away from the emphatic emotions.

In *Japanese Story* guilt (in the positive sense of taking responsibility and expressing remorse) is worked through in astute detail in the last third of the film (a part which has left some critics cold precisely because of its sustained indulgence of grief rather than catharsis). One way of thinking about this section of the film might be to revisit the Kleinian notion of mourning as a work of reparation that moves the subject from numbness to affect, from guilt to love. Sandy begins this journey of reparation not through the affair with Hiromitsu, but through taking on the full weight of responsibility for his body. The film makes us feel this dead weight, literally, as Sandy struggles to lift his body into the back of the four-wheel drive. When she reaches a town and finds that the coolroom is the only morgue, she has no words for what has happened. Back in Perth others take over the arrangements, telling Sandy to take a break – she's done a good job. However, her work of bearing witness to Hiromitsu's death is not done until she formally admits her guilt and remorse to Hiromitsu's wife, Yukiko, adopting a modicum of Yukiko's composure (and a few halting phrases in Japanese) to do so. This scene takes place between the two women as Hiromitsu's body is being loaded onto the plane. The film avoids a transcendent ending by making its final setting the departure lounge at the airport. Sandy has to struggle against protocol and against pragmatic arrangements in order to create a moment when she can step forward, take responsibility and express remorse. The film shows how easy it would be not to take that step.

Sandy's inchoate struggle to meet her social obligation to show remorse and accept guilt resonates with the post-*Mabo* politics of reconciliation. How does a nation reconcile with its colonial past, with its exclusionary White Australia policy as the very basis of nationhood at Federation in 1901? Gibson argues that a mature citizenship 'attains composure' through a process of mourning, through 'processes of realisation' which enable participation 'in the complex dynamics of social and historical obligation'.[27] Sandy breaks a pattern in Australian cinema, overcoming the tradition of tight-lipped resistance to the indulgence of those painful emotions which must accompany full acknowledgment, through sustained grief, of the injustices endured by Indigenous Australians.

Departing from Trauma: *Dreaming in Motion*

Each of the five films in *Dreaming in Motion* attests to a traumatic colonial history of which the films themselves are a symptom.[28] As a package, *Dreaming in Motion* contributes to a tentative, post-colonial imaginary whose traumatic past, in Felman's words, has 'not yet settled into collective remembrance'.[29] Introducing an anthology of essays on trauma and testimony, Cathy Caruth defines trauma (in its literal, belated and latent aspects) as a symptom of history: 'The traumatized . . . become themselves the symptom of a history that they cannot entirely possess.'[30] She adds: 'To listen to the crisis of a trauma . . . is to not only listen for the event, but to hear in the testimony the survivor's departure from it.'[31] It is precisely this sense of departing from crisis (rather than moving on from the past) that defines these films as post-colonial grief-work. As spectators of *Dreaming in Motion* (2003), we participate in the desire to depart from a traumatic history. Listening to the filmmakers' attempts to depart from traumatic events, we look at images that evoke crisis. The stimulation of involuntary memory by these images has the potential to startle the spectator, to reveal the lived experience behind the traumatic testimony found in television documentaries such as *Black Chicks Talking* (Leah Purcell, 2002). The kinds of images and stories offered to the film spectator by *Dreaming in Motion* are different in *affect* from the stories offered to the television viewer by Purcell. Rather than a spirited assertion of pride in Aboriginal identity, *Dreaming in Motion* is more interested in exploring and overcoming the shame and injury attached to Indigenous identity by the violence of colonialism (discussed in Chapter 9).

Shit Skin (writer/director Nicholas Boseley) deals directly with the traumatic experience of the Stolen Generations. It is a return home film which takes the form of an interrupted road trip to Central Australia, undertaken by a grandmother, Nina, with her grandson, Luke, in the driver's seat. Alternating between Nina and Luke, *Shit Skin* deftly evokes the long-term impact of historical trauma on a family over four generations. The repetitive nature of traumatic experience becomes evident in flashbacks, delayed in time only to be unleashed by sensory experience in the present. Nina's involuntary memories of a ruptured childhood are provoked not only by photographs and household objects but also by the scent and touch and taste of place. Deliberately understating the melodramatic potential of Nina's belated return home (sixty-two years after being taken away) the film enables a laconic revisiting of the past, at the same time drawing Nina and Luke forward into a more reconciled future. The pain of return impacts on Nina through the senses, transforming the meaning of both time and place. The scent of a twig from a tree and the splash on her face of fresh water released from its hiding place under the gravelly desert recalls Nina to her childhood self, awakening a sense of belonging which she tries to deny to her grandson, Luke: 'I'm glad they took me away. These people, they can't let go, they're hopeless.' When Nina and Luke address each other with rough affection as 'half-caste' and 'shit skin' at the end of the film, there is a sense that their shared return to the original place of loss allows memory to settle into a less traumatised, more connected sense of belonging, of being able (as Jimmy Little sings over the closing titles) to 'bring yourself home'. *Shit Skin* quietly, yet insistently, evokes the pain of return, and also its necessity, no matter how belated.

The presence of the past, and the necessity of return, are also structural themes in *Black Talk* (writer/director Wayne Blair). The film takes the form of a conversation between Scott and Tim, two cousins waiting to go into church as various relatives and friends arrive for a funeral. Seated under a tree, the cousins share childhood memories and a skylarking sense of humour, as well as feelings of loss and shame. Their affectionate banter turns serious when Scott, who remained behind with his community, asks city-boy Tim where he will find his soul once his assimilated, consumer lifestyle has finished sucking it out of him. Tim's ambivalence towards home resolves itself into grief as the two cousins enter the small country church for the funeral. As Tim walks up the aisle alone to view the body in the coffin, we realise with a shock that this is Scott's funeral and that the conversation outside the church took place between the living and the dead: that Tim has returned home for a final conversation with Scott. We learn that despite his material success Tim knows he's been in the wrong place, but we are left to guess at the reasons for Scott's untimely death. Perhaps there is no right place to be in terms of country, kinship and culture at this moment in post-colonial history. The film ends with an overwhelming sense that the past is never dead, but (like Scott) still present and waiting for recognition.

In *Flat* (writer/director Beck Cole), the routine, everyday present where 'nothing happens' is brought into view, literally, through the viewfinder of a digital camera given to fifteen-year-old Marnie by her unreliable dad, glimpsed briefly through the video lens at the local TAB. Marnie, like Cole herself, uses her camera to telling effect. *Flat* invites us to contemplate the difference between the unblinking gaze of the film image as Cole's camera frames Marnie on a swing against a brick wall, and the softer, more intimate video image as Marnie uses her camera to pick out an old woman sitting on a chair or a neighbour wrapping beer bottles in newspaper before putting them in the garbage bin. This slice-of-life film shares feminism's preoccupation with female self-image and identity, as Marnie lies on her bed and turns the camera on her own face and body. However, the final, more telling image is of a sign painted on the wall of the pawn shop: 'loved goods go cheap'. This mute comment on Marnie's circumscribed world is recorded as the last image on the video cassette before she embraces the inevitable loss – pawning the video camera to cover her father's losses at the TAB. A quality of stoicism, evident in Marnie's laconic exchanges with her little sister and a casual boyfriend, pervades the film, pointing to an austere ethic of survival as the bedrock of daily life. A glimpse of the desert landscape captured on video through the bus window is the only indicator of a time and place whose vast scale is lost to modernity, a loss of vision and connection signified by the ubiquity and disposability of film and video images.

A pervasive sense of loss is undercut in all the films by a sense of humour so dry you can hear the grass crackle underfoot. The final two films in the package bring this crackling humour to the fore, confronting modernity's conundrum of sex, gender and race with shrewd wit. *Turn Around* (writer/director Samantha Saunders) is a gentle romantic comedy which plays with the genre's central device of recognition/misrecognition between 'right' and 'wrong' partners. A feminist twist gives the controlling moves to the woman, who educates the man into recognising her in her own right. A road trip takes the would-be lovers on three detours. Each stopover educates the man into essential knowledge of the woman's qualities (respect for elders and culture; sensual affinity with nature; cool control of the pool table). These qualities, which value everyday encounters (a cup of tea with a respected uncle is an understated highlight), provide a strong contrast with the glossy-magazine appeal of his fantasy woman. When she drives off, leaving him to pursue his fantasy (or not, as the case may be) he has to make his own way home. In an act of comic recognition he returns to wash her car, acknowledging her wheels as the vehicle of his education into sexual equality. *Turn Around* replaces romantic comedy's upper-class settings (of city nightclubs, designer apartments and ocean liners) with country pubs, weatherboard houses and a Ford with radiator problems. This 'trading down' of the genre's glamorous middle-class settings extends our expectations of the reach of romantic comedy, at the same time enlarging the frame through which Aboriginal experience becomes recognisable in cinema.

The four films above undermine the entrenched portrayal of Aboriginal characters in cinema as objects of an ignorant, investigative or sympathetic white gaze. Non-Indigenous characters are sidelined in favour of the experiences and perceptions of Aboriginal characters. The final film, *Mimi* (writer/director Warwick Thornton), breaks this pattern by engaging directly with the whiter-than-white world of the cosmopolitan investor in Aboriginal art. *Mimi* begins as a send-up of yuppie aspiration and consumerism, then quickly turns into an acutely observed comedy-horror film by combining the scene-stealing comic talents of Sophie Lee, Aaron Pederson and David Gulpilil. Their star turns, however, are upstaged by the wickedly animated Mimi, who wreaks havoc before being lured into a stainless steel fridge and unceremoniously dumped in a waterhole by Gulpilil, who declares, 'Whitefellas aren't ready for you yet, Mimi.' Nothing is what it appears to be in this film, which delights in improvised mimesis. A plastic-wrapped chook from the supermarket becomes a magpie goose with a feather stuck in its breast. A red cocktail dress and cosmetic cream become a makeshift traditional costume for ceremonially smoking Mimi out of the hall cupboard. A 'real Aborigine' is revealed as an errant grandson, more interested in chasing white girls than learning his grandfather's culture. An Australian collector of Aboriginal art knows so little about where she lives that she dials 911 in an emergency, imitating the terrorised blondes dialling 911 in scary American movies. *Mimi* takes pleasure in using comic-horror conventions to joke about authenticity, upsetting expectations and undoing pretensions in an original display of visual and verbal wit. Although the delightful spirit-world Mimi is returned to the outback waterhole, there is a sense in which the film imagines something beyond the return home, or the occasional reconciled moment between past and present, or even the stoic survival of everyday life as suitable endings for Indigenous stories. *Mimi* proposes a spirited quick-wittedness as an inventive, ethical response to the dilemmas posed by black and white encounters within modernity. The distance between Sophie Lee's personal watercooler and David Gulpilil's outback waterhole is imaginatively traversed in this film, with Aaron Pederson mediating a playful space for unpredictable conversations between Indigenous tradition and Australian modernity. The past is present in *Mimi* in ways that enable the film's characters (and the spectator) to engage in imaginative acts of problem-solving, suggesting that there may be ways in which the time *after Mabo* and the time *after* colonialism (for Indigenous and settler peoples alike) are currently being experienced as mimetic spaces for inventing the future, creatively sustained by a keen sense of departing from (but not forgetting) a traumatic colonial history.

Notes

1 Ross Gibson, *Seven Versions of an Australian Badland*, Brisbane: University of Queensland Press, 2002.
2 ibid., p. 179.
3 Andreas Huyssen, 'Present pasts: media, politics, amnesia'. In Arjun Appadurai (ed.), *Globalization*, Durham & London: Duke University Press, 2001, p. 69.
4 ibid., pp. 57–8.
5 Thomas Elsaesser, *New German Cinema: A History*, Macmillan, 1989.
6 This section draws on an earlier account of Woodward's concept of 'grief-work' in Felicity Collins, 'Death and the face of the mother in the auto/biographical films of Rivka Hartman, Jeni Thornley and William Yang', *Metro*, 126, 2001, pp. 48–54.
7 Kathleen Woodward, 'Freud and Barthes: theorizing mourning, sustaining grief', *Discourse*, (13)1, 1990–91, pp. 97–9.
8 ibid., p. 101.
9 ibid.
10 Kathleen Woodward, 'Grief-work in contemporary American cultural criticism', *Discourse*, (15)2, 1992–93, p. 94.
11 ibid., p. 97.
12 ibid.
13 See Julia Kristeva, *Black Sun: Depression and Melancholia*, transl. Leon S. Roudiez, New York: Columbia University Press, 1989.
14 Woodward, 'Grief-work', pp. 98–9.
15 ibid., p. 99.
16 ibid., p. 97.
17 Takeo Doi, *The Anatomy of Dependence*, Kodansha International, Tokyo, 1971, cited in Chris Berry, 'Where is the love? The paradox of performing loneliness in Ts'ai Ming-Liang's Vive L'Amour'. In Lesley Stern and George Kouvaros (eds), *Falling For You: Essays on Cinema and Performance*, Sydney: Power, 1999, pp. 163–4.
18 Berry, 'Where is the love?', pp. 162–3.
19 ibid., p. 164.
20 This section draws on a review by Felicity Collins of *Japanese Story* published in *Senses of Cinema*, 29, 2003.
21 ibid., p. 165.
22 See *An Ordinary Woman* (Sue Brooks, 1989) and *The Road to Nhill* (Sue Brooks, 1996).

23 Minor characters in *Japanese Story* and *Heaven's Burning* register an unforgiving memory of wartime enmity with Japan, despite economic and cultural acceptance of Japanese investment and tourism in postwar Australia.

24 Gibson, *Seven Versions of an Australian Badland*, p. 93.

25 ibid., pp. 93–4.

26 ibid., p. 94.

27 ibid., pp. 160–1.

28 This section draws on a review by Felicity Collins of *Dreaming in Motion* published in *Senses of Cinema*, 27, 2003.

29 Shoshana Felman, 'Education and crisis, or the vicissitudes of teaching'. In Cathy Caruth, *Trauma: Explorations in Memory*, Baltimore: Johns Hopkins University Press, 1995, p. 16.

30 ibid., p. 5.

31 ibid., p. 10.

Bibliography

Acland, C., *Youth, Murder, Spectacle: The Cultural Politics of 'Youth in Crisis'*, Boulder CO: Waterview Press, 1995.

Akerman, P., 'Black man's burden', *Daily Telegraph Mirror*, 6 June 1995, p. 11.

Akerman, P., 'Artistic licence spoils this saga', *Sunday Telegraph*, 3 March 2002, p. 89.

Alessi, J., '*Head On*: A select bibliography', *Metro*, 127–128, 2001, pp. 46–9.

Alomes, S., *A Nation at Last? The Changing Character of Australian Nationalism, 1880–1988*, Sydney: Angus & Robertson, 1988.

Altman, R., 'What can genres teach us about nations?' In *Film/Genre*, BFI, London, 1999, pp. 195–206.

Anderson, B., *Imagined Communities*, 2nd edn, London: Verso, 1991.

Anderson, I., 'Black bit, white bit'. In Grossman, *Blacklines*, 2003, pp. 44–51.

Ansara, M., 'On the poetry of madness: an encounter with Dennis O'Rourke', *Metro*, 126, 2001, pp. 26–33.

Arendt, H. (ed.), *Illuminations*, transl. H. Zohn, New York: Schocken, 1992.

Bancks, T., 'Big screen/small screen', *Metro*, 137, 2003, pp. 82–5.

Bayet-Charlton, F., 'Overturning the doctrine: Indigenous people and wilderness – being Aboriginal in the environmental movement'. In Grossman, *Blacklines*, 2003, pp. 171–80.

Beckett, J., 'The Murray Island land case and the problem of cultural continuity'. In Sanders, *'Mabo' and Native Title*, 1994, pp. 7–24.

Benjamin, W. 'Theses on the philosophy of history'. In Arendt, *Illuminations*.

Benjamin, W., *The Origin of German Tragic Drama*, transl. J. Osborne, intro. George Steiner. London: Verso, 1977.

Benjamin, W., 'A small history of photography'. In *One-Way Street and Other Writings*, transl. E. Jephcott & K. Shorter. London: New Left Books, 1979, pp. 240–57.

Benjamin, W., 'On language as such and the language of man'. In P. Demetz (ed.), *Reflections: Essays, Aphorisms, Autobiographical Writings*, transl. Edmund Jephcott. New York: Schocken Books, 1986, pp. 314–32.

Benjamin, W., '"N" (re: the theory of knowledge, theory of progress)', transl. L. Hafrey & R. Sieburth. In G. Smith (ed.), *Benjamin: Philosophy, Aesthetics, History*, University of Chicago Press, 1989, pp. 43–82.

Benjamin, W., 'On Some Motifs in Baudelaire'. In Arendt, *Illuminations*, pp. 152–96.

Benjamin, W., 'The storyteller: reflections on the works of Nikolai Leskov'. In Arendt, *Illuminations*, pp. 83–107.

Benjamin, W., 'The work of art in the age of mechanical reproduction'. In Arendt, *Illuminations*, pp. 211–44.

Benjamin, W., 'Theses on the philosophy of history'. In Arendt, *Illuminations*, pp. 245–55.

Berlant, L., Editorial, *Critical Inquiry*, 24(2) 1998, pp. 281–8.

Berry, C., 'Heterogeneity as identity', *Metro*, 91, 1992, pp. 48–51.

Berry, C., 'Australia in Asia/Asia in Australia: an interview with Teck Tan', *Metro*, 94, 1993, pp. 42–4.

Berry, C., *A Bit on the Side: East–West Topographies of Desire*, Sydney: EM Press, 1994.

Berry, C., 'Not necessarily the Sum of Us: Australian not-so-queer cinema', *Metro*, 101, 1995, pp. 12–16.

Berry, C., 'The importance of being Ari', *Metro*, 118, 1999, pp. 34–7.

Berry, C., 'Where is the love? the paradox of performing loneliness in Ts'ai Ming-Liang's *Vive L'Amour*'. In L. Stern & G. Kouvaros (eds), *Falling For You: Essays on Cinema and Performance*, Sydney: Power, 1999, pp. 147–75.

Bertrand, I. (ed.), *Cinema in Australia: A Documentary History*, Sydney: UNSW Press, 1989.

Bertrand, I., & D. Collins, *Government and Film in Australia*, Sydney: Currency Press, and Melbourne: Australian Film Institute, 1981.

Birch, T., '"Nothing has changed": the making and unmaking of Koori culture'. In Grossman, *Blacklines*, 2003, pp. 145–58.

Blainey, G., 'Drawing up a balance sheet on our history', *Quadrant*, 37(7–8) 1993, pp. 10–15.

Blonski, A., B. Creed and F. Freiberg (eds), *Don't Shoot Darling! Women's Independent Filmmaking in Australia*, Melbourne: Greenhouse Publications, 1987.

Boland, M., 'Everyone's looking for Alibrandi', *Cinema Papers*, May 2000, pp. 22–4.

Bottomley, G., 'Post-multiculturalism? The theory and practice of heterogeneity', *Culture and Policy*, 6, 1994, pp. 139–52.

Breen, M. P., 'National mythology on film and television: The Australian experience', *Continuum*, 11(3) 1989, pp. 163–76.

Browning, D., 'Ivan Sen interview', *Message Stick*, ABC Radio, 24 May 2002.

Bunbury, S., 'Luhrmann says his film's strictly Australian-made', *Age*, 11 May 2001, p. 3.

Butler, A., 'New film histories and the politics of location', *Screen*, 33(4) 1992, pp. 86–93.

Butler, J. 1997, *Excitable Speech – A Politics of the Performative*, New York and London: Routledge, 1997.

Cameron, J. (ed.), *Changing Places: Re-imagining Australia*, Sydney: Longueville Books, 2003.

Capp, R., 'Monica Pellizari's short black look at the Australian-Italian experience', *Artlink*, 13(1) 1993, pp. 15–16.

Capp, R., 'Romancing the stone: outback adventures of a different kind in *Japanese Story*', *Metro*, 138, 2003, pp. 28–32.

Capp, R., & A. Villella, 'Interview with Leah Purcell', *Senses of Cinema*, 22, 2002. Online journal, <http://www.sensesofcinema.com>

Caputo, R., 'Review – *The Last Days of Chez Nous*', *Cinema Papers*, 90, 1992, pp. 52–53.

Caputo, R., 'Coming of Age: Notes toward a re-appraisal', *Cinema Papers*, 94, 1993, pp. 12–16.

Caputo, R., & G. Burton (eds), *Second Take: Australian Filmmakers Talk*, Sydney: Allen & Unwin, 1999.

Caputo, R., & G. Burton (eds), *Third Take: Australian Filmmakers Talk*, Sydney: Allen & Unwin, 2002.

Carroll, J., 'National identity'. In J. Carroll (ed.), *Intruders in the Bush: the Australian Quest for Identity*, Melbourne: Oxford University Press, 1982.

Carruthers, A., 'Substantial ways of reading cultural difference in the mainstream Australian media', *Media Information Australia*, 77, 1995, pp. 86–93.

Caruth, C., 'Unclaimed experience: trauma and the possibility of history', *Yale French Studies*, 79, 1991, pp. 181–92.

Caruth, C. (ed.), *Trauma: Explorations in Memory*, Baltimore and London: Johns Hopkins University Press, 1995.

Caruth, C., An Interview with Jean Laplanche, *Postmodern Culture* 11(2) 2001. <http://muse.jhu/edu/journals/postmodern_culture/vol11/11.2caruth.html>

Casey, M., 'After *Mabo*: What's at stake?' *Australian Screen Education*, 32, 2003, pp. 107–12.

Chau, S. K., 'A half-opened door: Australian perspectives on Asia', *Cinemaya*, Autumn–Winter 1992, pp. 17–18.

Chau, S. K., 'Reel neighbourly: the construction of Southeast Asian subjectivities', *Media Information Australia*, 70, 1993, pp. 28–33.

Clarke, A., *Making Priscilla*, Melbourne: Penguin, 1994.

Clarke, A., *The Lavender Bus: How A Hit Movie Was Made and Sold*, Sydney: Currency Press, 1999.

Collins, D., *Hollywood Down Under: Australians at the Movies: 1896 to the Present Day*, Sydney: Angus & Robertson, 1987.

Collins, F., 'Film'. In Barbara Caine (ed.), *Australian Feminism: A Companion*, Melbourne: Oxford University Press, 1998, pp. 107–115.

Collins, F., 'The experimental practice of history in the filmwork of Jeni Thornley', *Screening the Past*, 3, 1998. Online journal, <http://www.screeningthepast?>

Collins, F. 1999, 'Bringing the ancestors home: dislocating white masculinity in *Floating Life, Radiance* and *Vacant Possession*'. In Verhoeven, *Twin Peeks*, 1999, pp. 107–16.

Collins, F., 'Comedy'. In I. Bertrand, G. Mayer & B. McFarlane (eds), *Oxford Companion to Australian Film*, Melbourne: Oxford University Press, 1999, pp. 74–6.

Collins, F., *The Films of Gillian Armstrong*, Australian Teachers of Media, in association with Australian Film Institute and Deakin University School of Visual, Performing and Media Arts, Melbourne, 1999.

Collins, F., '*Heaven's Burning* aka You don't know what love is', *Senses of Cinema*, 9, 2000. Online journal, <http://www.sensesofcinema.com>

Collins, F., '*Strange Planet*: Contemporary Australian cinema – a symposium', compiled by F. Villella, *Senses of Cinema*, 9, 2000. Online journal, <http://www.sensesofcinema.com>

Collins, F., 'Death and the face of the mother in the auto/biographical films of Rivka Hartman, Jeni Thornley and William Yang', *Metro*, 126, 2001, pp. 48–54.

Collins, F., 'Memory in ruins: the woman filmmaker in her father's cinema', *Screening the Past*, 13, 2001. Online journal, <http://www.screeningthepast>

Collins, F. 2002, 'God Bless America (and Thank God for Australia)', *Metro*, 131–132, 2002, pp. 14–24.

Collins, F., 'Brazen brides, grotesque daughters, treacherous mothers: women's funny business in Australian cinema from *Sweetie* to *Holy Smoke*'. In Lisa French (ed.), *Womenvision: Women and the Moving Image in Australia*, Melbourne: Damned Publishing, 2003, pp. 167–82.

Collins, F., '*Dreaming in Motion*: five films from five new filmmakers', *Senses of Cinema*, 27, 2003. Online journal, <http://www.sensesofcinema.com>

Collins, F., '*Japanese Story*: a shift of heart', *Senses of Cinema*, 29, 2003. Online journal <http://www.sensesofcinema.com>

Collins, F., and S. Turnbull, 'Old Dogs, New Tricks: Beyond Simpson LeMesurier and the comic transformation of Australian drama series', *Media International Australia*, 100, 2001, pp. 33–48.

Cordaiy, H., '*Lantana* – A story of men and women', *Metro*, 129–30, 2001, pp. 54–63.

Cordaiy, H., 'An independent vision: an interview with Rolf de Heer', *Metro*, 134, 2002, pp. 24–8.

Cordaiy, H., 'The truth of the matter: an interview with Phillip Noyce', *Metro*, 131–132, 2002, pp. 126–32.

Cordaiy, H., '*Walking on Water*', *Metro*, 133, 2002, pp. 62–69.

Craven, I., 'Cinema, postcolonialism and Australian suburbia', *Australian Studies*, 9, 1995, pp. 45–69.

Craven, I. (ed.), *Australian Cinema in the 1990s*, London: Frank Cass Publishers, 2001.

Creed, B., 'Mothers and lovers: Oedipal transgressions in recent Australian cinema', *Metro*, 91, 1992, pp. 14–22.

Creed, B., J. Davies, F. Freiberg, D. Hanan & K. Montgomery (eds), *Papers and Forums on Independent Film and Asian Cinema: First Australian Screen Studies Association Conference Melbourne 1982*, Sydney: Australian Screen Studies Association & Australian Film and Television School, 1983.

Cunningham, S., 'The decades of survival: Australian film 1930–1970'. In Moran & O'Regan, *The Australian Screen*, 1989.

Cunningham, S., *Featuring Australia: The Cinema of Charles Chauvel*, Sydney: Allen & Unwin, 1991.

Cunningham, S., *Framing Culture: Criticism and Policy in Australia*, Sydney: Allen & Unwin, 1992.

Cunningham, S., & G. Turner (eds), *The Media in Australia: Industries, Texts, Audiences*, Sydney: Allen & Unwin, 1993.

Curtis, R., & C. Gray (eds), *Get The Picture: Essential Data on Australian Film, Television, Video and New Media*, 4th edn, Sydney: Australian Film Commission, 2002.

Daly, A., 'The rules of being Australian', *Senses of Cinema*, 25, 2003. Online journal <http://www.sensesofcinema.com>

Davies, P., '"Between fact and fiction": speculating on the documentary with John Hughes', *Metro*, 136, 2003, pp. 108–11.

Davis, T., 'The name and face of Mabo: questions of recognition', *Metro*, 127–128, 2001, pp. 24–8.

Davis, T., *The Face on the Screen: Death, Recognition and Spectatorship*, Bristol and Portland: Intellect, 2004.

Dawson, J., 'The fourth wall returns: *Moulin Rouge* and the imminent death of cinema', *Senses of Cinema*, 14, 2001. Online journal <http://www.sensesofcinema.com>

Dawson, J., 'All those in favour of little green oases: *Crackerjack*', *Metro*, 135, 2003, pp. 16–21.

Deane, Sir William, 'Australia Day message 2000'. In Grattan, *Reconciliation*, 2000, pp. 9–11.

Dermody, S., & E. Jacka, *The Screening of Australia: Anatomy of a National Cinema*, 2 vols, Sydney: Currency Press, 1987 and 1988.

Dermody, S., & E. Jacka (eds), *The Imaginary Industry: Australian Film in the Late '80s*, Sydney: Australian Film, Television and Radio School, 1988.

Dillon, M., '*Lantana* – a tangled web', *Metro*, 129–30, 2001, pp. 46–53.

Dillon, M., '*The Dish* – waxing nostalgic', *Metro*, 131–32, 2002, pp. 26–35.

Dixson, M., 'Identity: history, the nation and the self'. In J. Damousi & R. Reynolds (eds), *History on the Couch: Essays in History and Psychoanalysis*, Melbourne University Press, 2003, pp. 119–29.

Dodson, M., 'The end in the beginning: re(de)finding Aboriginality'. In Grossman, *Blacklines*, 2003, pp. 25–42.

Dodson, M., 'Indigenous Australians'. In Manne, *The Howard Years*, 2004, pp. 119–43.

Dodson, P., 'Lingiari: until the chains are broken'. In Grattan, *Reconciliation*, 2000, pp. 264–74.

Doyle, J., B. Van Der Heide & S. Cowan (eds), *Our Selection of Writings on Cinemas' Histories: Selected Papers from the Seventh Australian History and Film Conference*, (National Film and Sound Archive & ANU, Canberra, 20 November–2 December 1995), Canberra: National Film and Sound Archive & Australian Defence Force Academy, 1998.

Dzenis, A., '*Vacant Possession* – film review', *Cinema Papers*, 110, 1996, pp. 52, 54.

Dzenis, A., '*Australian Rules*', *Metro*, 134, 2002, pp. 36–41.

Elsaesser, T., *New German Cinema*, London: BFI, and Basingstoke: Macmillan, 1989.

Elsaesser, T. 'Specularity and engulfment: Francis Ford Coppola and *Bram Stoker's Dracula*'. In S. Neale & M. Smith (eds), *Contemporary Hollywood Cinema*, London: Routledge, 1998, pp. 191–208.

Elsaesser, T., 'Postmodernism as mourning work', *Screen*, 42(2) 2001.

Enker, D., 'Australia and Australians'. In Murray, *Australian Cinema*, 1994.

Felman, S., 'Education and crisis, or the vicissitudes of teaching'. In Caruth, *Trauma*, 1995.

Ferber, S. (ed.), *Beasts of Suburbia: Reinterpreting Culture in Australian Suburbs*, Melbourne University Press, 1994.

Flannery, T., 'Beautiful lies: population and environment in Australia', *Quarterly Essay*, no. 9, 2003.

Freeman, M., 'Caught in the Web: Ray Lawrence's *Lantana*', *Senses of Cinema*, 16, 2001. Online journal <http://www.sensesofcinema.com>

Freeman, M., 'Packaging Australia: Working Dog's *The Dish*', *Senses of Cinema*, 12, 2001. Online journal <http://www.sensesofcinema.com>

Freiberg, F., 'Lost in Oz? Jews in the Australian cinema', *Continuum*, 8(2) 1994, pp. 45–69.

Frontier Conflict: The Australian Experience, Canberra: National Museum of Australia, 2003.

Ghandi, Leela, 'Friendship and postmodern utopianism', *Cultural Studies Review*, 9(1) 2003, pp. 12–22.

Gibson, R., 'Formative landscapes'. In Murray, *Back of Beyond*, 1988.

Gibson, R., *South of the West*, Bloomington and Indianapolis IN: Indiana University Press, 1992.

Gibson, R., *Seven Versions of an Australian Badland*, Brisbane: University of Queensland Press, 2002.

Gilbert, Alan, 'The roots of Australian anti-suburbanism'. In Goldberg and Smith, *Australian Cultural History*, 1988, pp. 33–49.

Gillard, G., 'Quirkiness in Australian cinema', *Australian Screen Education*, 29, 2002, pp. 30–7.

Gillett, S., 'Never a native: deconstructing home and heart in *Holy Smoke*', *Senses of Cinema*, 5, 2000. Online journal <http://www.sensesofcinema.com>

Given, J., 'Dealing in culture: Australia/US free trade agreement', *Metro*, 138, 2003, pp. 100–103.

Glynn, S., 'Urbanisation in Australian History'. In G. Whitlock & D. Carter (eds), *Images of Australia*, Brisbane: University of Queensland Press, 1992.

Goldberg, S. L., & F. B. Smith (eds), *Australian Cultural History*, Cambridge University Press, 1988.

Goldsmith, B., 'Cultural diversity, cultural networks and trade: international cultural policy debate', *Media International Australia*, 102, 2002, pp. 35–53.

Goot, M., & T. Rowse (eds), *Make A Better Offer – The politics of Mabo*, Sydney: Pluto Press, 1994.

Graham, T., *Mabo – Life of an Island Man, Original Screenplay*, Sydney: Currency Press, 1999.

Grattan M. (ed.), *Reconciliation: Essays on Australian Reconciliation*, Melbourne: Black Inc., 2000.

Grech, J., 'Redeeming *Cunnamulla* or avoiding reality', *Metro*, 126, 2001, pp. 12–25.

Greer, G., 'Whitefella jump up: the shortest way to nationhood', *Quarterly Essay*, no. 11, 2003.

Grossman, M. (coordinating ed.), *Blacklines: Contemporary Critical Writing by Indigenous Australians*, Melbourne University Press, 2003.

Grunberg, S., 'Australia, from the desert to Hollywood', *Metro*, 100, 1994, pp. 27–31.

Gunew, S., & F. Rizvi (eds), *Culture, Difference and the Arts*, Sydney: Allen & Unwin, 1994.

Hammett-Jamart, J., 'Context for international coproduction', *Metro*, 140, 2004, pp. 122–6.

Hansen, M., 'America, Paris, the Alps: Kracauer and Benjamin on cinema and modernity'. In L. Charney & V. Schwartz (eds), *Cinema and the Invention of Modern Life*, Berkeley and Los Angeles: University of California Press, 1995.

Hansen, M. 'The mass production of the senses: classical cinema as vernacular modernism', *Modernism/Modernity*, 6(2) 1999, pp. 59–77.

Haynes, R., *Seeking the Centre: The Australian Desert in Literature, Art and Film*, Cambridge University Press, 1998.

Higson, A., 'The concept of national cinema', *Screen*, 30(4) 1989, pp. 36–46.

Hinde, J., *Other People's Pictures*, Sydney: Australian Broadcasting Corporation, 1981.

Hodge, B., & V. Mishra, *The Dark Side of the Dream*, Sydney: Allen & Unwin, 1991.

Hodson, B., *Straight Roads and Crossed Lines: The Quest for Film Culture in Australia from the 1960s?* Shenton Park, WA: Bernt Porridge Group, 2001.

Horrocks, R., 'New Zealand cinema: cultures, policies, films'. In Verhoeven, *Twin Peeks*, 1999, pp. 129–37.

Howard, J., 'Practical reconciliation'. In Grattan, *Essays on Australian Reconciliation*, 2000, pp. 88–96.

Hudson, W., & D. Carter (eds), *The Republicanism Debate*, Sydney: New South Wales University Press, 1993.

Hughes, P., 'A way of being engaged with the world: the films of John Hughes', *Metro*, 93, 1993, pp. 46–55.

Human Rights and Equal Opportunity Commission, *Bringing Them Home*, Report of the National Inquiry into the separation from their families and communities of Aboriginal and Torres Strait Islander children, Canberra, 1997.

Huntington, S., 'A *Black and White* history of Australian race relations', *Metro*, 134, 2002, pp. 42–6.

Huyssen, A., 'Present pasts: media, politics, amnesia'. In A. Appadurai (ed.), *Globalization*, Durham & London: Duke University Press, 2001.

Jacka, E., 'Australian cinema: An anachronism in the '80s'. In Dermody & Jacka, *The Imaginary Industry*, 1988.

Jacka, E., *The ABC of Drama: 1975–1990*, Sydney: Australian Film, Television and Radio School, 1992.

Jacka, E., 'Globalisation and Australian film and television'. In A. Moran (ed.), *Tuned: An Australian Broadcast Reader*, Sydney: Allen & Unwin, 1992.

Jacka, M., 'Making a difference', *Metro*, 134, 2002, pp. 142–7.

Jayamanne, L., 'Love me tender, love me true, never let me go . . . a Sri Lankan reading of Tracey Moffatt's *Night Cries*', *Framework*, 38–39, 1992, pp. 87–94.

Jayamanne, L., *Toward Cinema and its Double: Cross-Cultural Mimesis*, Bloomington IN: Indiana University Press, 2001.

Jennings, K. U., *Sites Of Difference: Cinematic Representations Of Aboriginality And Gender*, Melbourne: Australian Film Institute, 1993.

Johnson, C. (Mudrooroo), 'Chauvel and the centering of the Aboriginal male in Australian film', *Continuum*, 1(1) 1987, pp. 47–56.

Jones, D., 'Waltzing out of the outback into the ballroom'. In Baz Luhrmann & Craig Pearce (eds), *Strictly Ballroom: From a Screenplay by Baz Luhrmann and Andrew Bovell*, Sydney: Currency Press, 1992.

Karena, C., 'The power of three: an interview with Sue Brooks, Sue Maslin and Alison Tilson', *Metro*, 138, 2003, pp. 34–7.

Kaufman, T., 'Glenys Rowe: SBS Independent beating a path to the creative film-maker's door', *Metro*, 134, 2002, pp. 148–51.

Keating, P., 'The Redfern Park Speech'. In Grattan, *Reconciliation*, 2000, pp. 60–4.

Kennedy, F., 'Racists desecrate Mabo's gravestone', *Australian*, 6 June 1995, p. 1.

Kristeva, J., *Black Sun: Depression and Melancholia*, transl. Leon S. Roudiez, New York: Columbia University Press, 1989.

Langton, M., *"Well, I Heard it on the Radio And I Saw it on the Television": An Essay for the Australian Film Commission on the Politics and Aesthetics of Filmmaking by and about Aboriginal People and Things*, Sydney: Australian Film Commission, 1993.

Langton, M., 'Correspondence: Whitefella jump up', *Quarterly Essay*, no. 12, 2003, pp. 77–83.

Laplanche, J., 'Notes on afterwardsness'. In J. Fletcher & M. Stanton (eds), *Jean Laplanche: Seduction, Translation, Drives*, London: ICA, 1992.

Laseur, C., '*beDevil*: Colonial images, Aboriginal memories', *Span*, 37, 1993, pp. 76–88.

Lattas, A., 'Aborigines and contemporary Australian nationalism: primordiality and the cultural politics of Otherness'. In J. Marcus (ed.), *Writing Australian Culture, Social Analysis*, Adelaide: Dept. of Anthropology, University of Adelaide, 1990.

Lewis, J., *The Road to Romance and Ruin: Teen Films and Youth Culture*, New York and London: Routledge, 1992.

Lewis, R., *Study Guide: Message from Moree*, Sydney: ATOM, 2003.

Loos, N., & K. Mabo, *Edward Koiki Mabo: His Life and Struggle for Land Rights*, Brisbane: University of Queensland Press, 1996.

Macken, D., 'So superlatively superficial', *Australian Financial Review*, 26 May 2001, p. 2.

Malone, P., *In Black and White and Colour: Aborigines in Australian Feature Films, A Survey*, Jabiru, NT: Nelen Yubu Missiological Unit, 1988.

Malone, P., *Myth and Meaning: Australian Film Directors in their Own Words*, Sydney: Currency Press, 2001.

Malouf, D., 'Made in England: Australia's British inheritance', *Quarterly Essay*, no. 12, 2003.

Manne, R., 'In denial: the stolen generations and the right', *Quarterly Essay*, no. 1, 2001.

Manne, R., 'The colour of prejudice', *Sydney Morning Herald*, 23 February 2002, Spectrum, pp. 4–7.

Manne, R. (ed.), *Whitewash: On Keith Windschuttle's Fabrication of Aboriginal History*, Melbourne: Black Inc, 2003.

Manne, R., 'The Howard years: a political interpretation'. In Manne, *The Howard Years*, Melbourne: Black Inc. Agenda, 2004, pp. 3–53.

Marks, L. U., 'A Deleuzian politics of hybrid cinema', *Screen*, 35(3) 1994, pp. 244–64.

Marks, L. U., *The Skin of the Film: Intercultural Cinema, Embodiment, and the Senses*, Durham and London: Duke University Press, 2000.

Martin, A., 'Nurturing the next wave: what is cinema?'. In Murray, *Back of Beyond*, 1988.

Martin, A., 'More than Muriel', *Sight and Sound*, 5(6) 1995, pp. 30–32.

Martin, A., 'Review of *Moulin Rouge*', *Age*, Today Section, 24 May 2001, p. 5.

Martin, A., *The Mad Max Movies*, Sydney: Currency Press, and Canberra: ScreenSound Australia, 2003.

Martin, F., *Situating Sexualities: Queer Representation in Taiwanese Fiction, Film and Public Culture*, Hong Kong University Press, 2003.

Matheson, V., 'TV Extra', *Sunday Herald Sun* (Melbourne), 9 November 1997, p. 3.

Mellencamp, P., 'Haunted history: Tracey Moffatt and Julie Dash', *Discourse*, 16(2) 1994, pp. 127–63.

McFarlane, B., *Australian Cinema 1970–1985*, Melbourne: Heinemann, 1987.

McFarlane, B., & G. Mayer, *New Australian Cinema: Sources And Parallels in American and British Film*, Cambridge University Press, 1992.

McFarlane, B., G. Mayer and I. Bertrand (eds), *The Oxford Companion to Australian Film*, Melbourne: Oxford University Press, 1999.

Michaels, Eric, *For a Cultural Future: Francis Jupurrurla Makes TV at Yuendumu*, Melbourne: Artspace, 1987.

Miller, T. 'Exporting truth about Aboriginal Australia: "Portions of our past become present again, where only the melancholy light of origin shines"', *Media Information Australia*, 76, 1995, pp. 7–17.

Mills, J., 'Truth and the rabbit-proof fence', *Real Time*, 48, Apr.–May 2002, p. 15.

Macintyre, S., & A. Clark, *The History Wars*, Melbourne University Press, 2003.

McKee, A., *Australian Television: A Genealogy of Great Moments*, Melbourne: Oxford University Press, 2001.

McKenna, M., 'Different perspectives on black armband history', *Australian Parliamentary Library Research Paper*, no. 5, 1997–98.

McKenna, M., *Looking for Blackfellas Point: An Australian History of Place*, Sydney: UNSW Press, 2002.

McMurchy, M., & J. Stott (eds), *Signs of Independents: Ten Years of the Creative Development Fund*, Sydney: Australian Film Commission, 1988.

Moran, A., *Projecting Australia: Government Film Since 1945*, Sydney: Currency Press, 1991.

Moran, A., *Film Policy: An Australian Reader*, Brisbane: Griffith University, 1994.

Moran, A., & T. O'Regan (eds), *An Australian Film Reader*, Sydney: Currency Press, 1985.

Moran, A., & T. O'Regan (eds), *The Australian Screen*, Melbourne: Penguin, 1989.

Morden, T., 'Documentary. Past. Future?' In P. Holland, J. Spence & S. Watney (eds), *Photography/Politics II*, London: Comedia & Photography Workshop, 1986.

Morris, M., 'Fate and the family sedan', *East–West Film Journal*, 4(1) 1989, pp. 1, 113–34.

Morris, M., 'The very idea of a popular debate (or, not lunching with Thomas Keneally)', *Communal/Plural*, 2, 1992, pp. 153–67.

Morris, M., 'Beyond assimilation: Aboriginality, media history and public memory', *Aedon*, 4(1) 1996, pp. 12–26.

Morris, M., *Too Soon Too Late: History in Popular Culture*, Bloomington IN: Indiana University Press, 1998.

Mortimer, L., '*The Castle*, the garbage bin and the high-voltage tower: home truths in the suburban grotesque', *Meanjin*, 57(1) 1998, pp. 116–24.

Muecke, S., 'Narrative and intervention in Aboriginal filmmaking and policy', *Continuum*, 8(2) 1994, pp. 248–58.

Muecke, S., '*Backroads*: From identity to interval', *Senses of Cinema*, 17, 2001. Online journal <http://www.sensesofcinema.com>

Murray, S. (ed.), *The New Australian Cinema*, Melbourne: Thomas Nelson Australia, in assoc. with Cinema Papers, 1980.

Murray, S. (ed.), *Back of Beyond: Discussing Australian Film and Television*, Sydney: AFC-UCLA-ABA, 1988.

Murray, S. (ed.), *Australian Cinema*, Sydney: Allen & Unwin, in assoc. with Australian Film Commission, 1994.

Murray, S. (ed.), *Australian Film 1978–1994: A Survey of Theatrical Features*, Melbourne: Oxford University Press, in assoc. with the Australian Film Commission & Cinema Papers, 1995.

Myers, D. A., *Bleeding Battlers from Ironbark: Australian Myths in Fiction and Film, 1890s–1980s*, Rockhampton, Qld: Capricornia Institute, 1987.

Nelson, A., 'We want to put our culture out to the world: *Yolngu Boy*, the latest in Aboriginal and youth cinema', *Metro*, 131–132, 2002, pp. 118–25.

Nettheim, G., 'Native Title, fictions and "convenient falsehoods"'. *Law.Text.Culture*, 4(1) 1998, pp. 70–80.

Newspoll, Saulwick & Muller, and H. Mackay, 'Public opinion on reconciliation'. In M. Grattan (ed.), *Reconciliation: Essays on Reconciliation*, Melbourne: Black Inc & Bookman Press, 2000, pp. 33–52.

Niski, D., 'No man is an island', *Sunday Age*, 27 July 1997, C5.

Nowra, L., *Walkabout*, Sydney: Currency Press, and Canberra: ScreenSound Australia, 2001.

Nowra, L., & R. Perkins, '"Let the turtle live!" a discussion on adapting "Radiance" for the screen', *Metro*, 135, 2003, pp. 34–41.

Noyce, P., 'Rabbit-proof defence', *Sunday Telegraph*, 10 March 2002, p. 99.

O'Regan, T., *Australian National Cinema*, London: Routledge, 1996.

Pearson, N., 'Mabo: towards respecting equality and difference'. In G. Cowlishaw and B. Morris (eds), *Race Matters: Indigenous Australians and 'Our' Society*, Canberra: Aboriginal Studies Press, 1997.

Pearson, N., 'Aboriginal disadvantage', in Grattan, *Essays on Australian Reconciliation*, 2000, pp. 165–75.

Petro, P., 'After shock/between boredom and history'. In P. Petro (ed.), *Fugitive Images: From Photography to Video*, Bloomington IN: Indiana University Press, 1995, pp. 265–84.

Petro, P., *The Historical Film: History and Memory in Media*, New Brunswick NJ: Rutgers University Press, 2001.

Pierce, P., *The Country of Lost Children: An Australian Anxiety*, Cambridge University Press, 1999.

Pike, A., & R. Cooper, *Australian Film, 1900–1977: A Guide To Feature Film Production*, rev. edn, Melbourne: Oxford University Press, in assoc. with the Australian Film Institute, 1998.

Pilkington-Garimara, D., *Follow the Rabbit-Proof Fence*, Brisbane: University of Queensland Press, 1996.

Povinelli, E. A., 'The state of shame: Australian multiculturalism and the crisis of indigenous citizenship', *Critical Inquiry*, 24(2) 1998, pp. 575–610.

Quinn, K., 'Drags, dags and the suburban surreal', *Metro*, 100, 1994–95, pp. 23–6.

Radstone, S., *Memory and Methodology*, New York and Oxford: Berg, 2000, pp. 79–107.

Radstone, S. (ed.), 'Special Debate: Trauma and Screen Studies', *Screen*, 42(2) 2001, pp. 188–215.

Rathmell-Stiels, N., 'Serenades', *Metro*, 131–132, 2002, pp. 80–5.

Rattigan, N., *Images of Australia: 100 Films of the New Australian Cinema*, Dallas TX: Southern Methodist University Press, 1991.

Rayner, J. R., *Contemporary Australian Cinema: An Introduction*, Manchester University Press, 2000.

Reid, M. A., *Long Shots to Favourites: Australian Cinema Successes in the 90s*, Sydney: Australian Film Commission, 1993.

Reid, M. A., *More Long Shots: Australian Cinema Successes in the '90s*, Brisbane: Australian Key Centre For Cultural and Media Policy, and Sydney: Australian Film Commission, 1999.

Reis, B., *Australian Film: A Bibliography*, London: Mansell, 1997.

Reynolds, H., *Aboriginal Sovereignty: Reflections on Race, State and Nation*, Sydney: Allen & Unwin, 1996.

Roach, V., 'Dancing feet a sight to see', *Daily Telegraph*, Supplement, 24 May 2001, p. 8.

Robinson, C., & J. Given, 'Films, policies, audiences and Australia'. In Moran, *Film Policy*, 1994.

Robson, J., & B. Zalcock, *Girls' Own Stories: Australian and New Zealand Women's Films*, London: Scarlet Press, 1997.

Routt, W. D., 'Always already out of date: Australian bush comedy'. Paper presented at *Seriously Funny: 2004 National Screenwriters' Conference*, Melbourne, 2 April 2004.

Rowse, T., *After Mabo: Interpreting Indigenous Traditions*, Melbourne University Press, 1993.

Ryan, J., 'Mabo – Life of an Island Man', *Artery*, 6(8) 1997.

Ryan, T., 'Mabo – Life of an Island Man', *Sunday Age* (Melbourne), 10 August 1997, C2.

Sabine, J. (ed.), *A Century of Australian Cinema*, Melbourne: William Heinemann Australia, in assoc. with Australian Film Institute, 1995.

Sanders, W. (ed.), *'Mabo' and Native Title: Origins and Institutional Implications*, Canberra: Centre for Aboriginal Economic Policy Research, Australian National University, Research Monograph, no. 7, 1994.

Sanders, W., 'The owning of images and the right to represent', *Filmnews*, May, 1994, pp. 6–7.

Schembri, J., 'A portrait of the man who was the Mabo case', *Age*, 30 July 1997, p. 7.

Secomb, L., 'Interrupting mythic community', *Cultural Studies Review*, 9(1) 2003, pp. 85–100.

Sharp, N., *No Ordinary Judgement – Mabo, The Murray Islanders' Land Case*, Canberra: Aboriginal Studies Press, 1996.

Sheehan, P., '*Moulin Rouge* is all it was hyped up to be – and more', *Sydney Morning Herald*, 6 June 2001, p. 26.

Shirley, G., & B. Adams, *Australian Cinema: The First Eighty Years*, Sydney: Currency Press, 1983.

Siemienowicz. R., 'Globalisation and home values in new Australian cinema', *Journal of Australian Studies*, December 1999, p. 49.

Simpson, C., 'An Interview with Rachel Perkins – Director of *Radiance*', *Metro*, 120, 1999, pp. 32–4.

Simpson, C., 'Notes on the significance of home and the past in *Radiance*', *Metro*, 120, 1999, pp. 28–31.

Smaill, B., 'SBS Documentary and *Unfinished Business: Reconciling the Nation*', *Metro*, 126, 2001, pp. 34–40.

Smaill, B., '*The Tracker*', *Metro*, 134, 2002, pp. 31–3.

Smith, M., 'Mabo – Life of an Island Man', *Cinema Papers*, 119, 1997.

Speed, L., 'Tuesday's gone: the nostalgic teen film', *Journal of Popular Film and Television*, 26(1) 1998, pp. 24–32.

Squires, T., 'Remarkable life by "the fence" ends for Molly, 87', *Age*, 15 January 2004.

Stocks, I., 'The troubles of Dennis O'Rourke', *Senses of Cinema*, 13, 2001. Online journal <http://www.sensesofcinema.com>

Stratton, D., *The Last New Wave: The Australian Film Revival*, Sydney: Angus & Robertson, 1980.

Stratton, D., *The Avocado Plantation: Boom and Bust in the Australian Film Industry*, Sydney: Pan Macmillan, 1990.

Stratton, J. 1998, 'National identity, film and the narrativisation of multiculturalism and "Asians"'. In *Race Daze: Australia in Identity Crisis*, Sydney: Pluto Press, 1998.

Stratton, J., & I. Ang, 'Multicultural imagined communities: cultural difference and national identity in Australia and the USA', *Continuum*, 8(2) 1994, pp. 124–58.

Tacey, D., 'Spirit place'. In Cameron, *Changing Places*, 2003, pp. 243–48.

Taussig, M., *Defacement: Public Secrecy and the Labour of the Negative*, Palo Alto CA: Stanford University Press, 1999.

Taussig, M., *Mimesis and Alterity: A Particular History of the Senses*, New York: Routledge, 1993.

Thomas, S., 'Whatever happened to the social documentary', *Metro*, 134, 2002, pp. 152–60.

Tsiolkas, C., *Loaded*, Sydney: Vintage, 1995.

Tsiolkas, C., 'Through clouds: a discussion of *Kandahar* and *Beneath Clouds*', *Senses of Cinema*, 20, 2002. Online journal <http://www.sensesofcinema.com>

Tudball, L., *Study Guide: Mabo – Life of an Island Man*, Sydney: ATOM, 1997.

Tulloch, J., *Australian Cinema: Industry, Narrative and Meaning*, Sydney: Allen & Unwin, 1982.

Turner, G., 'The genres are American: Australian narrative, Australian film and the problem of genre', *Literature-Film Quarterly*, 21(2) 1993, pp. 102–12.

Turner, G., *Nation, Culture, Text: Australian Culture and Media Studies*, London: Routledge, 1993.

Turner, G., *National Fictions: Literature, Film, and the Construction of Australian Narrative*, Sydney: Allen & Unwin, 1986.

Turner, G., *Making it National: Nationalism and Australian Popular Culture*, Sydney: Allen & Unwin, 1994.

Turner, G., 'Whatever happened to national identity? Film and the nation in the 1990s', *Metro*, 100, 1994, pp. 32–5.

Verevis, C., '*Head On*: A (too) personal view', *Senses of Cinema*, 9, 2000. Online journal <http://www.sensesofcinema.com>

Verhoeven, D. (ed.), *Twin Peeks: Australian and New Zealand Feature Films*, Melbourne: Damned Publishing, 1999.

Villella, F. A., 'Long road home: Phillip Noyce's *Rabbit-Proof Fence*', *Senses of Cinema*, 19, 2001. Online journal, <http://www.sensesofcinema.com>

Villella, F. A., 'Review – *Yolngu Boy*', *Senses of Cinema*, 13, 2001. Online journal, <http://www.sensesofcinema.com>

Ward, Russel, *The Australian Legend*, Melbourne: Oxford University Press, 1958.

Walker, J., 'Trauma cinema: false memories and true experience', *Screen*, 42(2) 2001, pp. 194–214.

Walker, R., 'Blood on the tracks', *Metro*, 133, 2002, pp. 12–17.

Watson, D., 'Rabbit syndrome: Australia and America', *Quarterly Essay*, no. 4, 2001.

Williams, D., *Mapping the Imaginary: Ross Gibson's Camera Natura*, Australian Teachers Of Media, in assoc. with Australian Film Institute and Deakin University School of Visual, Performing and Media Arts, Melbourne, 1996.

Williams, E., 'Enough redemption already', *Weekend Australian*, Review, 19 July 1997, p. 11.

Wilson, J., 'Looking both ways: *The Tracker*', *Senses of Cinema*, 24, 2003. Online journal <http://www.sensesofcinema.com>

Woodward, K., 'Freud and Barthes: theorizing mourning, sustaining grief', *Discourse*, 13(1) 1990–91.

Woodward, K., 'Grief-work in contemporary American cultural criticism', *Discourse*, 15(2) 1992–93.

Wyatt, J., *High Concept: Movies and Marketing in Hollywood*, Austin TX: University of Texas Press, 1994.

Zion, L., 'Short cuts', *Age*, 30 January 2003, A3, p. 8.

Index